P9-BVG-320

THE
ELEMENTS
OF
JOURNALISM

ALSO BY THESE AUTHORS:

Warp Speed: America in the Age of Mixed Media

THE
ELEMENTS
OF
JOURNALISM

What Newspeople Should Know
and the Public Should Expect

COMPLETELY UPDATED AND REVISED

Bill Kovach & Tom Rosenstiel

 THREE RIVERS PRESS • NEW YORK

Copyright © 2001, 2007 by Bill Kovach and Tom Rosenstiel

All rights reserved.
Published in the United States by Three Rivers Press, an imprint of the Crown
Publishing Group, a division of Random House, Inc., New York.
www.crownpublishing.com

Three Rivers Press and the Tugboat design are registered trademarks of
Random House, Inc.

Grateful acknowledgment is made to Cable News Network, Inc. (CNN)
for permission to reprint a text excerpt from the show *Crossfire* (October 15, 2004).
Reprinted by permission of Cable News Network, Inc. (CNN).

Originally published in hardcover in the United States by
Crown Publishers, an imprint of the Crown Publishing Group,
a division of Random House, Inc., New York, and subsequently published
in paperback by Three Rivers Press, New York, a division of the Crown
Publishing Group, an imprint of Random House Inc., New York, in 2001.

Library of Congress Cataloging-in-Publication Data
Kovach, Bill.
The elements of journalism : what newspeople should know and the public should
expect/Bill Kovach and Tom Rosenstiel. –1st ed., completely updated and rev.
Includes bibliographical references and index.
1. Journalistic ethics. 2. Journalism–United States.
I. Rosenstiel, Tom. II. Title.

PN4756.K67 2007
070.40973–dc22
2006023159

ISBN 978-0-307-34670-4

Printed in the United States of America

Design by Maria Elias

10

First Revised Edition

For Lynne
&
For Beth and Karina

CONTENTS

S ince the first edition of this book was published in 2001, the relationship between journalism and technology has evolved considerably. The disaggregation of the audience that consumes the news has accelerated, and the crisis of confidence among journalists who produce the news has heightened. These changes leave us even more persuaded, however, that the elements of journalism remain fundamental and enduring.

To survive, journalism must adapt in form and style to reflect changes in culture, politics, taste, and technology. But as journalism changes, those who produce the news also must keep in mind the purpose and principles of producing accurate information on behalf of the citizens. Those principles and that purpose, which form the theory and function of news in civil society, are what this book tries to outline.

Many things have occurred in the last five years that seem at first glance to stand in the way of journalism's resurgence. At the turn of the millennium, first fear of change and then the dot-com bust made journalists too leery of the new medium of the Web, and it delayed their engagement with technological developments that by early 2006 had spawned countless forms of self-publishing and editing.

In 1999, a California company called Pyra Labs launched Blogger .com, a publishing system that allowed technically unsophisticated users to create and publish their own content on the Internet. These sites were known as "weblogs" or "blogs," and many citizens seized the opportunity to become their own editors. Blogs were but one factor in a spate of technology that allowed citizens to control information. Developments in digital photography and other portable electronics made laptops, cameras, and music players more versatile and more affordable. As more people acquired the technology, Web upstarts found ways to integrate the innovations, and by 2002 people were displaying their own text, photos, audio, and video on the Internet.

While these advances were occurring, the events of September 11, 2001, played an important role in bringing millions of people online for news, community, and a chance to debate the country's future.[1] Internet dependency soared to new heights and hasn't dropped since. Citizens involved in the political and social dialogue helped along the notion of citizen journalism, whose early advocates foresaw a future in which anyone could create and distribute information.

Adding to the challenges facing traditional media are news aggregators like Yahoo! and Google, which launched news services that produced no original content but carried stories reported by traditional organizations around the world. While most blogs were little more than personal diaries, some emerged as opinion leaders across the American political spectrum. For example, in late 2002, bloggers helped unseat Trent Lott from his position as leader of the Senate Republicans by widely circulating a racist remark that the Mississippi senator had made at Strom Thurmond's 100th birthday party.[2] Traditional media had all but ignored the episode.

By 2004, blogs were playing a role in the presidential primaries and nearly helped nominate a dark horse candidate in Howard Dean. That same year, a 10-minute video envisioning the media landscape of 2014 was developed by two young journalists who met at the Poynter Institute in St. Petersburg, Florida. This future was dominated by a Google spin-off called EPIC that produced "a custom content package for each user, using his choices, his consumption habits, his interests, his demographics, his social network—to shape the product." Most journalists now see the scenario as plausible.

At the same time, mainstream journalism has been racked by a series of scandals seemingly at every level. The fabrications and plagiarism of a young reporter on a fast track at the *New York Times* named Jayson Blair not only exposed deeper problems in the newsroom but also triggered a staff revolt that led to the forced ousting of the paper's executive editor–an embarrassment without precedent for the nation's most important newspaper.[3] The desire for scoops at *USA Today*, the nation's largest-circulation newspaper, and the inability of the paper's culture to produce them properly, allowed a rogue foreign correspondent named Jack Kelley to make up lies, put them in the paper, and be protected by top editors along the way, despite concerns from below. Other controversies have cast shadows on the motives of Pulitzer Prize winners like Judith Miller and Bob Woodward. And elsewhere journalists less well known, but holding great responsibility, have also been exposed for their serious sins. On that list are Stephen Dunphy at the *Seattle Times*, fired for plagiarism,[4] or Diana Griego Erwin at the *Sacramento Bee*, who resigned after editors found forty-three different people she had quoted whose existence could not be substantiated,[5] or Chris Cecil, a young managing editor at the Cartersville (Georgia) *Daily Tribune News*, who was fired after his bosses at the 8,000-circulation daily learned that he had plagiarized columns from a syndicated Pulitzer Prize winner.[6] It is impossible to determine whether such transgressions were on the rise or the monitoring of the press was merely exposing more of them–or both.

There were signs of hope along the way as well. In 2005, the BBC harnessed the power of citizens in its coverage of the July London bombings, running amateur video, witness accounts, and pictures snapped with cellphone cameras. Just weeks later American news organizations proved able to provide regularly updated information and use citizen-produced content when Hurricane Katrina struck New Orleans. Outside the traditional media, citizens gathered in chat rooms dedicated to breaking news and created perpetually updating resources, pulling information from all sources and editing each other's content to fix errors and add depth.

The ability of almost anybody to produce and disseminate text, video, and audio has also increased user demand to personalize the content they consume from other sources and preferably store it all on one site or manage it with one piece of software. In April 2006, the *New York Times* was putting the finishing touches on My Times, a service that "lets you create a personalized page with what you like best in *The*

New York Times and your favorite sites and blogs from all over the Web," and was launching blogs by editors and reporters that combined reported news with opinions and links to material produced by others.

The news is becoming less of a prepared lecture and more of an open-mike conversation, with all the pluses and minuses that implies.

The technology has continued to foment tensions between media and citizens. Journalists are under intense scrutiny from bloggers, and many organizations are struggling to integrate their online operations into the newsroom without lowering standards of reporting and verifying information. Much of that pressure is healthy. Clear away the rhetoric and animus of those who yearn for the annihilation of traditional journalism (the hated "MSM," or mainstream media), and journalism will be better for the scrutiny that the blogosphere offers.

This flurry of activity online would not have been possible without an explosion of infrastructure. Internet penetration in American homes by 2006 stood at more than 70 percent, and more than 74 million people used broadband connections—a nearly fourfold growth since 2002. These broadband users, regardless of age, tend to consume a lot more news online than do other groups.[7]

This newly updated edition of *The Elements of Journalism* tries to capture the effect of these developments. This work is also enriched by deeper insights that have resulted from discussions with journalists in hundreds of newsrooms around the country through the Committee of Concerned Journalists Traveling Curriculum, a training program based on the first edition. In addition, we have been able to more finely craft the lessons of journalism history and to correct some errors of fact brought to our attention by people who have read the book as well as journalism educators who have used it in their classrooms.

Readers will find changes throughout. Many of the examples have been replaced by newer ones. In other cases, newer developments have been added to the existing incidents because they build on one another and tell a more complex story together.

The chapter on allegiance and business has been recast to accommodate several changes—the failure of several major mergers since 2001, as well as the loss of leverage newspeople have in their companies and the further accumulation of influence by accountants. We little imagined so much would change in such a short time, given how long the battle over the soul of news companies has been going on.

Some of the changes are more obvious and predictable. Among them, the press now must not only accommodate itself to a new competitive atmosphere but also must understand and adjust to the newly amplified voice of the citizen.

Other chapters have been fleshed out as the thinking of journalists and our own reflections on certain concepts have deepened. Turning to the tools by which journalists pursue their purpose, the chapter on verification, perhaps more than any other chapter in the book, has benefited from conversations with hundreds of journalists and journalism educators in newsrooms and classrooms around the country. The treatment of objectivity has especially benefited from these discussions. As a result we feel we have come closer to describing the original understanding of objectivity as a unity of method rather than aim. In particular, the idea of transparency has gained much greater prominence in the vocabulary of journalism since the first edition appeared, and the concept continues to evolve as the interactivity of the Internet opens the process by which journalism is practiced to greater public examination. And, finally, these discussions have made it much clearer to us, and we hope to the readers of this edition, how a transparent method of verification becomes the most important tool for managing the thorny problem of bias, both useful and troubling, that plagues journalists and journalism.

Each of the remaining chapters benefits likewise from our newsroom conversations on how the various roles journalism assumes in a self-governing community are impacted as news becomes an abundantly available commodity.

In the chapter on journalism as a public forum, not only has the nature of that forum exploded with the concept of "we media," but our sense is that the Argument Culture and polarization of the media have entered a new stage, where argument weighed equally to create fireworks is giving way to something new—the promise of answers, or affirmation, a more one-sided but in some ways more settled Argument Culture. The chapter on conscience in the news also has changed markedly in the wake of scandals and upheavals large and small.

Perhaps most notably, readers will notice a new element of journalism here. In the first paperback edition of this book we had added A Citizen's Journalism Bill of Rights. In this new edition, the interactive relationship developing between journalism and the public has convinced us that the question of the citizen's role rises to the status of a tenth principle, The Citizen's Rights and Responsibilities.

As we approach the end of the first decade of this century, the need for structural change in the press is more widely accepted than it was five years ago. The signs of understanding are not across the board. Local TV news, for instance, does not appear to be building a future online the way network news is. In turn, some newspapers are moving more seriously online than others.

Readers may also notice that many questions remain unresolved. One question is whether the news industry has waited too long, letting too many opportunities slip by, including offers years ago to buy startup companies that now are major new-media rivals. Another question is whether consumers will care about the values that the old press embodies, or the brands—such as CBS News or the *New York Times*—that represent these values. A third question, and perhaps the most important one, is whether journalists have sufficiently mastered the principles that have sustained them over generations to ensure their place in the future.

How news is gathered is becoming more open and accessible to the public. The reaction of many journalists in the past was to tell themselves: "Never let them see how the sausage is made." The fact that this notion was never expressed openly suggested its hypocrisy even then, and the transparency of today has made it unthinkable.

Nothing since the confusion and doubt that inspired the Progressive movement early in the twentieth century has required journalists to think more deeply and creatively about what they do, how they do it, and why it is crucial to an informed democracy. The voices speaking in this book, as well as the research that supplements those voices, reveal how journalists today are returning to the issues that thinkers of that earlier era grappled with as they redefined journalism for a new century.

We hope this updated edition of *The Elements of Journalism* adds light to that discussion.

Bill Kovach and Tom Rosenstiel

ENDNOTES

1. PEW Internet and American Life Project, "The Commons of the Tragedy," October 10, 2001; available at www.pewinternet.org/ppf/r/46/report_display.asp.
2. Olivia Burkeman, "Bloggers Catch What Washington Post Missed," *The Guardian*, December 21, 2002; available at www.guardian.co.uk/international/story/0,863964,00.html.
3. CNN.com, "Top New York Times Editors Quit," March 1, 2004; available at www.cnn.com/2003/US/Northeast/06/05/nytimes.resigns/.
4. Poynter online, "Encouraging Transparency in Reporting," February 15, 2005; available at www.Poynter.org/column.asp?id=31&aid=78491.
5. Sacbee.com, "Rick Rodriguez: Griego Erwin Resigns Amid Internal Enquiry into Her Columns," May 12, 2005; available at www.sacbee.com.
6. Poynter online, "Georgia Newsman Fired After Lifting from Columnist Pitts," June 3, 2005; available at www.Poynter.org/column.asp?id=45&aid=83351.
7. PEW Internet and American Life Project, "Online News," March 22, 2006; available at www.pewinternet.org/ppf/r/178/report_display.asp.

THE

ELEMENTS

OF

JOURNALISM

W hen anthropologists began comparing notes on the world's few remaining primitive cultures, they discovered something unexpected. From the most isolated tribal societies in Africa to the most distant islands in the Pacific, people shared essentially the same definition of what is news. They shared the same kind of gossip. They even looked for the same qualities in the messengers they picked to gather and deliver their news. They wanted people who could run swiftly over the next hill, accurately gather information, and engagingly retell it. Historians have pieced together that the same basic news values have held constant through time. "Humans have exchanged a similar mix of news ... throughout history and across cultures," historian Mitchell Stephens has written.[1]

How do we explain the mystery of this consistency? The answer, historians and sociologists have concluded, is that news satisfies a basic human impulse. People have an intrinsic need—an instinct—to know what is occurring beyond their direct experience.[2] Being aware of events we cannot see for ourselves engenders a sense of security, control, and confidence. One writer has called it "a hunger for awareness."[3]

One of the first things people do when meeting a friend or acquaintance is to share information. "Have you heard about...?" We want to know if they've heard what we have, and if they heard it the same way. There is a thrill in a shared sense of discovery. We form relationships, choose friends, and make character judgments based partly on whether someone reacts to information the same way as we do.

When the flow of news is obstructed, "a darkness falls" and anxiety grows.[4] The world, in effect, becomes too quiet. We feel alone. John McCain, the U.S. senator from Arizona, writes that in his five and a half years as a prisoner of war in Hanoi, what he missed most was not comfort, food, freedom, or even his family and friends. "The thing I missed most was information—free uncensored, undistorted, abundant information."[5]

Call it the Awareness Instinct.

We need news to live our lives, protect ourselves, bond with each other, identify friends and enemies. Journalism is simply the system societies generate to supply this news. That is why we care about the character of the news and journalism we get: they influence the quality of our lives, our thoughts, and our culture. Writer Thomas Cahill, the author of several popular books on the history of religion, has put it this way: you can tell "the worldview of a people . . . the invisible fears and desires . . . in a culture's stories."[6]

At a moment of revolution in communications, what do the stories we tell say about our worldview—our fears, desires, and values?

This book began on a rainy Saturday in June 1997, when twenty-five journalists gathered at the Harvard Faculty Club. Around the long table sat editors of several of the nation's top newspapers, as well as some of the most influential names in television and radio, several of the top journalism educators, and some of the country's most prominent authors. They were there because they thought something was seriously wrong with their profession. They barely recognized what they considered journalism in much of the work of their colleagues. Instead of serving a larger public interest, they feared, their profession was damaging it.

The public, in turn, increasingly distrusted journalists, even hated them. And it would only get worse. By 1999, just 21 percent of Americans would think the press cared about people, down from 41 percent in 1987.[7] Only 58 percent would respect the press's watchdog role, a drop from 67 percent in 1985. Less than half, just 45 percent, would think the press protected democracy. That percentage had been nearly ten points higher in 1985.[8] By 2005 some of these numbers saw slight improvements–28 percent of Americans believed the press cared about people.[9]

What was different that day in Cambridge was that many of the journalists in the room–and around the country–were beginning to agree with the public. "In the newsroom we no longer talk about journalism," said Maxwell King, then editor of the *Philadelphia Inquirer.* "We are consumed with business pressure and the bottom line," agreed another editor. News was becoming entertainment and entertainment news. Journalists' bonuses were increasingly tied to the company's profit margins, not to the quality of their work. Finally, the late Columbia University professor James Carey offered what many recalled as a summation: "The problem is that you see journalism disappearing inside the larger world of communications. What you yearn to do is recover journalism from that larger world."

Implied in that was something more important. If journalism–the system by which we get our news–was being subsumed, what would replace it? Advertising? Entertainment? E-commerce? Propaganda? Online news aggregators? Some new hybrid of all these? And what would the consequence be?

The answers matter to the public and newspeople alike. Journalism provides something unique to a culture: independent, reliable, accurate, and comprehensive information that citizens require to be free. A journalism that is asked to provide something other than that subverts democratic culture. This is what happens when governments control the news, as in Nazi Germany or the Soviet Union. We're seeing it again in places like Singapore, where news is controlled to encourage capitalism but discourage participation in public life. Something akin to this may be taking root in the United States in a more purely commercial form, as when news outlets owned by larger corporations are used to promote their conglomerate parent's products, to engage in subtle lobbying or corporate rivalry, or are intermingled with advertising to boost profits. The issue isn't just the loss of journalism. At stake is whether, as citizens, we have access to the independent information that makes it possible for us to take part in governing ourselves.

In the years since 1997, when the group met in Cambridge, those pressures have only increased. During the administration of George W.

Bush, the president and other top aides openly dismissed the press as nothing more than another interest group in society with its own private agenda.[10] While that pose may have been partly political, and the president in early 2005 would back away from that position with an endorsement of the independence of the press, these politicians were articulating something the public increasingly felt already. [11]

The administration also went further than either the Clinton or the previous Bush administration in creating government-produced media. It distributed deceptive video news releases to local TV stations. It paid a company to place one-sided stories, written by the American military, in Iraqi media. It also paid columnists in the United States to produce material that supported policies on education and marriage.[12] And it tried to criminalize whistleblowing with investigations into press revelations about extra-legal domestic wiretapping and secret prisons overseas. [13]

Technology did not only help the government's efforts to create and distribute material. When blogs achieved mainstream notoriety in 2004, people increasingly began to publish on their own websites. This citizen journalism movement may have helped wash away any particular fear of the idea that government was creating its own official journalism.

In 1997, the group of journalists who met in Cambridge on the cusp of these changes decided on a plan: engage journalists and the public in a careful examination of what journalism was supposed to be. We set out to answer two questions. If newspeople thought journalism was somehow different from other forms of communication, how was it different? If they thought journalism needed to change but that some core principles needed to endure, what were those principles?

Over the next two years, the group, now calling itself the Committee of Concerned Journalists, organized the most sustained, systematic, and comprehensive examination ever conducted by journalists of news gathering and its responsibilities. We held twenty-one public forums attended by 3,000 people and involving testimony from more than three hundred journalists. We partnered with a team of university researchers who conducted more than a hundred 3½-hour interviews with journalists about their values. We produced two surveys of journalists about their principles. We held a summit of First Amendment and journalism scholars. With the Project for Excellence in Journalism we produced nearly a dozen content studies of news reporting. We studied the history of those journalists who came before us and have conducted training in newsrooms nationwide. This book is the fruit of that examination. It is not an argument. It is, rather, a description of the theory and culture of journalism that emerged from three years of listening to citizens and journalists, from our empirical studies, and from our reading of the history of the profession as it evolved in the United States.

We learned, among other things, that society expects journalists to apply this theory, and citizens to understand it, though it is seldom studied or clearly articulated. This lack of clarity, for both citizens and newspeople, has weakened journalism and is now weakening democratic society. Unless we can grasp and reclaim the theory of a free press, journalists risk allowing their profession to disappear. In that sense, the crisis of our culture, and our journalism, is a crisis of conviction.

There are, we have distilled from our search, some clear principles that journalists agree on—and that citizens have a right to expect. They are principles that have ebbed and flowed over time, but they have always in some manner been evident. They have survived because journalists have been able to adapt the principles to the demands of new platforms and ways of doing their basic work of informing the people. But they have adapted their work—not their principles—just as the public has adapted to the way they receive their news. These are the principles that have helped both journalists and the people in self-governing systems to adjust to the demands of an ever more complex world. They are the elements of journalism. The first among them is that the purpose of journalism is to provide people with the information they need to be free and self-governing.

To fulfill this task:

1. Journalism's first obligation is to the truth.
2. Its first loyalty is to citizens.
3. Its essence is a discipline of verification.
4. Its practitioners must maintain an independence from those they cover.
5. It must serve as an independent monitor of power.

6. It must provide a forum for public criticism and compromise.
7. It must strive to make the significant interesting and relevant.
8. It must keep the news comprehensive and in proportion.
9. Its practitioners have an obligation to exercise their personal conscience.
10. Citizens, too, have rights and responsibilities when it comes to the news.

Why these ten? Some readers will think items are missing here. Where is fairness? Where is balance? After synthesizing what we learned, it became clear that a number of familiar and even useful ideas—including fairness and balance—are too vague to rise to the level of essential elements of the profession. Others may say that this list is nothing new. To the contrary, we discovered that many ideas about the elements of journalism are wrapped in myth and misconception. That journalists should be protected by a wall between business and news is one myth. That independence requires journalists to be neutral is another. The concept of objectivity has been so mangled it now is usually used to describe the very problem it was conceived to correct.

Nor is this the first moment that the way we get news has gone through momentous transition. It has happened each time there is a period of significant social, economic, and technological change. It occurred in the 1830s and 1840s with the arrival of the telegraph, in the 1880s with the drop in the price of paper and the influx of immigrants. It occurred again in the 1920s with the invention of the radio and the rise of the tabloids and the culture of gossip and celebrity. And it occurred with the invention of television and the arrival of the Cold War.

It is occurring now with the advent of cable, followed by the Internet. The collision this time may be more dramatic. For the first time in our history, the news increasingly is produced by companies outside journalism, and this new economic organization is important. We are facing the possibility that independent news will be replaced by rumor and self-interested commercialism posing as news. If that occurs, we will lose the press as an independent institution, free to monitor the other powerful forces and institutions in society.

In the new century, one of the most profound questions for a democratic society is whether an independent press survives. The answer will depend on whether journalists have the clarity and conviction to articulate what an independent press means and whether, as citizens, the rest of us care.

This book is intended as a first step in helping journalists articulate those values and helping citizens demand a journalism connected to the principles that spawned the free press in the first place. Some may ask whether there is a specific program laid out here to do that, to "fix" journalism's problems. Our answer to that comes in two parts.

The first answer is that the yearning for a single moment, the bold action, or the formulaic solution, is not how history works. Nor is it how journalism grew up or came to be in its current predicament in the early twenty-first century. Journalism evolves continually. At any given moment, one can point to trends of improvement and disorientation simultaneously.

In 2006, there are maybe more young people observing their world and sharing what they find in a journalistic way, complete with a higher sense of public mission and public ethics, than at any other time in history. And there are self-appointed pragmatists—people in corporate settings—who are convinced that the current economics of journalism prove that quality and commitment to the public interest are quaint notions and naïve ideas that knowledgeable realists must forgo.

The second answer—the reason one will not find a five- or ten-point program to solve the problems of journalism's role in society—is that our collective experience of more than seventy years in this business suggests a clearer lesson on how to find that solution.

The answer will be found in those who produce the news mastering the principles of journalism and rigorously applying them to the way they work and think every day. The solution will be found the same way that athletes perfect performance: in the repetition of doing, until these elements become second nature. This is what will breed clarity of purpose, confidence of execution, and public respect.

The key to this, first, is to distinguish between the principles that guide journalism's purpose and the techniques that one generation develops in a specific medium to fulfill those principles. Only by recognizing the primacy of principle can journalism change ethically and come out the other side still fulfilling the same democratic purpose for a new century, a new technology, and a new kind of information–wired citizen.

ENDNOTES

1. Mitchell Stephens, *A History of News* (Fort Worth, TX: Harcourt Brace College Publishers, 1996), 27.
2. Harvey Molotch and Marilyn Lester, "News as Purposive Behavior: On the Strategic Use of Routine Events, Accidents and Scandal," *American Sociological Review,* 39 (February 1974), 101–12.
3. Stephens, *History of News,* 12.
4. Ibid.
5. John McCain, with Mark Salter, *Faith of My Fathers* (New York: Random House, 1999), 221.
6. Thomas Cahill, *The Gift of the Jews: How a Tribe of Desert Nomads Changed the Way Everyone Thinks and Feels* (New York: Nan A. Talese/Anchor Books, 1998), 17.
7. Committee of Concerned Journalists (CCJ) and the Pew Research Center for the People and the Press, "Striking the Balance: Audience Interests, Business Pressures and Journalists' Values," March 1999, 79.
8. Ibid.
9. Pew Research Center for the People and the Press, "Public More Critical of Press, But Goodwill Persists," June 26, 2005; available at http://people-press.org.
10. Ken Auletta, "Fortress Bush," *The New Yorker,* January 19, 2004; available at www.newyorker.com/fact/content/articles/040119fa_fact2.
11. Associated Press, "Bush to Agencies: Don't Hire Columnists to Promote Agendas," *USA Today,* January 26, 2005; available at www.usatoday.com.
12. Susan Goldenberg, "Bush Payola Scandal Deepens as Third Columnist Admits Being Paid," *The Guardian,* January 29, 2005; David Folkernflik, "Video News Releases Find News Airtime," National Public Radio, March 25, 2005; David S. Cloud, "Quick Rise for Purveyors of Propaganda in Iraq," *New York Times,* February 15, 2006; Gail Russell Chaddock, "Bush Administration Blurs Media Boundary," *Christian Science Monitor,* February 17, 2005; available at www.guardian.co.uk.
13. Scott Shane, "Criminal Inquiry Opens into Spying Leak," *New York Times,* December 31, 2005; Walter Pincus, "Prosecution of Journalists is Possible in NSA Leaks," *Washington Post,* May 22, 2006.

1

What Is
Journalism For?

On a gray December morning in 1981, Anna Semborska woke up and flipped on the radio to hear her favorite program, *Sixty Minutes Per Hour (60MPH)*. Semborska, who was seventeen, loved the way the comedy revue pushed the boundaries of what people in Poland could say out loud. Though it had been on the air for some years, with the rise of the labor union Solidarity, *60MPH* had become much more bold. Sketches like one about a dim-witted communist doctor looking vainly to find a cure for extremism were an inspiration to Anna and her teenage friends in Warsaw. The program showed her that other people felt about the world the way she did but had never dared express. "We felt that if things like these can be said on the radio then we are free," she would remember nearly twenty years later.[1]

But when Anna ran to the radio to tune in the show on December 13, 1981, she heard only static. She tried another station, then another. Nothing. She tried to call a friend and found no dial tone. Her mother called her to the window. Tanks were rolling by. The Polish military government had declared martial law, outlawed Solidarity, and put the clamps back on the media and on speech. The Polish experiment with liberalization was over.

Within hours, Anna and her friends began to hear stories that suggested something this time was different. In a little town called Świdnik near the Czech border, there were the dogwalkers. Every night at 7:30, when the state-run television news came on, nearly everyone in Świdnik went out and walked his or her dog in a little park in the center of town. It became a daily silent act of protest and solidarity. We refuse to watch. We reject your version of truth.

In Gdansk, there were the black TV screens. People there began moving their television sets to the windows—with the screens pointed out to the street. They were sending a sign to one another, and the government. We, too, refuse to watch. We also reject your version of truth.

An underground press began to grow, on ancient hand-crank equipment. People began carrying video cameras and making private documentaries, which they showed secretly in church basements. Soon, Poland's leaders acknowledged that they were facing a new phenomenon, something they had to go west to name: the rise of Polish public opinion. In 1983, the government created the first of several institutes to study public opinion. Similar institutes would soon sprout up throughout Eastern Europe. But public opinion was something totalitarian officials could not dictate. At best, they could try to understand it and then manipulate it, not unlike Western democratic politicians. They would not succeed.

Afterward, leaders of the movement toward freedom would look back and think that the end of communism owed a good deal to the coming of the new information technology and the effect it had on human souls. In the winter of 1989, the man who shortly would be elected Poland's new president visited journalists in Washington. "Is it possible for a new Stalin to appear today who could murder people?" Lech Walesa asked rhetorically. No, he answered himself, in the age of computers, satellites, faxes, VCRs, "it's impossible." Technology now made information available to too many people, too quickly. And information created democracy.[2] We may look back and think Walesa was caught up in the euphoria of the moment. But his sentiment was less a reflection of naivete than a burst of optimism coming from a part of the world that was just discovering technology and its power to do good and inspire people to fight for their freedom.

What is journalism for? For the Poles and others in the emerging democracies of Eastern Europe, the question was answered with action. Journalism was for building community. Journalism was for citizenship. Journalism was for democracy. And as Czech president Vaclav Havel told a group of journalists gathered in Prague in 1991, journalism was for taking back the language from a government that had subverted it with propaganda that undermined freedom of thought itself. Millions of people, empowered by a free flow of information, became directly involved in creating a new government and new rules for the political, social, and economic life of their country. Is that always journalism's purpose? Or was that true for one moment, in one place?

In the United States for the last half century or so the question "What is journalism for?" has rarely been asked, by citizens or journalists. You owned a printing press or a broadcasting license and you produced journalism. In the United States journalism has been reduced to a simple tautology: it is whatever journalists say it is. As Maxwell King, the former editor of the *Philadelphia Inquirer*, has said, "We let our work speak for itself." Or, when pressed, journalists take it as a given that they work in the public interest.[3]

This simplistic answer is no longer sufficient—if it ever really was to an increasingly skeptical public. Not now that the new communications technology means anyone with a modem and a computer can claim to be "doing journalism." Not now that the technology has created a new economic organization of journalism in which the norms of journalism are being pulled and redefined, and sometimes abandoned.

Perhaps, some suggest, the definition of journalism has been exploded by technology so that now anything is seen as journalism. But on closer examination, as the people of Poland demonstrated, the purpose of journalism is not defined by technology, nor by journalists or the techniques they employ. As we will show, the principles and purpose of journalism are defined by something more basic: the function news plays in the lives of people.

For all that the face of journalism has changed, indeed, its purpose has remained remarkably constant, if not always well served, since the notion of "a press" first evolved more than three hundred years ago. And for all that the speed, techniques, and character of news delivery have changed, and are likely to continue to change ever more rapidly, there exists a clear theory and philosophy of journalism that flows out of the function of news that has remained consistent and enduring.

The primary purpose of journalism is to provide citizens with the information they need to be free and self-governing.

As we listened to citizens and journalists, we heard that this obligation to citizens encompasses several elements. The news media help us define our communities as well as help us create a common language and common knowledge rooted in reality. Journalism also helps identify a community's goals, heroes, and villains. "I've felt strongly for a long time that we proceed best as a society if we have a common base of information," then NBC anchorman Tom Brokaw told our academic research partners.[4] The news media serve as a watchdog, push people beyond complacency, and offer a voice to the forgotten. "I want to give voices to people who need the voice ... people who are powerless," said Yuen Ying Chan, a former reporter for the *New York Daily News* who created a journalism training program in Hong Kong.[5] The late James Carey, one of the founders of our committee, has put it this way in his own writing: perhaps in the end journalism simply means carrying on and amplifying the conversation of people themselves.[6] The rise of the Internet, blogs, and citizen journalism obviously make that purpose seem more relevant.

This definition has held so consistent through history, and proven so deeply ingrained in the thinking of those who produce news through the ages, that it is in little doubt. It is difficult, in looking back, even to separate the concept of journalism from the concept of creating community and later democracy. Journalism is so fundamental to that purpose that, as we will see, societies that want to suppress freedom must first suppress the press. They do not, interestingly, have to suppress capitalism. At its best, as we will also show, journalism reflects a subtle understanding of how citizens behave, an understanding that we call the Theory of the Interlocking Public.

Yet the longstanding theory and purpose of journalism are being challenged today in ways not seen before, at least in the United States. Technology is shaping a new economic organization of information companies, which is subsuming journalism within it. The threat is no longer simply from government censorship. With new technology, government is more likely to try to subvert the press by trying to discredit its integrity and dilute its influence. It has more tools to do that in the twenty-first century, creating pseudo-journalism in the form of faux news websites, video news releases, subsidies to "media personalities" willing to accept money to promote policy, and more. Government will inevitably also try to imitate citizen journalism as it evolves further. And the threat from government is compounded by a new danger that independent journalism may be dissolved in the solvent of commercial communication and synergistic self-promotion: corporatism. The real meaning of the First Amendment—that a free press is an independent institution—is threatened for the first time in our history, even without government meddling.

There are some who will contend that defining journalism is dangerous. To define journalism, they argue, is to limit it. Maybe doing so violates the spirit of the First Amendment: "Congress shall make no law . . . abridging the freedom of speech or of the press." This is why journalists have avoided licensing, like doctors and lawyers, they note. They also worry that defining journalism will only make it resistant to changing with the times, which probably will run it out of business.

Actually, the resistance to definition in journalism is not a deeply held principle but a fairly recent and largely commercial impulse. Publishers a century ago routinely championed their news values in front-page editorials, opinion pages, and company slogans, and just as often publicly assailed the journalistic values of their rivals. This was marketing. Citizens chose which publications to read based on their styles and their approaches to news. It was only as the press began to assume a more corporate, more homogenous, and monopolistic form that it became more reticent. Lawyers advised news companies against codifying their principles in writing for fear that they would be used against them in court. Thus, avoiding definition was a commercial strategy. It was not born of the meaning of the First Amendment.

On the other side, some will argue that not only should journalism's purpose be unchanging but its form should be constant as well. They see changes in the way journalism looks from when they were young, and they fear that, in the memorable phrase of Neil Postman, we are "amusing ourselves to death." They miss another fact. Every generation creates its own journalism. But the purpose and the underlying elements of journalism, we have found, are the same.

Though journalists are uncomfortable defining what they do, they fundamentally agree on their purpose. When we set out in 1997 to chart the common ground of newspeople, this was the first answer we heard: "The central purpose of journalism is to tell the truth so that people will have the information that they need to be sovereign." It came from Jack Fuller, an author, novelist, lawyer, and then president of the Tribune Publishing Company, which produces the *Chicago Tribune*.[7]

Even people who resist the label of journalist, who work on the Web, offer a similar goal. Omar Wasow, a self-described "garage entrepreneur" who founded a website called New York Online, told us at one forum that his aim, in part, was to help create citizens who are "consumers, devourers and debunkers of media . . . an audience who have engaged with the product and can respond carefully."[8]

Were these just disparate voices? Not really. In collaboration with the Pew Research Center for the People and the Press, we asked journalists what they considered the distinguishing feature of journalism. Those working in news volunteered this democratic function by nearly two to one over any other answer.[9] Open-ended, in-depth interviews with a hundred more journalists conducted by developmental psychologists at Stanford, Harvard, and the University of Chicago with whom we collaborated came to the same conclusion. "News professionals at every level . . . express an adamant allegiance to a set of core standards that are striking in their commonality and in their linkage to the public information mission," they write.[10]

Ethics codes and journalism mission statements bear the same witness. The goal is "to serve the general welfare by informing the people," says the code of the American Society of Newspaper Editors, the largest association of print newsroom managers in North America. "Give light and the people will find their own way," reads the masthead of Scripps Company newspapers. Indeed, every newspaper mission statement on file with the American Society of Newspaper Editors names advancing self-government as the primary goal of the news organization.[11]

Those outside journalism, too, understand a broader social and moral obligation for journalism. Listen to Pope John Paul II in June 2000: "With its vast and direct influence on public opinion, journalism cannot be guided only by economic forces, profit, and special interest. It must instead be felt as a mission in a certain sense sacred, carried out in the knowledge that the powerful means of communication have been entrusted to you for the good of all."[12]

This democratic mission is not just a modern idea. The concept of creating sovereignty has run through every major statement and argument about the press for centuries, not only from journalists but also from the revolutionaries who fought for democratic principles, both in America and in virtually every developing democracy since.

THE AWARENESS INSTINCT

Historian Mitchell Stephens studied how news has functioned in people's lives throughout history, and he found the remarkable consistency that we talked about at the beginning of this book. "The basic topics with which . . . news accounts have been concerned, and the basic standards by which they evaluate newsworthiness, seem to have varied very little," he writes. "Humans have exchanged a similar mix of news with a consistency throughout history and cultures that makes interest in this news seem inevitable, if not innate."[13] Various scholars have identified the reason for this. People crave news out of basic instinct—what we call the Awareness Instinct. They need to know what is going on over the next hill, to be aware of events beyond their direct experience. Knowledge of the unknown gives them security; it allows them to plan and negotiate their lives. Exchanging this information becomes the basis for creating community, making human connections.

News is that part of communication that keeps us informed of the changing events, issues, and characters in the world outside. In time, historians have suggested, rulers used news to hold their societies together. It provided a sense of unity and shared purpose. It even helped tyrannical rulers control their people by binding them together around a common threat.

History reveals one other important trend. The more democratic the society, the more news and information it tends to have. As societies first became more democratic, they tended toward a kind of pre-journalism. The earliest democracy, ancient Greece, relied on an oral journalism in the Athens marketplace in which "nearly everything important about the public's business was in the open," journalism educator John Hohenberg writes.[14] The Romans developed a daily account of the Roman Senate and political and social life, called the *acta diurna*, transcribed on papyrus and posted in public places.[15] As European societies became more authoritarian and violent in the Middle Ages, communication waned and written news essentially disappeared.

THE BIRTH OF JOURNALISM

As the Middle Ages ended, news came in the form of song and story, in news ballads sung by wandering minstrels.

What we might consider modern journalism began to emerge, in the early seventeenth century, literally out of conversation, especially in public places. In England, the first newspapers grew out of coffeehouses—numerous enough for some to be known for specializing in certain kinds of information. They became so popular that scholars complained that "nothing but news and the affairs of Christendome is discussed."

Later, in America, journalism grew out of pubs, or publick houses. Here, the bar owners, called publicans, hosted spirited conversations about information from travelers who often recorded what they had seen and heard in log books kept at the end of the bar. The first newspapers evolved out of these coffeehouses when enterprising printers began to collect the shipping news, tales from abroad and more gossip, and political arguments from the coffeehouses and to print them on paper.

With the evolution of the first newspapers, English politicians began to talk about a new phenomenon, which they called public opinion. By the beginning of the eighteenth century, journalists/printers began to formulate a theory of free speech and free press. In 1720, two London newspapermen writing, under the pen name "Cato," introduced the idea that truth should be a defense against libel. At the time, English common law had ruled the reverse: not only that any criticism of government was a crime but that "the greater the truth, the greater the libel," since truth did more harm.[16]

Cato's argument had a profound influence in the American colonies, where discontent against the English Crown was growing. A rising young printer named Benjamin Franklin was among those who republished Cato's writings. When a printer named John Peter Zenger went on trial in 1735 for criticizing the royal governor of New York, Cato's ideas became the basis for his defense. People had "a right ... both of exposing and opposing arbitrary power ... by speaking and writing the truth," argued Zenger's lawyer, who was paid by Franklin, among others. The jury acquitted Zenger, shocking the colonial legal community, and the meaning of a free press in America began to take formal shape.

The concept became rooted in the thinking of the Founders, finding its way into the Virginia Declaration of Rights written partly by James Madison, the Massachusetts constitution written by John Adams, and most of the new colonial statements of rights. "No government ought to be without censors & where the press is free, no one ever will," Thomas Jefferson would tell George Washington.[17] Neither Franklin nor Madison thought such language was necessary in the federal Constitution, but two delegates, George Mason of Virginia and Elbridge Gerry of Massachusetts, walked out of the convention, and with men like Thomas Paine and Samuel Adams, they agitated the public to demand a written bill of rights as a condition of approving the Constitution. A free press thus became the people's first claim on their government.

Over the next two hundred years the notion of the press as a bulwark of liberty became embedded in American legal doctrine. "In the First Amendment," the Supreme Court ruled in upholding the *New York Times's* right to publish the secret government documents called the Pentagon Papers in 1971, "the Founding Fathers gave the free press the protection it must have to fulfill its essential role in our democracy. The press was to serve the governed, not the governors."[18] The idea that was affirmed over and over by the courts, First Amendment scholar Lee Bollinger, then president of the University of Michigan, told us at one committee forum, is a simple one: out of a diversity of voices the people are more likely to know the truth and thus be able to self-govern.[19]

Even when journalism was in the hands of the yellow-press mavens at the turn of the twentieth century or the tabloid sheets of the 1920s, building community and promoting democracy remained a core value. At their worst moments, Joseph Pulitzer and William Randolph Hearst appealed to both the sensational tastes and the patriotic impulses of their audiences. Pulitzer used his front page to lure his readers in, but he used his editorial pages to teach them how to be American citizens. On election nights he and Hearst would vie to outdo each other, one renting Madison Square Garden for a free party, the other illuminating campaign results on the side of his newspaper's skyscraper.

Whether one looks back over three hundred years, or even three thousand years, it is impossible to separate news from community and, over time, even more specifically from democratic community.

A FREE PRESS IN AN ELECTRONIC AGE

At the beginning of the twenty-first century, what relevance does this have? Information is so free, the notion of journalism as a homogeneous entity might seem quaint. Perhaps the First Amendment itself is an artifact of a more restricted and elitist era.

Certainly, the notion of the press as a gatekeeper—deciding what information the public should know and what it should not—no longer strictly defines journalism's role. If the *New York Times* decides not to publish something, at least one of countless other websites, talk radio hosts, blogs, and partisans will. We now see examples of this regularly. When *Newsweek* delayed breaking the initial Lewinsky scandal, Matt Drudge went ahead and published. Or when traditional news media ignored Trent Lott's praise of Strom Thurmond's 1948 presidential bid centered on racial segregation, the blogs pounced hard, eventually leading to Lott's stepping down as leader of the Senate Republicans.

The rise of the Internet, the blogosphere, the concepts of "citizen journalism," "we media," and the democratization of broadband, do not mean, as some have suggested, that the idea of applying judgment to the news—of trying to decide what people need and want to know to self-govern—is obsolete. On the contrary, they make the need all the greater.

Technology is transforming citizens from passive consumers of news produced by professionals into active participants who can assemble their own journalism from disparate elements. As people Google for information, graze across a seemingly infinite array of outlets, and read blogs or write them, they are becoming their own editors, researchers, and even correspondents. What was called journalism is only one part of the mix, and its role as intermediary and verifier, like the roles of other civic institutions, is weakening. We are witnessing the rise of a new and more active kind of American citizenship—with new responsibilities that are only beginning to be considered. The journalism of the twenty-first century must recognize this and help arm the public with the tools it needs to perform this more active form of citizenship.

John Seeley Brown, the former director of Xerox PARC, the legendary think tank in Silicon Valley, saw early on that rather than rendering the democratic public service notion of journalism moot, technology has instead changed how journalists fulfill it. "What we need in the new economy and the new communications culture is sense making. We have a desperate need to get some stable points in an increasingly crazy world." This means, Brown explained, that journalists need "the ability to look at things from multiple points of view and the ability to get to the core" of matters.[20] Futurist Paul Saffo described this task as applying journalistic inquiry and judgment "to come to conclusions in uncertain environments."[21]

The new journalist is no longer deciding what the public should know—this was the classic role of gatekeeper. He or she is helping audiences make order out of it. This does not mean simply adding interpretation or analysis to news reporting. The first task of the new journalist/sense maker, rather, is to verify what information is reliable and then order it so people can grasp it efficiently.

In an era when anyone can be a reporter or commentator on the Web, the journalist becomes "a forum leader," or a mediator rather than simply a teacher or lecturer, Seeley Brown suggested.[22] The audience becomes not consumers but "pro-sumers," a hybrid of consumer and producer.

Some advocates of "we media" believe that no one controls information anymore, thus the need for journalists per se may become obsolete. Since citizens can communicate with each other more easily, they will be closer to real truth and more accurate information. No doubt they can communicate more easily. Millions read blogs, although the data suggest that those numbers may already be stabilizing. But one must also ask a series of questions. Do these citizens have the time, the motivation, and the skills this requires? If not, then do those who try to cover the news professionally have the skills and the will to help citizens gain these tools?

Whether or not the end result is more verified and truthful information will depend on the degree of commitment to those goals that the "we media" culture develops. The driving force of the Age of Enlightenment, out of which grew the notion of individual worth and a public press, was the search for truthful information. This information freed the public from control by the kind of centralized dictatorial or dogmatic power we see developing in our society today. If the journalism of verification is to survive in the new Information Age, then it must become a force in empowering citizens to shape their own communities based on verified information.

It is an epochal transformation, at least as momentous as the invention of the telegraph or the television. The former created the capacity for people divided by great distance to learn things at the same time; the latter added the ability for people to see the news for themselves.

Today, people go from passive consumers to proactive assemblers of their own journalism and views of the world. Among other things, people have the ability to interact with the news itself as well as the professionals delivering it. Some use the Web to present their own accounts of events, complete with photographs, video, or audio. Some contact the journalists covering a story through e-mail or feedback forms to either correct the record or offer new facts. And some participate in discussions about the process that brought forth the news, building an almost immediate record of press criticism and scrutiny.

If citizens have a problem with the news, they know whom to e-mail to correct the record (papers increasingly print e-mail addresses and websites put authors' names in hypertext, making it simple to contact writers, editors, and publishers). Audiences expect their new facts to become part of the record. The dialogue with the audience is thus an integral part of the story as it evolves.

This kind of high-tech interaction is a journalism that resembles conversation again, much like the original journalism that occurred in the publick houses and coffeehouses four hundred years ago. Seen in this light, journalism's function is not fundamentally changed by the digital age. The techniques may be different, but the underlying principles are the same. The journalist is first engaged in verification.

How does this role—whether offered by an idealist writer from the Age of Enlightenment or a theoretician from Silicon Valley—really work in practice? How does the free press actually work as a bulwark of liberty? Does it work at all?

THE JOURNALIST'S THEORY OF DEMOCRACY

Journalists don't usually consider these questions explicitly. It may seem slightly ridiculous to ask: what is the theory of democracy that drives your TV news operation or your newspaper? We have the freest press imaginable, and yet over the last thirty years the number of Americans who can even name their congressman is often as low as three out of ten.[23] Fewer than half of Americans vote—even in presidential elections—far fewer than in countries without a First Amendment.[24] Most people get their news from local television, a medium that largely ignores the process of governing.[25] Only 42 percent said they read a daily newspaper the day before, and people know no more about the outside world than they did fifty years ago.[26] Maybe, when you look hard, the idea that the press provides the information necessary for people to self-govern is an illusion. Maybe people don't care. Maybe we don't, in reality, actually self-govern at all. The government operates, and the rest of us are largely bystanders.

This argument flared briefly in the 1920s in a debate of ideas between journalist Walter Lippmann and philosopher John Dewey. It was a time of pessimism about democracy. Democratic governments in

Germany and Italy had collapsed. The Bolshevik revolution loomed over the West. There was a growing fear that police states were employing new technology and the new science of propaganda to control public will.

Lippmann, already one of the nation's most famous journalists, argued in a best-selling book called *Public Opinion* that democracy was fundamentally flawed. People, he said, mostly know the world only indirectly, through "pictures they make up in their heads." And they receive these mental pictures largely through the media. The problem, Lippmann argued, is that the pictures people have in their heads are hopelessly distorted and incomplete, marred by the irredeemable weaknesses of the press. Just as bad, the public's ability to comprehend the truth even if it happened to come across it was undermined by human bias, stereotype, inattentiveness, and ignorance. In the end, Lippmann thought citizens are like theatergoers who "arrive in the middle of the third act and leave before the last curtain, staying just long enough to decide who is the hero and who is the villain."[27]

Public Opinion was an enormous success and gave birth, according to many, to the modern study of communication.[28] It also deeply moved the nation's most famous philosopher, Columbia professor John Dewey. Reviewing *Public Opinion* in Lippmann's own magazine, *The New Republic*, Dewey called Lippmann's analysis about the limits of human perception "the most effective indictment of democracy... ever penned," and he acknowledged that Lippmann had diagnosed some serious weaknesses about the press and the public.[29]

But Dewey, who later expanded his critique in his own book, *The Public and Its Problems*, said Lippmann's definition of democracy was fundamentally flawed. The goal of democracy, Dewey said, was not to manage public affairs efficiently. It was to allow people to develop to their fullest potential. Democracy, in other words, was the end, not the means. It was true that the public could only be an "umpire of last resort" over government, usually just setting the broad outlines of debate. That, however, was all the Founders ever intended, Dewey argued, for democratic life encompassed so much more than efficient government. Its real purpose was human freedom. The solution to democracy's problems was not to give up on it, but to try to improve the skills of the press and the education of the public.

Dewey sensed something easier to see today, after the fall of fascism and communism in the twentieth century. He believed that if people were allowed to communicate freely with each other, democracy was the natural outgrowth of the human interaction. It was not a stratagem for making government better.

Eighty years later the debate is still relevant—and unresolved. The increasingly interactive relationship between journalist and citizen has raised questions in newsrooms about whether journalists still have a role as agenda setters—trying to signal to the audience what news is important, the top stories. While that role is changing, it seems clear to us it does not disappear. Those who cover the news still have to decide how to deploy resources, which stories to cover, which to cover at length, and which to consider something that can be handled in brief, and a thousand more decisions every day.

In making those choices, journalists are also engaged in something larger than it might seem on the surface. Whenever editors lay out a page or website, or people decide what angle or element of an event or issue to emphasize and explore, they are guessing at what readers want or need to know. However unconscious, as they do so they are operating by some theory of democracy—some theory of what drives politics, citizenship, and how people make judgments. Our purpose here is to lay out a theory that we think lies implicit, and often unrecognized, in the journalism that serves us best as citizens.

A number of critics argue that Lippmann's view dominates too much of how journalists operate today.[30] Studies show that newspapers and TV have aimed their coverage at elite or other more narrow demographics, ignoring much of the citizenry.[31] Policy and ideas are ignored or presented as sport, or are couched in the context of how a certain policy position is calculated to gain someone power over a rival.[32] Even the practice of reporters' interviewing voters in political campaigns, reporters admit, is a vanishing art. We have developed "a journalism that justifies itself in the public's name but in which the public plays no role, except as an audience," writes James Carey.[33] Citizens have become an abstraction, something the press talks about but not to.

No doubt the rise of citizen media and the empowering of consumers are helping address this problem. The public is forcing itself into the conversation. The journalists with their own political agendas are more likely to be quickly exposed. The journalists whose attempts at verifying the news are scant are more likely to be found out. The journalists who claim to know what citizens care about may quickly find out they are wrong.

Yet obviously this does not solve the problem for journalists of discerning what it is citizens want and what they need. It calls instead for an even clearer theory of democracy and citizenship for the press.

As we examine the new interactive relationship between journalists and citizens, in the websites, blogs, community newspapers, and public-access television, we see a more complicated and fluid vision of the public than the traditional debates usually offer. We think this vision holds a key to how both citizens and many journalists really operate.

THE THEORY OF THE INTERLOCKING PUBLIC

Dave Burgin, who edited newspapers from Florida to California, epitomized this vision in the way he taught scores of journalists to lay out pages. Imagine, he would say, that no more than roughly 15 percent of your readers would want to read any one story on the page. Your job was to make sure each page had a sufficient variety of stories that every member of the audience would want to read one of them.[34]

Implicit in Burgin's theory of a diverse page is the idea that everyone is interested and even expert in something. The notion that people are simply ignorant, or that other people are interested in everything, is a myth. As we listened to journalists and citizens talk, we realized this is a more realistic description of how people interact with the news to form a public. We call this the Theory of the Interlocking Public.

For the sake of argument let's say there are three broad levels of public engagement on every issue, each with even subtler gradations. There is an involved public, with a personal stake in an issue and a strong understanding. There is an interested public, with no direct role in the issue but that is affected and responds with some firsthand experience. And there is an uninterested public, which pays little attention and will join, if at all, after the contours of the discourse have been laid out by others. In the interlocking public, we are all members of all three groups, depending on the issue.

An autoworker in suburban Detroit, for instance, may care little about agriculture policy or foreign affairs, and may only sporadically buy a newspaper or watch TV news. But he will have lived through many collective bargaining debates and know a good deal about corporate bureaucracy and workplace safety. He may have kids in local schools and friends on welfare, and know how pollution has affected the rivers where he fishes. To these and all other concerns he brings a range of knowledge and experience. On some matters he is the involved public; on others, the interested; and on still others, remote, unknowledgeable, and unengaged.

A partner in a Washington law firm will similarly defy generalization. She is a grandmother, avid gardener, and news junkie who looks from a distance like a classic member of the involved "elite." A leading expert on constitutional law who is quoted often in the press, she is also fearful of technology and bored by and ignorant of investing and business. Her children grown, she no longer pays attention to news about local schools or even local government.

Or imagine a housewife in California with a high school education who considers her husband's career her own. Her volunteer work at children's schools gives her keen ideas about why the local paper is wrong in its education coverage, and she has an intuitive sense from her own life about people.

These sketches are obviously made up, but they bring the complex notion of the public down to earth. The sheer magnitude and diversity of the people is its strength. The involved expert on one issue is the ignorant and unconcerned member of the public on another. The three groups—which themselves are only crude generalizations—work as a check on one another so that no debate becomes merely a fevered exchange between active interest groups. What's more, this mix of publics is usually much wiser than the involved public alone.

Listen to some journalists talk about the audience they imagine as they work and you will hear a sense of the interlocking public. Byron Calame, public editor of the *New York Times*, heard it when he interviewed colleagues. "Several editors, including Suzanne Daley, who just became national editor after a stint as education editor, noted that they must keep two kinds of readers in mind. 'One is an expert on whatever subject we are writing about, someone who will read this story no matter what, but who will be highly judgmental. . . . The other is your basically curious person, but without a lot of time, who is, in my mind, the real challenge. He or she might read the story. But it has to hook them. The game in my head is: Okay, how do we write this so that it is accurate and has weight, but is still fun to read for someone who really doesn't care much about say, college dorms or tutoring?'"[35]

Looked at this way, the public is far more able than Lippmann dreamed, and the press does not have as daunting a job of delivering "truth" to a passive public as he imagined. The job of the news media, as we will discuss more in the next chapter, is to give this more complex and dynamic public what it needs to sort out the truth for itself over time.

Yet this more complex understanding of the public carries with it an indictment of the modern press as well. A journalism that focuses on the expert elite—the special interests—may be in part responsible for public disillusionment. Such a press does not reflect the world as most people live and experience it. Political coverage that focuses on tactical considerations for the political junkie and leaves the merely interested and the uninterested behind is failing in the responsibilities of journalism. A journalism in which every story is aimed at the largest possible audience—all O.J. all the time—actually leaves most of the audience behind.

In short, this more pluralistic vision of the interlocking public suggests that the requirements of the old press, of serving the interests of the widest community possible, remain as strong as ever. At the same time, trends developing in the first decade of this century make it clear that recognizing the needs of the more complex interlocking public will be more difficult than ever. The conservative momentum evident in the first two national elections of the twenty-first century have been seen by many analysts to be fueled by a large body of citizens marginalized by trends of previous decades that historian Anatol Lieven concluded left them "profoundly alienated, and yearning for a 'return' to an idealized version of the country of their youth, or possibly by now their parents' youth."[36]

The failure of so many Americans to "even understand" the causes of their alienation suggests that at least part of the problem has been the way the press covered these issues as they developed and the political strategies and rhetoric they inspired that favored extreme positions. Too often in coverage of the great social issues of the latter half of the twentieth century–civil rights, the sexual revolutions, anti–Vietnam War sentiment, immigration, and globalization–the press employed labels and stereotypes and depended on spokespeople for the extremes. These stereotypes and labels became the lingua franca of the public debate and prevented the press from stopping to ask to what extent these positions were widely held, or even what they meant. If journalists work for citizens of a democratic society, then the responsibility of journalism is to facilitate the understanding that allows the sort of compromise on which governance of a complex interlocking public depends.

The Theory of the Interlocking Public also casts a shadow over the concept of niche marketing in journalism. Many of the niches created by the new information delivery platforms are much harder to define than the artificial categories identified by marketing research may imply. Television aimed at women eighteen to thirty four, or Generation X, or soccer moms, or football fans is likely to alienate larger numbers of the very group at which it is aimed. People are simply more complex than the categories and stereotypes we create for them.

THE NEW CHALLENGE

If the Theory of the Interlocking Public reinforces the notion that journalism should enhance democratic freedom, the profession may face its greatest threat yet at the beginning of the twenty-first century. We are seeing for the first time the rise of a market-based journalism increasingly divorced from the idea of civic responsibility.

Consider modern media baron Rupert Murdoch's comment when his company won television rights in Singapore:

Singapore is not liberal, but it's clean and free of drug addicts. Not so long ago it was an impoverished, exploited colony with famines, diseases, and other problems. Now people find themselves in three-room apartments with jobs and clean streets. Material incentives create business and the free market economy. If politicians try it the other way around with democracy, the Russian model is the result. Ninety percent of the Chinese are interested more in a better material life than in the right to vote.[37]

The notion of a modern publisher's advocating capitalism without democracy has no meaningful precedent in American journalism history. Yet there is a growing list of other examples of ownership subordinating journalism to other commercial interests. The day Time Inc. was acquired by Internet service provider America Online, Time Warner chairman Gerald Levin exulted that, "This really completes the digital transformation of Time Warner. . . . These two companies are a natural fit."[38] The fact that one company had a journalistic mission and the other had none, or that journalists at *Time*, CNN, *Fortune*, or the rest might now have conflicting loyalties when trying to cover the Internet, cable, and a host of other areas seemed incidental. Steve Case, the CEO from America Online who acquired Time Warner, enumerated for the public the great benefits it would receive from the newly merged companies. Although the new company would contain several of the nation's most powerful journalism organizations, he only mentioned entertainment, online shopping, and person-to-person communication. Six years later, Case regarded the AOL–Time merger as a failure and said in late 2005 that the "one company" strategy never got off the ground.

"Each division 'did its own thing,'" Case wrote in a *Washington Post* op-ed. "While that staved off turf wars, it did nothing to drive innovation." Case argued for the company to split into four separate entities: Time Warner Cable, Time Warner Entertainment, Time Inc., and AOL.

Other mergers at the same time evoked similar conflicts. Shortly after acquiring ABC News, Disney CEO Michael Eisner said he didn't think it appropriate that "Disney cover Disney."[39] In other words, in the mind of the man who runs the conglomerate in which ABC News is embedded, the news organization had not only lost its distinctive identity but now has to struggle with whether and how it can cover the "Wonderful World of Disney," a $23 billion corporation whose global operations range from sports teams and theme parks to cable channels and Internet portals.[40]

The Disney acquisition also failed from an economic standpoint, at least for the journalistic enterprises inside ABC. Not long before the acquisition from Capital Cities, then ABC News president Roone Arledge told his staff that ABC News programs were No. 1 in every time slot in which they competed—morning, evening news, Sunday morning, and even its prime-time news magazine programs.[41] Under Disney's stewardship, along with Arledge's forced retirement as a manager difficult to control,[42] ABC saw virtually all of its news programs falter, a decline that may have culminated in the effort by Disney executives in 2002 to replace *Nightline* with the *David Letterman Show* from CBS. ABC eventually succeeded in driving Ted Koppel and his executive producer Tom Bettag out of the network late in 2005.

Three key forces are causing this shift away from journalism connected to citizen building. The first is the nature of the new technology. The Internet has begun to disassociate journalism from geography and therefore from community as we know it in a political or civic sense. It is easier to see how to serve the Web's commerce- and interest-based communities than its political community.[43] At the same time, technology offers the potential for citizens not connected through geography to interact directly with each other—a prospect that presents possibilities and challenges, which we will discuss later in the book.

The second major factor is conglomeration. Critics have long railed against the rise of news chains—companies that own outlets across different communities. A. J. Liebling, *The New Yorker* press critic, complained about it in the 1940s. We've also seen the rise of companies that owned across different mediums before. The Tribune Company in Chicago still owns radio, TV, and newspapers in the same city—something the federal government would eventually outlaw in the middle of the twentieth century and is looking to relax again. Even with publicly owned chains, however, these outlets were clearly news companies. The chief criticism against them was mediocrity or homogeneity. Gannett owned some ninety newspapers, but it was a newspaper company, led by newsmen who articulated company-wide news values, and even were able to create a set of Principles of Ethical Conduct for its newspaper division. The one exception was in the three traditional broadcast TV networks, where companies produced entertainment as well as news. For most of their history, however, network news divisions existed to meet public-interest requirements demanded by the government in exchange for use of the public airwaves. Profit making is a more recent requirement.

As the new century began, this tradition of news companies' owning journalism was breaking down. News was becoming a smaller component inside global conglomerates. ABC News represented less than 2 percent of the profits at Disney. News once accounted for most of the revenue of Time Inc., but it was just a fraction of that inside AOL-Time. NBC News provided less than 2 percent of the profits of General Electric.[44]

Even newer major players in the news business were not news gatherers at all, but sources like Google News and Yahoo! News, which largely aggregated the work other people produced. Google's news service, launched in 2002, did this compiling and prioritizing without human editors. The work was done by computer algorithms.

The managers of the news subsidiaries will fight and protest for their independence, but history suggests that the shift will likely alter the nature of their journalism. "We look at the 1930s and we see steel and chemical industries starting to buy up the journalism of Europe," says James Carey. That altered how the press of Europe saw the rise of fascism. Militarism was good business. Today, he says, American journalism is beginning to be "bought up by the entertainment business—and e-commerce. Entertainment and e-commerce are today what the steel and chemical industries were in the 1930s."[45]

The notion of freedom of the press is rooted in independence. Only a press free of government censors could tell the truth. In a modern context, that freedom was expanded to mean independence from other institutions as well—parties, advertisers, business, and more. The conglomeration of the news business threatens the survival of the press as an independent institution as journalism becomes a subsidiary inside large corporations more fundamentally grounded in other business purposes.

This conglomeration and the idea behind much corporate synergy in communications—that journalism is simply content, or all media are indistinguishable—raise another prospect. The First Amendment ceases to imply a public trust held in the name of a wider community. Instead it lays claim to special rights for an industry akin to the antitrust exemption for baseball. In this world, the First Amendment becomes a property right establishing ground rules for free economic competition, not free speech. This is a fundamental and epic change with enormous implications for democratic society. As Michael Sandel, professor of philosophy at Harvard University, has said, "There should be a nagging voice in us all asking: Is democracy going to be bought up too?"[46]

The third factor driving the new market journalism is globalization. As companies, especially communication companies, become corporations without borders, the notion of citizenship and traditional community becomes in a commercial sense obsolete.

Globalization changes the content these companies produce. It is one thing when Hollywood makes more action movies now because pyrotechnics require no translation and make more money in foreign sales. It is another to consider the implications for journalism of news decisions based on a similarly simplified set of cultural cues. The first reaction to globalization was to favor stories with iconic news values—about celebrities, disaster, and tragedy—that play across borders both regional and national. These included the murder trial of O. J. Simpson, the death of Princess Diana, or the plane crash of John F. Kennedy Jr.

But September 11 proved that globalization does not occur in a vacuum. The hijacked planes crashing into the World Trade Center introduced a steady diet of hard news stories of a different nature that transcended national borders: the train bombings in Madrid and London, the widespread protests over cartoons of Prophet Muhammad, and violence throughout the Middle East. While these were now distributed through a global media system, the coverage often had a strongly nationalist flavor. The coverage on Fox and CNN of these events is hardly the same as on Al Jazeera.

The question is not whether this new global media system will lose its national character. Rather, the question is to what extent can citizens rely on this new subsidiary press inside global conglomerates to monitor the powerful interests in society? Can we rely on a few large companies to sponsor that monitoring—even when it is not in their own corporate interests? In the end, the question is this: can journalism sustain in the twenty-first century the purpose that forged it in the three and a half centuries that came before? Doing so begins with identifying what the purpose is. The next step is understanding the principles that allow those who gather the news to sustain that purpose on behalf of the rest of us.

ENDNOTES

1. Anna Semborska, interview by Dante Chinni, January 2000.
2. Thomas Rosenstiel, "TV, VCR's, Fan Fire of Revolution: Technology Served the Cause of Liberation in East Europe," *Los Angeles Times*, January 18, 1990, A1.
3. Maxwell King, at founding meeting of Committee of Concerned Journalists (CCJ), Chicago, June 21, 1997.
4. Tom Brokaw, interview by William Damon, Howard Gardner, and Mihaly Csikszentmihalyi; unpublished interviews conducted for the book *Good Work: When Excellence and Ethics Meet* (New York: Basic Books, 2001).
5. Yuen Ying Chan, interview by William Damon, Howard Gardner, and Mihaly Csikszentmihalyi, ibid.
6. James Carey, *James Carey: A Critical Reader*, ed. Eve Stryker Munson and Catherine A. Warren (Minneapolis and London: University of Minnesota Press, 1997), 235.
7. Jack Fuller, at CCJ Forum, Chicago, November 6, 1997.
8. Omar Wasow, at CCJ Forum, Ann Arbor, MI, February 2, 1998.
9. CCJ and the Pew Research Center for the People and the Press, "Striking the Balance: Audience Interests, Business Pressures and Journalists' Values," March 1999, 79; available at www.journalism.org.
10. William Damon and Howard Gardner, "Reporting the News in an Age of Accelerating Power and Pressure: The Private Quest to Preserve the Public Trust," academic paper, November 6, 1997, 10.
11. In total, all twelve of the ethics codes on file with the American Society of Newspaper Editors that mention purpose describe this as journalism's primary mission. Four of the twenty-four that don't mention purpose include it inside the texts of their ethics codes.
12. Associated Press, report of Pope John Paul II's declaration of the Vatican's Holy Year Day for Journalists, by Ellen Knickmeyer, June 4, 2000; available at Associated Press Worldstream, via LexisNexis.
13. Mitchell Stephens, *History of News* (Fort Worth, TX: Harcourt Brace College Publishers, 1996), 27.
14. John Hohenberg, *Free Press, Free People: The Best Cause* (New York: Free Press, 1973), 2.
15. Stephens, *History of News*, 53–59. The creation of this government-sponsored daily newspaper was the first formal act of Julius Caesar on becoming consul of Rome, 60 B.C.
16. Hohenberg, *Free Press*, 38. The writers were John Trenchard and William Gordon.

17. Thomas Jefferson, letter to George Washington, September 9, 1792. Retrieved from www.about.com.

18. *New York Times Co. v. United States*, 439 U.S. 713 (1971).

19. Lee Bollinger, at CCJ Forum, Ann Arbor, MI, February 2, 1998.

20. John Seeley Brown, expressed to author Rosenstiel at a meeting to discuss the future of journalism curriculum, sponsored by Columbia University Graduate School of Journalism, Menlo Park, CA, June 15–16, 2000.

21. Paul Saffo, expressed to author Rosenstiel, same meeting.

22. Brown, expressed to author Rosenstiel, same meeting.

23. CBS News/New York Times poll (October 1994), "Do you happen to know the name of the representative in Congress from your district? (If yes, ask:) What is your representative's name?" Data provided by the Roper Center for Public Opinion Research.

24. This datum refers to the 1996 presidential election. In the 1998 off-year congressional races, only 36 percent voted.

25. The idea that most people get their news from local television is drawn from Nielsen Media Research data; the idea that local television ignores government coverage is drawn from "Project for Excellence in Journalism Local TV Project," in *Columbia Journalism Review*, January 1999, November 1999, November 2000; available at www.journalism.org.

26. The percentage of people who read newspapers is from Pew Research Center for the People and the Press's biennial survey of media consumption, June 2004. The level of knowledge about public life is inferred from work done by Michael Delli Carpini and Scott Keeter for their article "Stability and Change in the U.S. Public's Knowledge of Politics," in *Public Opinion Quarterly*, Winter 1991, 583–612.

27. Walter Lippmann, *The Essential Lippmann*, ed. Clinton Rossiter and James Lare (New York: Random House, 1963), 108.

28. Carey, *A Critical Reader*, 22.

29. John Dewey, review of *Public Opinion* by Walter Lippmann, *The New Republic*, 3 (May 1922), 286.

30. Two authors have notably made this argument: Carey in *A Critical Reader*, and Christopher Lasch in *The Revolt of the Elites and the Betrayal of Democracy* (New York/London: W. W. Norton, 1995).

31. Lou Urenick, "Newspapers Arrive at Economic Crossroads," *Nieman Reports*, special issue (Summer 1999), 3–20.

32. Several researchers have found this tendency in political coverage over the years. Some recent examples include Joseph N. Cappella and Kathleen Hall Jamieson in *Spiral of Cynicism: The Press and the Public Good*, Thomas E. Patterson in *Out of Order: How the Decline of the Political Parties and the Growing Power of the News Media Undermine the American Way of Electing Presidents*, and the Project for Excellence in Journalism in "In the Public Interest: A Content Study of Early Press Coverage of the 2000 Presidential Campaign," February 2, 2000; available at www.journalism.org.

33. Carey, *A Critical Reader*, 247.

34. David Burgin was Rosenstiel's editor in 1980 and 1982 at the *Peninsula Times*

Tribune in Palo Alto, CA, where he taught the author this theory of laying out newspaper pages.

35. Byron Calame, "Turning the Tables: What the Times News Staff Thinks of You," *New York Times*, October 9, 2005; available at www.nytimes.com.
36. Anatol Lieven, "Taking Back America," *London Review of Books*, 26 (December 2, 2004).
37. Ralf Dahrendorf, *After 1989: Morals Revolution and Civil Society* (London: Macmillan, in association with St. Antony's College, Oxford, 1997), 98.
38. Seth Sutel, "AOL to Buy Time Warner for About $166 Billion," January 10, 2000; available at Associated Press online, via LexisNexis.
39. Rico Gagliano, "Lockout Blackout," *L.A. Weekly*, December 18, 1998; available at http://home.pacbell.net/one-11/Nabet.html.
40. Walt Disney Company, 1999 Annual Report. Revenues are based on fiscal year 1999.
41. Co-author Rosenstiel was on the conference call during which Arledge made this statement in January 2002. Rosenstiel was researching his book *Strange Bedfellows*.
42. Peter Johnson, "Pioneering TV Executive Roone Arledge Dies," *USA Today*, December 6, 2002.
43. After struggling with the issue of Internet sales taxes for years, Congress agreed on a three-year ban on Internet access taxes. This agreement, reached in 2004, also ensured that products bought online would neither be taxed by more than one state nor be taxed differently from other goods in the state of purchase. Both the Senate and the House are looking to make the ban permanent. Although online shoppers are required to pay tax, many sites don't add them to the purchase total. This system and the slow legislative progress have seriously eroded local revenue used to help support roads, fire departments, schools, government, and the like.
44. Thomas Friedman, "Corporations on Steroids," *New York Times*, February 4, 2000, A29; available at www.nytimes.com.
45. Profit estimates for ABC and NBC news are from Marc Gunther, "The Transformation of Network News: How Profitability Has Moved Networks Out of Hard News," *Nieman Reports*, special issue (Summer 1999), 28–29. In 1998, ABC News earned a pretax profit of $55 million while Disney earned $4 billion. NBC News earned a pretax profit of $200 million in 1998 while General Electric earned $13.5 billion.
46. Carey made this remark at a CCJ steering committee meeting in Washington, DC, June 19, 2000.

2

Truth: The First
and Most
Confusing
Principle

A few days after John F. Kennedy was murdered, the man who succeeded him as president, Lyndon Johnson, sent for the secretary of defense. Johnson wanted to know what was really going on 10,000 miles across the globe, in the tiny country called Vietnam. Johnson didn't trust what he'd been told as vice president. He wanted his own information. So Defense Secretary Robert McNamara flew to Saigon and spent three days talking to all the generals and touring the various battle zones.

On his way back, McNamara gave a press conference at Tan Son Nhut Airport, and reported that he was greatly encouraged. Progress was noteworthy. South Vietnamese forces were taking an ever-greater role. Viet Cong casualties were increasing. When he landed at Andrews Air Force Base the next day, he gave another press conference to say much the same thing. Then he took a helicopter to the White House lawn to report to Johnson personally, and the world heard nothing more about the secretary's visit or his report to President Johnson.

Eight years later, the *New York Times* and the *Washington Post* published a secret government-written history about what the government leaders really knew and thought about the Vietnam War. Buried inside these documents, which came to be called the Pentagon Papers, was the substance of what McNamara in fact had reported to the president. Things were going to hell in Vietnam. Viet Cong reinforcements were outpacing Viet Cong casualties. More American troops were going to be needed, not fewer. All in all, it was a complete repudiation of everything he had said in his two public press conferences. "What might have happened," Benjamin C. Bradlee, the former executive editor of the *Washington Post*, would wonder two decades later, "had the truth emerged in 1963 instead of 1971. . . ."[1]

We use the words every day—*truth* and *lies*, *accurate* and *false*—and we think they convey something meaningful. McNamara *lied* during his press conferences. The Pentagon Papers revealed the *truth* of what he thought and reported to Johnson. The story even involves layers of truth and falsity. The press reported accurately what McNamara said in his press conferences, but did not get at the truth of what he knew.

Over the last three hundred years, news professionals have developed a loose set of principles and values to fulfill the function of providing news—the indirect knowledge by which people come to form their opinions about the world. Foremost among these principles is this:

Journalism's first obligation is to the truth.

On this there is absolute unanimity and also utter confusion: everyone agrees journalists must tell the truth, yet people are befuddled about what "the truth" means.

When asked what values they consider paramount, 100 percent of journalists interviewed for a survey by the Pew Research Center for the People and the Press and the Committee of Concerned Journalists answered "getting the facts right."[2]

In long interviews with our university research partners, journalists from both old and new media similarly volunteered "truth" overwhelmingly as a primary mission.[3] In forums, even ideological journalists gave the same answer. "What we're saying is you cannot be objective because you're going to go in with certain biases," said Patty Calhoun, the editor of the alternative weekly paper *Westword*. "But you can certainly pursue accuracy and fairness and the truth, and that pursuit continues."[4]

The desire that information be truthful is elemental. Since news is the material that people use to learn and think about the world beyond themselves, the most important quality is that it be usable and reliable. Will it rain tomorrow? Is there a traffic jam ahead? Did my team win? What did the president say? Truthfulness creates, in effect, the sense of security that grows from awareness and is at the essence of news.

This basic desire for truthfulness is so powerful, the evidence suggests it is innate. "In the beginning was the Word" is the opening line of the Gospel of St. John in the New Testament. The earliest journalists—messengers in preliterate societies—were expected to recall matters accurately and reliably, partly out of need. Often the news these messengers carried was a matter of survival. The chiefs needed accurate word about whether the tribe on the other side of the hill might attack.

It is interesting that oppressive societies tend to belittle literal definitions of truthfulness and accuracy, just as postmodernists do today, though for different reasons. In the Middle Ages, for instance, monks held that there was actually a hierarchy of truth. At the highest level were messages that told us about the fate of the universe, such as whether heaven existed. Next came moral truth, which taught us how to live. This was followed by allegorical truth, which exclaimed the moral of stories. Finally, at the bottom, the least important, was the literal truth, which the theorists said was usually empty of meaning and irrelevant. As one fourteenth-century manual explained, using logic similar to what we might hear today from a postmodern scholar or a Hollywood producer, "Whether it is truth of history or fiction doesn't matter, because the example is not supplied for its own sake but for its signification."[5]

Modern political operatives are enamored of similar notions and often preach the idea that in public life perception is reality. The operatives around Richard Nixon in 1968 extolled such notions to aggrandize their role in that election.[6]

The tools for such information management arguably are even greater today. The technology that creates the idea of citizen journalism also empowers political powers to control their image to the public. Consider what an anonymous advisor to George Bush told

Ron Suskind for his report in *The New York Times Magazine* about how the government tries to control information in the new world: "[Journalists] are in what we call the reality-based community.... That's not the way the world really works anymore.... When we act, we create our own reality. While you are studying that reality ... we'll act again, creating other new realities, which you can study too."[7]

This is nothing new. The goal of the medieval thinkers, as it is for political operatives today, was not enlightenment so much as control. They didn't want literal facts to get in the way of political or religious orthodoxy. An accurate understanding of the day threatened that control—just as today, it is a weapon against oppression and manipulation.

As the modern press began to form with the birth of democratic theory, the promise of being truthful and accurate quickly became a powerful part of even the earliest marketing of journalism. The first identifiable regular newspaper in England proposed to rely "on the best and most certain intelligence." The editor of the first paper in France, though his enterprise was government owned, promised in his maiden issue, "In one thing I will yield to nobody—I mean in my endeavor to get at the truth." Similar promises to accuracy are found in the earliest papers in America, Germany, Spain, and elsewhere.[8]

The earliest colonial journalism was a strange mix of essay and fact. The information about shipping and cargoes was accurate. The political vitriol was less so, yet it was also obviously more opinion or speech than strict information. Even the worst scandalmonger of the age, James Callender, who made his reputation with sex exposés of Alexander Hamilton and Thomas Jefferson, did not make his stories up, historians have concluded, but trafficked in facts mixed with rumor.[9]

As it disentangled itself from political control in the nineteenth century, journalism sought its first mass audience in part by relying on sensational crime, scandal, thrill seeking, and celebrity worship, but also by writing the news in plain language for regular people. The move away from party affiliation began with the *New York Sun* in the 1830s, and journalism gained new heights of popularity and sensation at the end of the century. These were the years of William Randolph Hearst and Joseph Pulitzer, and "yellow journalism." Yet even the Lords of the Yellow Press sought to assure readers that they could believe what they read, even if the pledge was not always honored. Hearst's *Journal*, which was guilty more of sensationalism than of invention, claimed it was the most truthful paper in town. Pulitzer's *World* operated under the motto "Accuracy, Accuracy, Accuracy" and was more reliable than is usually credited.[10]

It was to assure his readers they could believe what they read that, in 1913, at the *New York World*, Pulitzer created a Bureau of Accuracy and Fair Play. In a 1984 article in the *Columbia Journalism Review*, Cassandra Tate described how the *World*'s first ombudsman noticed a pattern in the newspaper's reporting on shipwrecks: each such story featured a cat that had survived. When the ombudsman asked the reporter about this curious coincidence, he was told:

> One of those wrecked ships had a cat, and the crew went back to save it. I made the cat a feature of my story, while the other reporters failed to mention the cat, and were called down by their city editors for being beaten. The next time there was a shipwreck, there was no cat but the other ship news reporters did not wish to take a chance, and put the cat in. I wrote the report, leaving out the cat, and then I was severely chided for being beaten. Now when there is a shipwreck all of us always put in the cat.[11]

The irony, of course, is that the embellishments were all put there to create a sense of realism.

By the beginning of the twentieth century, journalists were beginning to realize that realism and reality—or accuracy and truth—were not so easily equated. In 1920, Walter Lippmann used the terms *truth* and *news* interchangeably in "Liberty and the News." But in 1922, in *Public Opinion*, he wrote: "News and truth are not the same thing.... The function of news is to signalize an event," or make people aware of it. "The function of truth is to bring to light the hidden facts, to set them into relation with each other, and make a picture of reality upon which men can act."[12] By 1938, journalism textbooks were beginning to question how truthful the news could really be.[13]

Over the next fifty years, after decades of debate and argument, sometimes by political ideology and sometimes by postmodern deconstructionist academics, we came to the point where some deny that anyone can put facts into a meaningful context to report the truth about them. An epistemological skepticism has pervaded every aspect of our intellectual life, from art, literature, law, and physics to history. Columbia University historian Simon Schama has suggested that "the certainty of an ultimately observable, empirically verifiable truth" is dead.[14]

Truth, it seems, is too complicated for us to pursue. Or perhaps it doesn't even exist, since we are all subjective individuals. These are interesting arguments, maybe, on some philosophical level, even valid. But where does that leave journalism? Is the word *truth* now something adequate for everyday conversation but one that doesn't hold up to real scrutiny?

Clearly, there are levels. "The journalist at the *New York Times* told us the other day that the New York Giants lost a football game by a score of 20–8," journalist and press critic Richard Harwood told us at one committee forum. "Now that was a small piece of truth. But the story of why the Giants lost can be told in a hundred different ways— each story being written through a different lens that is fogged over by stereotypes and personal predilections."[15]

So what does a journalist's obligation to the truth mean? The usual efforts to answer this question, at seminars or in philosophical tracts, end up in a muddle. One reason is that the conversation is usually not grounded in the real world. Philosophical discussions of whether "truth" really exists founder in semantics.

Another reason is that journalists themselves have never been very clear about what they mean by truthfulness. Journalism by nature is reactive and practical rather than philosophical and introspective. The serious literature by journalists thinking through such issues is not rich, and what little there is, most journalists have not read. Theories of journalism are left to the academy, and many newspeople have historically devalued journalism education, arguing that the only place to learn is through osmosis on the job. As even highly respected TV journalist Ted Koppel once said, "Journalism schools are an absolute and total waste of time."[16]

The conventional explanations by journalists about how they get at the truth tend to be quick responses drawn from interviews or speeches or, worse, from marketing slogans, and they often rely on crude metaphors. The press is "a mirror" on society, says David Bartlett, former president of the Radio and Television News Directors Association. Journalism is "a reflection of the passions of the day," says Tom Brokaw. News is whatever is "most newsworthy on a given day," says a CNN producer.[17] These explanations make journalists seem passive—mere recorders of events rather than selectors or editors.[18] It's as if they think truth is something that rises up by itself, like bread dough. Rather than defend our techniques and methods for finding truth, journalists have tended to deny that they exist.

Whether it is secrecy or ineptness, the failure by journalists to articulate what they do leaves citizens suspicious that the press is either deluding itself or hiding something. This is one reason the discussion of journalistic objectivity has become such a trap. The term has become so misunderstood and battered, the discussion mostly goes off track. As we will discuss in more depth in Chapter 4, on verification, originally it was not the journalist who was imagined to be objective. It was his or her method. Today, however, in part because journalists have failed to articulate what they are doing, our contemporary understanding of objectivity is mostly confusion.

Despite the public's confusion, there is little doubt that journalists believe themselves to be engaged in pursuing truth, not just free speech or commerce. We have to be—for this is what society requires of us.

And, as we will see, "journalistic truth" is more than mere accuracy. It is a sorting-out process that takes place between the initial story and the interaction among the public, newsmakers, and journalists. This first principle of journalism—its disinterested pursuit of truth—is ultimately what sets journalism apart from all other forms of communication.

JOURNALISTIC TRUTH

To understand this sorting-out process, it is important to remember that journalism exists in a social context. Out of necessity, citizens and societies depend on accurate and reliable accounts of events. They develop procedures and processes to arrive at what might be called "functional truth." Police track down and arrest suspects based on facts. Judges hold trials. Juries render verdicts of guilty or innocent. Industries are regulated, taxes are collected, laws are made. We teach our children rules, history, physics, and biology. All of these truths—even the laws of science—are subject to revision, but we operate by them in the meantime because they are necessary and they work.

This is what journalism is after—a practical or functional form of truth. It is not truth in the absolute or philosophical sense. It is not the truth of a chemical equation. Journalism can—and must—pursue the truths by which we can operate on a day-to-day basis. "We don't think it's unreasonable to expect jurors to render fair verdicts, or teachers to teach honest lessons, or historians to write impartial history, scientists to perform unbiased research. Why should we set any lower goals for poor journalists," Bill Keller, then managing editor of the *New York Times*, told us at one committee forum. "Whether true objectivity is ever possible—I don't think that is what we're here for. . . . We strive for coverage that aims as much as possible to present the reader with enough information to make up his or her own mind. That's our fine ideal."[19]

Does this suggest that journalists should stick simply to accuracy, getting the names and dates right? Is that sufficient? The increasingly interpretative nature of most journalism today, and the answers of journalists at forums, in surveys, and in interviews tells us no. A journalism built merely on accuracy fails to get us far enough.

In the first place, mere accuracy can be a kind of distortion all its own. As long ago as 1947, the Hutchins Commission, a group of scholars who spent years producing a document that outlined the obligations of journalism, warned of the dangers of publishing accounts that are "factually correct but substantially untrue."[20] Even then, the commission cited stories about members of minority groups that, by failing to provide context or by emphasizing race or ethnicity pointlessly, reinforced false stereotypes. "It is no longer enough to report the fact truthfully. It is now necessary to report the truth about the fact."

Mere accuracy is also not what people are looking for. Journalist Jack Fuller, in his book *News Values*, explains that, according to philosophers, there are two tests of truth: one is correspondence, the other is coherence. For journalism, these tests roughly translate into getting the facts straight and making sense of the facts. Coherence must be the ultimate test of journalistic truth, Fuller decides. "Regardless of what the radical skeptics argue, people still passionately believe in meaning. They want the whole picture, not just part of it. . . . They are tired of polarized discussion, the 'McLaughlin Group' model of public discourse."[21]

Common sense tells us the same thing. Today, stories reporting simply that the mayor praised the police at the Garden Club luncheon seem inadequate—even foolish—if the police are in fact entangled in a corruption scandal; the mayor's comments are clearly political rhetoric, and they come in response to some recent attack by his critics.

This, however, does not mean that accuracy doesn't matter. On the contrary, accuracy is the foundation upon which everything else is built: context, interpretation, debate, and all of public communication. If the foundation is faulty, everything else is flawed. One of the risks of the new proliferation of outlets, talk programs, blogs, and interpretative reporting is that these forms have left verification behind. A debate between opponents arguing with false figures or purely on prejudice fails to inform. It only inflames. It takes the society nowhere.

It is more helpful, and more realistic, to understand journalistic truth as a process—or as a continuing journey toward understanding— that begins with the first story and builds over time. For instance, the first news stories signal a new event or trend. They may begin with an account of something simple—a meeting or a car accident. The time and place of the accident, the damage done, the types of vehicles, arrests, unusual weather or road conditions—in effect, the physical externalities of the case—are facts that can be recorded and checked. Once they have verified the facts, reporters try to convey a fair and reliable account of their meaning, valid for now, subject to further investigation. Journalist Carl Bernstein has described this as reporters' striving to provide "the best obtainable version of the truth."[22] The principles of the *Washington Post*, drafted by Eugene Meyer in 1933, describe telling "the truth as nearly as the truth may be ascertained."[23]

The individual reporter may not be able to move much beyond a surface level of accuracy in a first story. But the first story builds to a second, in which the sources of news have responded to initial mistakes and missing elements, and the second story to a third story, and so on. Context is added in each successive layer. In more important and complex stories, there are subsequent contributions on the editorial pages, discussions on the talk shows, in the op-ed opinions, viewpoints expressed on blogs and other Internet venues, and reactions in letters to the editor or calls to radio shows—the full range of public and private conversation. This practical truth is a protean thing that, like learning, grows like a stalactite in a cave, drop by drop, over time.

There are countless examples. Take the case of Abner Louima, the Haitian immigrant arrested for disorderly conduct outside a Brooklyn nightclub in 1997. The story at first looked like a police-blotter brief. But three days later, New York *Daily News* columnist Mike McAlary discovered Louima in the hospital and interviewed him. Louima revealed that police had brutalized and sodomized him with a toilet plunger handle. That same day, police removed two officers involved in the arrest from active duty. Two days later, in a second interview, Louima alleged that the arresting officers told him, "This is Giuliani time [in reference to Mayor Rudolph Giuliani]. It's not Dinkins time" [in reference to former Mayor David Dinkins, an African-American]. More officers are pulled off duty, and soon citizens stage protests in Brooklyn. Within days, the *New York Times* published an in-depth look, suggesting that the drop in crime in New York City coincided with systemwide increases in police harassment and brutality. The city focused anew on police treatment of suspects. A year later, Louima recanted his allegations about the "Giuliani time" statement, though not that he was brutalized. Several months later, the Manhattan Institute's *City Journal* published an article making the case that, despite high-profile incidents of police brutality, the New York Police Department has a relatively good record on the question of police brutality.[24]

The truth here, in other words, was a complicated and sometimes contradictory phenomenon, but seen as a process over time, journalism can get at it. It attempts to get at the truth in a confused world by first stripping information of any attached misinformation, disinformation, or self-promoting bias and then letting the community react, with the sorting-out process to ensue. The search for truth becomes a conversation.

This definition helps reconcile the way we use the words *true* and *false* every day with the way we deconstruct those words in the petri dish of a philosophical debate. This definition comes closer to journalists' intuitive understanding of what they do than the crude metaphors of mirrors and reflections that are commonly handed out.

We understand truth as a goal—at best elusive—and still embrace it. We embrace it the same way as Albert Einstein did when he said of science that it was not about truth but about making what we know less false. For this is how life really is—we're often striving and never fully achieving. As historian Gordon Wood has said about writing history: "One can accept the view that the historical record is fragmentary and incomplete . . . and that historians will never finally agree in their interpretations" and yet still believe "in an objective truth about the past that can be observed and empirically verified." This is more than a leap of faith. In real life, people can tell when someone has come closer to getting it right, when the sourcing is authoritative, when the research is exhaustive, when the method is transparent. Or as Wood put it, "Historians may never see and present that truth wholly and finally, but some of them will come closer than others, be more nearly complete, more objective, more honest, in their written history, and we will know it, and have known it, when we see it."[25]

Those who have worked in news or in public life say much the same thing: getting news that comes closer to a complete version of the truth has real consequences. In the first hours of an event, when being accurate is most difficult, accuracy is perhaps most important. It is during this time that public attitudes are formed, sometimes stubbornly, by the context within which the information is presented. Is it a threat to me? Is it good for me? Is it something I should be concerned about? The answer to these questions determines how carefully I follow a new event, how much verification of the facts I will look for. Based on his experience, Hodding Carter, a longtime journalist who served as assistant secretary of state for public affairs in the Carter administration's State Department, has said that this is the time in which the government can exercise its greatest control over the public mind: "If given three days without serious challenge, the government will have set the context for an event and can control public perception of that event."[26]

This is a point made potent by the lack of government action or reaction in the immediate aftermath of 2005's Hurricane Katrina. Because the government failed to set context, reports by frightened citizens and journalists defined the news. It took weeks for the government to get the story under its political control.

Over the years, some journalists have suggested substitutes for truthfulness. Probably the two most common substitutes are fairness and balance. Yet both, under scrutiny, are inadequate. Fairness is too abstract and, in the end, is more subjective than truth. Fair to whom? How do you test fairness? Truthfulness, for all its difficulties, at least can be tested.

Balance, also, is too subjective. Balancing a story by being fair to both sides may not be fair to the truth if both sides do not, in fact, have equal weight. Is global warming fact or fiction? The preponderance of scientists have argued for years that it exists, but press coverage has continued long past the time of the scientific debate to give equal weight to both sides. And in those many cases where there are more than two sides to a story, how does one determine which side to honor? Balance, if it amounts to false balance, becomes distortion.

In our book *Warp Speed*, we talked about how various forces were converging to weaken journalists' pursuit of truthfulness, despite the continuing allegiance most journalists profess to it. Without repeating those arguments at any length, it is sufficient to note that, in the new media culture of continuous news, the news has become more piecemeal; sources are gaining power over the journalists who cover them; varying standards of journalism are breaking down the gatekeeper function of the press; inexpensive, polarizing argument is overwhelming reporting; and the press is increasingly fixated on finding the "big story" that will temporarily reassemble the now-fragmented mass audience. Together, these new characteristics of what we called the Mixed Media Culture are displacing the classic function of sorting out a true and reliable account of the day's events. In the continuous news culture, journalists trying to shovel the latest information onto the air or the Web have little time to check things out. Often they are largely passing things along, creating what we have called a new journalism of assertion, which is overwhelming the old journalism of verification. And in the years since the first edition of this book was published, in 2001, we have seen the rise of a third model of media in the form of talk radio and in some cable news and elsewhere—a journalism of affirmation, whose appeal is not in verifying the facts skeptically but in affirming the preconceptions of the audience. On the Internet, too, websites that merely gather, often by machines using computer algorithms, are giving rise to yet a fourth model—a journalism of aggregation, which may or may not discriminate among rumor, fact, and speculation. That is for the user to sort out.

Despite these trends, journalists still believe in the importance of telling the truth. In our survey of core values, eight out of ten journalists working in national outlets, and more than seven out of ten working in local outlets, said they felt "there is such a thing as a true and accurate account of an event." The same was true for new media or Internet journalists, where seven out of ten believed that arriving at such a true and accurate account was possible.[27]

Seven in ten national and local journalists are confident that they can develop a professional method "to cover events in a disinterested and fair way." Almost as many, six in ten, new media people said so, too. Still, there is noticeable skepticism: roughly a quarter of all journalists, across all media, have doubts about whether this goal is practical—27 percent among local journalists and 31 percent among new media people.[28]

Perhaps because of these doubts, the conventional response of the so-called serious press to the new media culture has been that its place is to add more context and interpretation to the news. The idea is that this will help audiences sort through the information overload, giving the news more meaning. Yet this response to the new technology, we think, is poorly conceived. For one thing, it is impractical to imagine people sorting through reams of unfiltered information. While it is unquestionably true that Internet-connected consumers of the early twenty-first century have more news outlets than their counterparts did in the early twentieth century, there remains a finite amount of time people can devote to consuming news. In fact, despite the growth in the amount of available news, it is far from clear that people have expanded the amount of time they spend with the news.[29]

. . .

The instinct for truth is no less necessary today—in our age of new media and proliferating outlets—than it ever was. Peter Viereck, professor emeritus in history at Mt. Holyoke College, believes an instinct for truth is more necessary than ever. "I can think of nothing more gallant," Viereck says, "even though again and again we fail, than attempting to get at the facts; attempting to tell things as they really are. For at least reality, though never fully attained, can be defined. Reality is that which, when you don't believe it, doesn't go away."[30]

Ironically, finding the truth in some ways takes more work than it did precisely because there is so much information available. Call it the paradox of learning in the Information Age. When information is a commodity in oversupply—when there is so much more input—knowledge becomes more difficult to acquire, not easier. One must process more information to set things in order. The knowledge acquired may be deeper and better, but it will likely also be more specialized.

What's more, when the media become background noise, our capacity to focus is diminished. It becomes more difficult to rise above the din. If Winston Churchill was correct that "A lie gets halfway around the world before the truth has a chance to get its pants on," greater technology has only speeded up the process, aiding truth and falsehood alike.[31]

These factors help to explain why the new partisan journalism of our time, the journalism of affirmation, is even more appealing today for some audiences. It makes things easier. It is a way of achieving order in a more confusing world, without so much sifting and heavy lifting. It offers comfort. All the more, this situation adds to the challenge, and pushes the need for journalism that gets the facts right first. It is the foundation for everything else. More interpretation may only add to the cacophony and stray toward the softer levels of truth, the levels that need to be part of the sorting-out process after the facts have been established. It is a mistake to rush to the interpretative stage before sorting out what has actually occurred.

Rather than rush to add context and interpretation, the press needs to concentrate on synthesis and verification. Sift out the rumor, the innuendo, the insignificant, and the spin, and concentrate on what is true and important about a story. Give citizens identifiable sources and verify the information, highlighting what is important to know and filtering out what is not. Rather than expanding the time to sort through information themselves, people need sources that tell them what is true and significant. They need an answer to the question: "What here can I believe?" The role of the press, then, in this new age is to answer the question: "Where is the good stuff?" Verification and synthesis become the backbone of the new journalist; their role is that of "sense maker," as John Seeley Brown of Xerox PARC meant it in the previous chapter. In short, the need for truth is greater, not lesser, in the new century, for the likelihood of untruth has become so much more possible.

For truth to prevail, journalists must make clear to whom they owe their first loyalty. That is the next step.

ENDNOTES

1. Benjamin C. Bradlee, *Nieman Reports*, special issue (Winter 1990).
2. CCJ and the Pew Research Center for the People and the Press, "Striking the Balance: Audience Interests, Business Pressures and Journalists' Values," March 1999, 79; available at www.journalism.org and http://people-press.org.
3. Interviews by William Damon, Howard Gardner, and Mihaly Csikszentmihalyi with a number of journalists; unpublished interviews for the book *Good Work: When Excellence and Ethics Meet* (New York: Basic Books, 2001).
4. Patty Calhoun, at CCJ Forum, Chicago, November 6, 1997.
5. Peter Levine, *Living Without Philosophy: On Narrative, Rhetoric, and Morality* (Albany: State University of New York Press, 1998), 169.
6. This concept of image taking precedence over reality is most dramatically portrayed in Joe McGinniss, *The Selling of the President 1968* (New York: Trident Press, 1969).
7. Ron Suskind, "Without a Doubt," *New York Times Magazine*, October 17, 2004; available at www.nytimes.com.
8. John Hohenberg, *Free Press, Free People: The Best Cause* (New York: Free Press, 1973), 17.
9. Joseph Ellis, *American Sphinx: The Character of Thomas Jefferson* (New York: Alfred A. Knopf, 1997), 303.
10. Edwin Emery, *The Press in America*, 2d ed. (Englewood Cliffs, NJ: Prentice-Hall, 1962), 374.
11. Cassandra Tate, "What Do Ombudsmen Do," *Columbia Journalism Review* (May/June 1984), 37.
12. Ibid.
13. David T. Z. Mindich, *Just the Facts: How "Objectivity" Came to Define American Journalism* (New York and London: New York University Press, 1998), 115. Mindich says the first textbook to question objectivity was Curtis MacDougall's *Interpretative Reporting*, 8th ed. (New York: Macmillan, 1982).

14. Gordon Wood, "Novel History," *New York Review of Books*, June 27, 1991, 16.
15. Richard Harwood, at CCJ Forum, New York City, December 4, 1997.
16. Everette E. Dennis, "Whatever Happened to Marse Robert's Dream?: The Dilemma of American Journalism Education," *Gannett Center Journal* (Spring 1988).
17. Mindich, *Just the Facts*, 6–7. All three of these examples come from this book, but they are representative of statements we have heard from many journalists through the years.
18. Mindich makes this point as well in *Just the Facts*, 141.
19. Bill Keller, at CCJ Forum, New York City, December 4, 1997.
20. Robert D. Leigh, ed., *A Free and Responsible Press* (Chicago: University of Chicago Press, 1947), 23.
21. Jack Fuller, *News Values: Ideas for an Information Age* (Chicago and London: University of Chicago Press, 1996), 194.
22. Carl Bernstein has made this point on several occasions, in speeches, interviews, and conversation with the authors.
23. Eugene Meyer, "The Post's Principles," *Washington Post Deskbook on Style*, 2nd edition (New York: McGraw-Hill, 1989), 7.
24. Heather MacDonald, "America's Best Urban Police Force," *City Journal* (Summer 2000).
25. Wood, "Novel History," 16.
26. Hodding Carter, interview by author Kovach, April 1998.
27. CCJ and the Pew Research Center, "Striking the Balance," 53.
28. Ibid., 54.
29. John Robinson and Geoffrey Godbey, *Time for Life: The Surprising Ways Americans Use Their Time*, 2d ed. (University Park, PA: Pennsylvania State University Press, 1999), 143. In *Public Opinion*, Lippmann used research from 1900 to 1920 to show that the amount of time people spent with the newspaper had held steady at slightly over 15 minutes. By 1965 studies by University of Maryland sociologist John Robinson found that people were still spending about 15 minutes with the newspaper. Furthermore, when he went back to look at those figures ten years later, he found that the increased presence of television news had not led to more time spent with the news, but rather "the loss in newspaper-reading time was almost directly mirrored in the increased diary time spent watching local news programs." These numbers are even more telling when one takes into account the increase in spare time that Americans have experienced over the last 100 years.
30. Tom Reiss, "The First Conservative: How Peter Viereck Inspired—and Lost—a Movement," *The New Yorker*, October 23, 2005, 42.
31. Variations on this quote have been used by many politicians, writers, and journalists. Mark Twain is often quoted as having said "A lie can travel halfway around the world while the truth is putting on its shoes."

3

Who Journalists
Work For

At the close of each year, top news executives around the country await a new professional verdict: how good a job did they do, and how much will they be paid? Often a significant portion of their income is at stake. The verdict, however, is no longer based simply on the quality of their journalism. Quality factors often make up half or less of the decision criteria. The bonuses of newsroom executives today are based in large part on how much profit their companies make.[1]

All this may seem unremarkable. Many businesses have incentive bonus programs for their managers as a way of creating accountability. Yet tying journalists' pay to factors other than the quality of their journalism is a new trend, a feature of the last twenty years. The reasons for it seem sensible at face value. Journalism is a business, and managers have business responsibilities for keeping budgets and attracting customers.

These corporate incentive programs, however, mark a major shift in thinking at newsrooms. The trend formalizes a new theory of the journalist's responsibilities that are part of a larger change in the nature of the profession of delivering news.

By the end of the twentieth century, in deed if not in name, America's journalistic leaders had been transformed into businesspeople. Half of them now report that they spend at least a third of their time on business matters rather than on journalism.[2]

As citizens, we should be alarmed. Journalists, in turn, should understand that their position has been undermined. Largely unnoticed is how this change has weakened the link between citizens and news gatherers and how it contradicts the theory that has defined the modern press. The shift in emphasis has created confusion and morale problems inside news organizations and is restricting the ability of journalists to provide the news without fear or favor. It has been one of the key reasons citizens have lost confidence in the press, and it has made it more complicated for newsroom leaders to be advocates for the public interest in their own companies.

At this point, the notion that journalists must seek out the truth is clear, but that is not enough. What conditions are necessary for them to be able to know the truth, and also to communicate that truth to the public in a way that citizens will believe? The answer—the second principle of journalism—is loyalty.

No one questions that news organizations answer to many constituencies. Community institutions, local groups, parent companies, shareholders, advertisers, and many more interests must be considered and served by a successful news organization. Yet what newspaper publishers gradually came to understand in the nineteenth century—and have refined with significant hardship ever since—is that journalists (and usually owners as well) must have one allegiance above all others. And this commitment forms the second element of journalism:

Journalism's first loyalty is to citizens.

A commitment to citizens is more than professional egoism. It is the implied covenant with the public, which tells the audience that the movie reviews are straight, that the restaurant reviews are not influenced by who buys an ad, that the coverage is not self-interested or slanted for friends. The notion that those who report the news are not obstructed from digging up and telling the truth—even at the expense of the owners' other financial interests—is a prerequisite of telling the news not only accurately but also persuasively. It is the basis for why citizens believe a news organization. It is the source of the organization's credibility. It is, in short, the franchise asset of the news company and those who work in it.

Thus people who gather news are not like the employees of other companies. They have a social obligation that at times overrides their employers' immediate interests, and yet this obligation is the source of their employers' financial success.

The allegiance to citizens is the meaning of what we have come to call journalistic independence. As we will see, the phrase has often been used as a synonym for other ideas, including disengagement, disinterestedness, and detachment. But these terms create confusion and reflect a fuzzy understanding on behalf of newspeople. Journalists have contributed to their woes by passing that confusion on to the public, and citizens have understandably become skeptical, even angry, as a result.

Still, the idea that journalists serve citizens first remains deeply felt by those who produce the news. The question "For whom do you work?" elicited a particularly strong response among the journalists we interviewed. In a 1999 survey on values by the Pew Research Center for the People and the Press and the Committee of Concerned Journalists,[3] more than 80 percent listed "making the reader/listener/viewer your first obligation" as a "core principle of journalism." In separate open-ended in-depth interviews with developmental psychologists, more than 70 percent of journalists similarly placed "audience" as their first loyalty, well above their employers, themselves, their profession, or even their families.[4] "I always worked for the people who turned on the television set," says Nick Clooney, a former newscaster in Los Angeles, Cincinnati, and elsewhere. "Always. Whenever I was having a discussion with a general manager or a member of the board of directors, my bottom line was always, 'I don't work for you. You're paying my check, and I'm very pleased. But the truth of the matter is, I don't work for you, and if it comes down to a question of loyalty, my loyalty will be to the person who turns on the television set. . . . When I made that position clear, [it was] never questioned."[5]

This sense that the journalist has a loyalty beyond and above that to the employer is so deeply held that it manifests itself at the very best news organizations in dramatic, public rebellions of a sort inconceivable in other industries. In 2003, when reporters and editors at the *New York Times* felt that the two most powerful people in their newsroom–the executive editor and managing editor–had violated this loyalty in condoning the conduct of and then trying to avoid responsibility for Jayson Blair, a reporter who plagiarized and fictionalized, the newsroom's anger effectively forced the publisher to remove these editors.[6] When the publisher's handling of controversial reporter Judith Miller's involvement in a leak investigation in 2005 evoked similar concerns, *New York Times* reporters Don Van Natta Jr., Adam Liptak, and Clifford J. Levy were not shy about revealing these shortcomings in the paper.[7] And then in a very public warning to her boss, columnist Maureen Dowd threatened in the opinion pages that if Miller were allowed back on her beat, the public shouldn't trust the newspaper. Eventually, Miller resigned.

At the *Los Angeles Times*, reporter Henry Weinstein and others led a similar revolt after that paper engaged in a secret deal with owners of a new sports arena, the Staples Center, to share advertising revenues for an edition of the Sunday magazine devoted entirely to the arena's opening. Said editor John Carroll, who later was brought in from a sister paper in Baltimore to take over the *Times* newsroom, "there was a confrontation in the lunchroom with management that was so angry it verged on violence." The incident eventually prompted a full investigation of the paper's management and ultimately contributed to the sale of the company to the Tribune Company.

To those outside journalism, such public eruptions might signal a crisis of values in journalism. Without doubt, the transgressions that prompted these rebellions were serious. Yet the contrary is a more accurate reading of these cases. The ferocity and boldness of the reactions in the newsrooms, and their public nature, reveal how deeply and widely held the code of loyalty to the public is among those who work in this profession.

This kind of understanding did not come easily. Though the loyalty effort began a half century earlier, it was not until the latter part of the nineteenth century that a large number of leading daily newspaper publishers began to substitute editorial independence for political ideology. The most famous declaration of this intellectual and financial independence came in 1896, when a young publisher from Tennessee named Adolph Ochs bought the struggling *New York Times*. Ochs was convinced that a good many New Yorkers were tired of the tawdry sensationalism of William Randolph Hearst and Joseph Pulitzer, and they would welcome a more tasteful—and accurate—style of journalism. Under the simple headline "Business Announcement," Ochs published on his first day as owner the words that would become his legacy. It was his "earnest aim," he wrote, "to give the news impartially, without fear or favor, regardless of party, sect or interests involved."

Other publishers had made similar claims to independence, but as authors Alex Jones and Susan Tifft put it, Ochs "actually believed what he wrote."[8] Newspapers across the country reprinted the statement in full. As the *Times* went on to become the most influential paper in New York and then the world, others followed the Ochs model, staking the business plan on the idea that putting the audience ahead of political and immediate financial interests was the best long-term financial strategy. After buying the *Washington Post* in 1933, for instance, Eugene Meyer crafted a set of principles that stated, among other items, "In pursuit of the truth, the newspaper shall be prepared to make sacrifices of its material fortunes, if such a course be necessary for the public good."[9]

As owners began trumpeting editorial independence in their marketing, journalists seized upon it to upgrade their professionalism. A generation of early press critics emerged, such as Will Irwin, a former newspaper reporter and editor of *McClure's Magazine*, who in 1911 published a bracing fifteen-part series in *Collier's*, chronicling in bold detail the abuses of the press. Seizing on the new technology of the light bulb, Irwin called on a new public service role for journalism, "an electric light in a dark alley."[10] Newspaper editors in turn reacted to the rhetoric of their bosses and the rebukes of the critics, and they tried to professionalize as a group. Malcolm Bingay, a columnist for the *Detroit Free Press*, has traced the development to the genesis of the American Society of Newspaper Editors, the primary trade association for those who run America's newspaper newsrooms. In 1912, a group of editors had gathered to preview Glacier National Park one summer night in the Rockies:

> As they sat around a campfire they heard [Casper] Yost [editorial page editor of the *St. Louis Globe-Democrat*] discuss an idea which possessed him. His dream was the creation of an ethical organization of American newspaper editors. . . . Little Casper, tagged Arsenic and Old Lace by his contemporaries, might more appropriately be remembered as creating the modern concept of responsibility of the press, a concept often lost today in the more dramatic scuffles about press freedom.[11]

The organization's code of ethics placed editorial independence above all: "Independence: Freedom from all obligations except that of fidelity to the public interest is vital," it stated. "Promotion of any private interest contrary to the general welfare, for whatever reasons, is not compatible with honest journalism. . . . Partisanship, in editorial comment which knowingly departs from the truth, does violence to the best spirit of American journalism; in the news columns it is subversive of a fundamental principle of the profession."

No less a successful organization, or financially astute one, than the *Wall Street Journal* shows how the principle of serving the audience first has taken hold. When one of its columnists, Foster Winans, was caught engaging in insider trading in the 1980s, the newspaper felt compelled to publicly reexamine and rewrite its code of conduct. "The central premise of this code is that Dow Jones' reputation for quality and for the independence and integrity of our publications is the heart and soul of our enterprise." This was a financial premise, not a purely journalistic one, just as it is for other news organizations as well. "Dow Jones cannot prosper if our customers cannot assume that . . . our analyses represent our best independent judgments rather than our preference, or those of our sources, advertisers or information providers."[12]

Newspapers became monopolies in the 1960s and generally toned down such declarations, except—like the *Journal*—in times of crisis. But television journalism, which is far more commercially competitive, continued to market itself in the public's name. Throughout the 1990s, for instance, at the very time of rising suspicions about the press, "On

Your Side" and "Working 4 You" were two of the most popular slogans in local television news. Internal station research, as well as focus groups conducted by the Project for Excellence in Journalism, suggest they were also the most effective slogans.[13]

INDEPENDENCE TO ISOLATION

As with so many professional ideas, editorial independence has over time begun, in some quarters, to harden into isolation. As journalists tried to honor and protect their carefully won independence from party and commercial pressures, they sometimes came to pursue independence for its own sake. Detachment from outside pressures could bleed into disengagement from the community.

In part, ironically, this was a result of journalism's becoming professionalized. As journalists became better educated and the press organized itself into chains, companies began to use their newspapers and TV stations as farm systems to train journalists in small markets for assignments later in the bigger ones. By 1997, two-thirds of newspaper journalists, according to one survey, did not grow up in the community they were covering.[14] The majority of them felt "less involved" in their communities than other people who lived there, up markedly from only eight years earlier.[15] Journalists were becoming transients–residents only of the community of journalism, a class of "news Bedouins."

A second factor in the growing isolation was a change in journalism's tone. After Vietnam and Watergate, and later the advent of 24-hour cable news, journalism became noticeably more subjective and judgmental.[16] Coverage was focused more on mediating what public people were saying than simply reporting it. One notable study found that on television, for instance, the length of time for each candidate quote, or sound bite, on network nightly news programs during election years began to shrink, from an average of 43 seconds in 1968 to a mere 9 seconds in 1988.[17] At the same time, the stand-up closes, in which the reporters summarized the story, became longer and more judgmental.[18] In newspapers, as various studies have found, stories began to focus less on what candidates said and more on the tactical motives for their statements.[19] A study of the front pages of the *New York Times* and the *Washington Post* found that the number of "straight news" accounts decreased, and the number of interpretative and analytical stories grew. Often, these analytical stories were not labeled or identified as analysis.[20] Phrases designed to pull back the curtain of public life, including terms like "spin doctors" and "photo op," began to emerge in the press. In time this engendered a new jargon about the objectionable behavior of journalists—terms like "feeding frenzy" and "gotcha journalism."

In some hands, this more interpretative style serves the desire of journalists to create a public persona as much as anything else. In the year leading into the 2000 presidential campaign, political columnist Michael Kelly satirized Democrat Al Gore for playing up his rural background. The piece "Farmer Al" ridiculed the fact that Gore had spent more of his youth living in a Washington hotel while his father served in the U.S. Senate than he had in Tennessee.

> Al ran through the vast apartment. (The Gore farmhouse occupied six big rooms on the top floor of the Fairfax [Hotel] and Al was proud of that; there weren't many families in Washington whose penthouses boasted views of sunrise and sunset.) . . . He ate as he ran, just pausing to grab his trusty two-bladed ax from the umbrella stand.[21]

Kelly's thoroughly entertaining piece earned praise for exposing Gore's presumed hypocrisy. The problem was that twelve years earlier, before he had become a Washington columnist noted for his sharp edge, Kelly as a news reporter for the *Baltimore Sun* had presented the same facts as authentic rather than hypocritical:

> Down at the farm, at the insistence of his father and over the objections of his mother, life was different. "In the summer I would have to get up before dawn and help feed livestock," [Gore] says. "Then I would have to clean out the hog parlors. . . . Then I would work on the farm all day and feed the stock again at night before dinner." By all accounts, Mr. Gore was from early youth unusually serious and hardworking.[22]

Even some journalists had become concerned that too many of their colleagues had crossed a line from skepticism to cynicism, or even a kind of journalistic nihilism, the philosophy of believing in nothing. Phil Trounstein, then political editor of the *San Jose Mercury News*, was moved to write an essay on the subject for the Committee for Concerned Journalists. "It seems the worst thing a reporter or commentator can be accused of in certain circles is not inaccuracy or unfairness but credulousness."[23]

A key part of the problem, University of Pennsylvania professors Joseph N. Cappella and Kathleen Hall Jamieson argued in *The Spiral of Cynicism: The Press and the Public Good*, is the growing journalistic focus on the motives of public officials rather than their actions. By shifting from the "what" of public life to the "why," they argued, journalists "interiorized" public life, making it about the psyche and self of politicians and also making it less about the outcomes of public policy that actually affected citizens. This cynical focus tended to further disconnect journalists from citizens.

Finally, the creeping journalistic isolation coincided with a business strategy at many newspapers and later television stations to enhance profits by going after the most affluent or efficient audience rather than the largest. In television, that meant designing the news for women ages 18 to 49 who make most household buying decisions. In newspapers, that meant limiting circulation to the more affluent ZIP code areas, which cut the cost of production and distribution. Targeting the news meant a news company theoretically could get more out of less—higher advertising rates with a smaller audience. It also meant the paper or the TV station could ignore certain parts of the community in its coverage, which also saved money. Isolation, in other words, became a business plan. After the *Minneapolis Star Tribune* dropped in circulation by 4 percent in three years in the mid-1990s, publisher Joel Kramer told the *New York Times*, "We are a healthier business because we are charging readers more and accepting a somewhat smaller circulation."[24] Perhaps nothing illustrated the thinking better than the story of a Bloomingdale's executive who told Rupert Murdoch that the store did not advertise in his *New York Post* because "your readers are our shoplifters." Though it was probably apocryphal, the story became an urban legend within the newspaper business because it so succinctly framed the industry's prevailing modus operandi.

A BACKLASH AGAINST DETACHMENT

Though few realized it at the time, there began in the 1990s what amounted to a reconsideration of the independence of the newsroom. The initial cause was that the business strategy of targeted demographics began to backfire. Making money without growing circulation had worked because the journalism business was such a monopoly that it had been able to take its advertising base for granted. About 1989, with transforming shifts in American retailing and communications technology, that situation began to unravel. Grocery and department stores–the financial backbone of newspapers–were being rocked by bankruptcy, mergers, and debt. The discount retailers that replaced them didn't buy newspaper advertising, since, as everything was discounted every day, they didn't need to announce their specials. In the eleven years between 1980 and 1991, the amount of advertising space in big-city dailies dropped by 8 percent, according to Sanford C. Bernstein.[25] In 1991 alone, the industry suffered a 4.9 percent drop in retail advertising–the steepest one-year decline in history. A similar dislocation was affecting television, where the audience began to slip away to pseudo news programs, cable reruns, and eventually the Internet.

As the journalism business became more difficult, managers began to refashion how they operated. In newspapers, that largely meant cutting costs, not investing more in the news to expand its appeal. Between 1992 and 1997, smaller newspapers cut the percentage of their budgets going to news by 11 percent, and larger papers by 14 percent. In its place, the industry invested more in marketing.[26]

As they cut costs, business managers began to want more accountability from their editors. They also began to want the newspeople to begin justifying their journalism. The businesspeople had market research and all kinds of new technology–minute-by-minute ratings data in TV, focus group data, even infrared glasses that would track reader eye movements across a page. The hope was that if journalists used the technology more, they could do more to build circulation and not be so unpopular with the public.

A gulf began to form between businesspeople and newspeople–and worse, between reporters and news managers. Journalists saw the business side as challenging their journalistic independence and feared *accountability* was a code word for letting advertisers shape the news. The business side began to wonder, if the newsroom was so intransigent about change, maybe the fabled detachment of the newsroom was the root of their stagnation. A culture war began to boil in the news business.

"A lot of reporters think their editors have gone over the wall," Deborah Howell, then Washington bureau chief of Newhouse Newspapers, explained at a committee meeting of the American Society of Newspaper Editors in 1998.

At the same time, journalists who made a case for the public-interest obligation inside their companies could be labeled as naïve, old-fashioned, and difficult. "If you mention 'public service' with corporate, you will be branded as an idealist, as an unrealistic person and you will not be listened to," said John Carroll, who won a record thirteen Pulitzer Prizes in five years at the helm of the *Los Angeles Times* from 2000 to 2005 and then resigned after fighting with his corporate bosses at the Tribune Company in Chicago.

The two sides were often not as divided in reality as they were rhetorically. The real fight was not over values but over the nature of change. The advocates of change saw themselves as fighting for the industry's survival. The resisters saw themselves defending a professional ethic that was the basis of the industry's success.

Nonetheless, the schism had damaging consequences. One was that innovators were denounced. When Mike Fancher at the *Seattle Times* began in the early 1990s to suggest that editors gain more knowledge of business to protect themselves, he was shunned. The movement that came to be known as "public" or "civic" journalism similarly contained some fine ideas about trying to reconnect with community by using new techniques, such as finding out what voters cared about most and then asking political candidates to address those concerns. But inevitably not all experiments worked. There were instances when polling was followed too literally and allowed to dictate coverage; there were other times when the civic journalism banner was used as a marketing ploy. Many members of the elite national press seized on such instances as reason to resist change.

The second consequence of the chasm was that some business practices were put into the newsroom that ran counter to journalism's and the citizens' best interests. One of the most basic techniques to create more newsroom accountability was an incentive program called Management By Objective, or MBO. The concept, pioneered in the 1950s by management guru Peter F. Drucker, is simple: by setting goals and attaching rewards for achieving them, a company can create a coherent system for both coordinating and monitoring what its executives are doing.

Today, the vast majority of news executives in TV and print have MBOs.[27] A good many of them are structured in a way that unwittingly distorts and undermines the role of journalists or the needs of communities. In a survey by the State of the American Newspaper Project in 1998, 71 percent of editors said their companies employ such MBOs. Of those who do, half said they get 20 to 50 percent of their income from the programs. And the majority of these editors said that more than half of their bonus is tied to their paper's financial performance.

What is wrong with these practices? What good is journalism, after all, if it doesn't sell?

The problem is that tying a journalist's income to his organization's financial performance in effect changes the journalist's allegiance. The company is explicitly saying that a good portion of the journalist's loyalty must be to the corporate parent and to shareholders—ahead of readers, listeners, or viewers. What if an advertiser makes it clear that more income will come if the coverage of an issue begins to ease off, or if a certain reporter is fired or moved off a beat? When has an advertiser ever urged more coverage of business corruption or price-fixing? How do you tell the news without fear or favor when you are explaining to the editor that one of his key goals is making money this quarter? MBOs tied to the bottom line divide that loyalty.

Sandra Rowe, editor of Portland's *Oregonian,* captured the problem well. She has said it is fine to teach your journalists about business. The question is, what religion are your journalists practicing? Are they journalists who understand business? Or are they businesspersons who understand journalism? The distinction is a matter of loyalty. Is the corporate culture based on the belief that devotion to serving the citizen will lead to solvency? Or is the corporate culture based on a dedication to maximizing profit, even at the expense of what the citizen requires?

Confusing journalists about their loyalties has always had tangible consequences. When a Fox-affiliated TV news station in Tennessee was found promising in writing to provide positive coverage to those who advertised on the station, the discovery made the wire services. What didn't make news was that the practice is far more common than even many journalists realize. "It occurs all the time with a wink and nod . . . especially in small markets where revenue is harder to come by," said one former Fox executive, whose identity we want to protect so he can continue to work in commercial television. "What is even more common is that when you are working on a story about anything, there is an understanding the first interview will be with a sponsor."

The rationale is a classic, many news veterans admit. "We have to talk to somebody. It might as well be someone who sponsors our shows." Another technique is to cover commercial promotions by major sponsors, such as auto dealers, as live public events, sometimes using news personnel or just as often weather or sportscasters.

CITIZENS ARE NOT CUSTOMERS

Bringing business accountability to the newsroom involved bringing the language of business as well. In several companies, this meant applying the language of consumer marketing to news, with readers and viewers becoming "customers," understanding them becoming "marketing," and news becoming "customer service." "The best editors are marketers," says Bob Ingle, former executive editor of Knight Ridder's *San Jose Mercury News* and then president of Knight Ridder's new media operations. "That's what I tried to do as editor—get the bloody staff to listen to the audience. I wanted them to say about me, 'He's a terrific marketer.' "[28]

Few would argue that journalists must market, but here precision is important. The word *customer* is both too limiting and inaccurate. A customer, as the *American Heritage Dictionary of the English Language* puts it, is "one that buys goods or services." Most journalism is not a service bought. It is provided free—including most Internet news sites, many of the nation's weekly papers, radio news, and news on television. What's more, the metropolitan newspapers and magazines actually sell to their audience at a loss.

Rather than selling customers content, newspeople are building a relationship with their audience based on their values, judgment, authority, courage, professionalism, and commitment to the community. Providing this service creates a bond with the public, which the news organization then rents to advertisers.

The news audience is a consumer, but it is an oversimplification and a confusion to call it a customer. The relationship is deeper than that and is distinct from that of the true business customer of journalism—the advertiser.

In short, the business relationship of journalism is different from traditional consumer marketing, and in some ways it is more complex. That is, it is a triangle. The audience is not the customer buying goods and services—the advertiser is. Yet the customer/advertiser has to be subordinate in that triangle to the third figure, the citizen. Even entrepreneurial business magnates such as Henry Luce understood this triangular relationship. "If we have to be subsidized by anybody, we think that the advertiser presents extremely interesting possibilities," he told top aides in 1938. His goal, Luce said, was not to compromise "more than a small fraction of our journalistic soul."[29] Luce's boast was that "there is not an advertiser in America who does not realize that Time Inc. is cussedly independent."

THE WALL

If journalists are committed to the citizen first, what about the rest of the people who work in news companies—the ad salespeople, the circulation department, the truckers, the publisher, and the owner? What should citizens expect of them? What is their relationship to the newsroom?

Traditionally, journalists in the twentieth century often talked about there being a firewall between the news and the business sides of news companies. Editors at Time Inc. often hailed the idea that H. R. Luce talked about the separation in their company between church (news) and state (the business side). Robert McCormick, the famous and notorious publisher of the *Chicago Tribune,* early in the twentieth century created two separate banks of elevators inside his ornate Tribune Tower overlooking the Chicago River. He didn't want his advertising salesmen even to ride with his reporters.

Unfortunately, that notion of the journalist cloistered behind some wall in service to the audience while everyone else is committed freely to profit is a misguided metaphor. First, it encouraged the isolation we have described. Second, if the two sides of a news-providing organization are really working at cross purposes, the journalism tends to be on the side that is corrupted.

The scandal involving the *Los Angeles Times* and the Staples Center sports arena reveals how poor the wall metaphor really is. The paper arranged to share profits with arena owners in exchange for help selling ads. The arena owners sent stern letters to their subcontractors insisting that ads be bought. The stories assigned and written at the paper were all positive. The newsroom was not told of the arrangement. The wall, in other words, was kept intact. When the arrangement was discovered, both reporters and readers were outraged.

More than two hundred letters, e-mails, faxes, and phone messages poured onto the desk of reader representative Narda Zacchino in less than a week. When Sharon Waxman of the *Washington Post* went to interview Zacchino, she saw a log of phone messages lying on the desk, the main ideas from each one highlighted with a yellow marker. "Basically, readers are saying that this shakes their faith, their trust in the paper," Zacchino told Waxman. "People are questioning a lot of things. They are asking whether advertisers have influence in our stories. Questioning our integrity. What concerns me are these questions over whether our reporting is honest: 'Does such and such corporation have a deal with you?'"

Eventually, media reporter David Shaw would discover a growing pattern by Times management of exploiting the readership on behalf of its advertisers, all without letting the newsroom know. All of this had occurred after a former cereal company executive named Mark Willes, with little background and a shallow understanding of the economics of journalism, took over the Times Mirror company that owned the paper. The mythical wall, in other words, did little to protect anyone. The business side was selling the newsroom out and had enough power to circumscribe the newsroom without its knowing.

Tensions between the newsroom and the business side had been building for years. The 1970s were one point in this escalation. In reaction to the oil crisis, major state newspapers like the *Atlanta Journal-Constitution* or the *Des Moines Register* cut back drastically on their state-wide circulation because of the increased cost of delivery.

Another period of escalating tension started in 1989, when the industry faced an advertising recession and overall newspaper circulation began to fall in absolute terms for the first time, rather than just declining as a percentage of the population.[30] Major advertisers, like department stores and grocery chains, were going through a period of consolidation; as competition disappeared, so did the advertising it generated. Meanwhile, new retail rivals like Wal-Mart were not advertising in newspapers at all.

By the early nineties, most newspaper companies were publicly traded corporations. In response to the problems, the industry began to try to persuade Wall Street that they were getting tough with costs and shedding any remaining inefficiencies. Newsroom budgets were cut, and when the industry began to come back along with the economy, those cuts were not fully restored. That pattern was repeated in the next newspaper recession of 2001, when 2,000 jobs were lost and not restored in the good times that followed.[31]

As the business side began tightening its grip to make up for lost revenue, a series of academic studies continued to find a strong correlation between financial investment in the newsroom and quality journalism. Supporting news gathering, the studies argued, would create quality journalism, which in turn would drive up circulation and help the bottom line. The argument was never popular in boardrooms, however, where most of the debate occurred. For years this dispute was little but background noise for journalists and their public. Some scholars, such as Phil Meyer at the University of North Carolina, argued that the industry was being short-sighted, committing suicide in a death spiral of cuts to the product to maintain high profit margins. The cuts would only drive away more readers who had other choices for news, which in turn would lead to further cutbacks. It was, whether conscious or not, a strategy of liquidating the industry.

By 2005, the problems on the financial side seemed to worsen as readers began to move online.[32] The circulation losses accelerated, and the industry began to see significant job losses again—this time not attributable to economic cycles but wholly to industry fundamentals.[33] The companies that fared best were those that had taken a slower, more long-term approach, including fewer cuts and more newsroom investment. But by then, for companies that had not, time had run out. Investors in Knight Ridder, a company that had been among the most aggressive about cost cutting, were still not satisfied and forced the company up for sale. The buyer, the McClatchy Company, was one of the more long-term, investment-oriented rivals.

Five years ago, when the first edition of this book was published, people were still optimistic about ways to preserve the values of journalism in the corporate age. In 2000, Peter C. Goldmark Jr., then chairman and chief executive of the *International Herald Tribune,* suggested in a meeting at the Aspen Institute that corporations needed to do something "to cement the value of the journalistic enterprise within these huge corporate empires. . . . Every CEO understands they have a fiduciary obligation to their shareholders. In terms of journalism, I put more faith in corporate leadership that understands that they have an equally solemn fiduciary responsibility arising from their ownership of a news organization—that they hold a public trust."[34]

Goldmark offered four suggestions: have the CEO meet annually with those of similar organizations to assess the journalistic health of their companies; designate a member of the board of directors to assume special responsibility for protecting the independence of the news organization; invite an annual review or audit of the independence and vigor of the company's news function; jointly, with similar companies, fund an independent council to track, promote, examine, and defend the independence of the press.

In 2006, there was enough evidence to conclude that even more ground has been lost in this battle. In effect, at many old media companies, though not all, the decades-long battle at the top between the idealists and the accountants is over. The idealists have lost. The troubles of 2005, when more than 2,000 journalists lost their jobs at newspaper companies across the country, dealt a huge blow in this fight for journalism in the public interest.

An executive at one of the three broadcast networks told senior staff in a meeting last year, "the ethical anvil has been lifted," meaning the producers could dispense with traditional notions of journalistic propriety. Perhaps the most celebrated editor in the country, John Carroll of the *Los Angeles Times,* stepped down in frustration, but only after taking weeks to persuade his successor not to join him. Perhaps the most celebrated journalist still at ABC, Ted Koppel, left for cable, but only after announcing that neither cable news nor network news was amenable to the long-form work to which he aspired.

The most cogent explanation for why journalism in the public interest has lost leverage was probably offered by Polk Laffoon IV, the corporate spokesman of Knight Ridder: "I wish there were an identifiable and strong correlation between quality journalism . . . and newspaper sales," he said. "It isn't . . . that simple."[35] From here on, in many companies the fight on behalf of the public interest will come from the rank and file of the newsroom—with the news executive as mediator with the boardroom. At many new media companies, it is not clear if advocates for the public interest are present at all.

In the old media world, there are some notable exceptions to this situation, and journalists who work there today consider themselves lucky. They are organizations where there is no wall, but where the business side of the company has embraced the values of the newsroom as the soul of the operation. In these companies, independent public-interest journalism is the product and the value that the company is selling, with profit as a second priority, a predictable by-product that is strategically and necessarily required for long-term health.

In 2002, the Guardian Newspapers Limited in the United Kingdom responded to the challenge of developing a new relationship with its public when it launched a major effort in transparency, creating an annual audit called "Living Our Values." The purpose of the independently produced audit was to make clear to readers the special nature of the relationship between a commercial news organization and the citizens. The audit reports annually to the public in documented detail on the social and ethical behavior of the company and its promise to produce a "liberal, progressive, internationalist newspaper," as well as its behavior as a commercial business in such areas as its relationships with its employees, its business partners, and other institutions in the community and the world. Rather than presenting the company as two separate organizations, the Guardian audit describes how the values shared by the business and the news sides combine to serve a public interest.

One American newspaper company that escaped layoffs in 2005 was McClatchy, whose president and CEO believes that quality journalism is the cornerstone of the enterprise. In a speech to shareholders in 2005, Gary Pruitt emphasized this commitment, saying it made possible both the major achievements at the company's dozen newspapers and its financial success. And, Pruitt added, "Our focus on journalistic quality and continuous improvement certainly supports our strong performance in circulation." To that point, the McClatchy papers had grown in circulation steadily for twenty years.

In a profile of the company in 2003, the *American Journalism Review* ran Pruitt's 100-word definition of quality journalism: "Quality newspapers provide complete, thorough coverage of local, national and international news and features so that people can be fully informed, participate in civic life and just live a better life—from recipes to the actions of city councils and the United Nations. Newspapers are the sole remaining mass medium in each local market, so they are essential in not only informing readers but also in creating a sense of cohesion within a community. No other medium or institution, including government, can play that role given the fragmentation of audiences that has occurred in all other forms of media."[36]

Despite layoffs and a drop in stock prices, the New York Times Company had always maintained a commitment to quality journalism, best reflected by the flagship newspaper. Analysts have actually expressed a worry that the Times Company is too focused on newspapers and is not looking to diversify its revenue by investing in other products. "We are a company committed to journalism," Arthur Sulzberger Jr., the company chairman and publisher of the *New York Times*, told Ken Auletta of *The New Yorker* in 2005. "That is our core strength. That is our hedgehog. We are not in the education or cooking business. You are going to see us make journalism investments."[37]

If the mythical wall cannot protect the journalists' allegiance to citizens first, what will? The companies that have not yet been defeated by the pressure of the bottom line share similar characteristics when it comes to defining the relationship between news and business. Five key characteristics emerge.

1 • THE OWNER/CORPORATION MUST BE COMMITTED TO CITIZENS FIRST

Rather than cloister the newsroom from the rest of the organization, journalism works best when both sides are committed to the profession's values, not one side to business and the other to public service. History suggests that this works only when the owner of the company believes deeply in these core journalistic values.

Even some of the so-called defenders of the wall were, in reality, practitioners of this joint philosophy, with journalism predominant. Contrary to legend, there is scant evidence that Henry Luce actually talked about church and state, according to historian Tom Leonard. Rather, Luce believed the whole company needed to be "cussedly independent."

As he looked back on his own career, Tom Johnson, the former publisher of the *Los Angeles Times* and then president of the Cable News Network, came to the same conclusion as Luce had a generation earlier, or Ochs a generation before that:

> Media owners, or in the case of publicly traded companies, the board-elected CEO, ultimately decide the quality of the news produced by or televised by their news departments. It is they who most often select, hire, fire, and promote the editors, and publishers, top general managers, news directors, and managing editors—the journalists—who run their newsrooms. . . . Owners determine newsroom budgets, and the amount of time and space allotted to news versus advertising. They set the standards of quality by the quality of the people they choose and the news policies they embrace. Owners decide how much profit they should produce from their media properties. Owners decide what quality levels they are willing to support by how well or how poorly they pay their journalists.[38]

As publisher of the *Los Angeles Times*, the late Otis Chandler repeatedly demonstrated that he was cussedly independent, Johnson recalls.

Chandler provided the "heat shield" protecting his newspeople's independence from his family, his board of directors, and special interests–whether it was Chandler's mother who occasionally wanted the *Times* music critic fired, board members who had other pet peeves, or a host of others.

This position was easier to hold in the age of independent owners, a model that, with a handful of exceptions, no longer exists. If independence is the key asset of the news company–and the key meaning of the First Amendment–the challenge is how to maintain that independence in a corporate culture of, as Johnson puts it, the board-appointed CEO.

The historical protection for journalism, the benevolent patriarch, has disappeared, and the new corporation culture has done nothing to replace it. Corporations assume an obligation broader than that of their shareholders when they incorporate journalism in their portfolios. The key is that they begin to realize and articulate their responsibility to citizens, and take steps to protect it. Equally crucial is that the public understand its stake in this and demand that its democratic interests be recognized, not only by journalists but also by the corporate leadership to whom the journalists now answer. If this does not occur, journalism independent of corporate self-interest will disappear.

2 • HIRE BUSINESS MANAGERS WHO ALSO PUT CITIZENS FIRST

While the owner is the ultimate determiner of an institution's values, successful businesspeople also talk about hiring managers who share the mission, even if selling ads or building circulation is a different path from producing stories. Robert Dechard, the chairman and chief executive of A. H. Belo, the newspaper and television company, said that commitment and understanding should flow down the organization. "It comes down to selecting people who have good news judgment and experience in journalism and are sensitive to potential conflicts. I would prefer to have a person with that sound judgment."[39]

The *New York Times* has a similar model. Its advertising department, for instance, regularly turns away ads on days when events require a larger space for the news, such as on days of a presidential press conference or major speech. The advertising department knows that the paper's readers have come to expect full transcripts of such events, and that relationship will nurture the paper's business in the long run.

3 • SET AND COMMUNICATE CLEAR STANDARDS

Even if owners share the journalistic mission, many news companies feel they need clearly articulated standards down the ranks, as well as an atmosphere in which the businesspeople and newspeople, at least at certain levels, can talk to make sure they understand and appreciate each other's roles.

"You have to have clearly understood principles, have things in writing," said Jennie Buckner, then editor of the Knight Ridder–owned *Charlotte Observer*. The *Observer* in 1999 held a series of meetings at which employees from all departments were briefed on guidelines for handling potential conflicts between advertising and news. *Observer* editors sat in on ad department meetings to explain the news judgment process and to show, in Buckner's words, "We are open to ideas but not interference."[40]

The *Baltimore Sun* had similar sessions to clarify advertising and news relationships and to make sure all employees knew about them. "We discussed the fact that, on journalistic decisions, the newsroom has to have the integrity to make the final call," said then managing editor William Marimow.[41]

Yet meetings and codes represent a first step that goes only so far. These have to be living policies that stand up to the pressures of a crisis and that manifest everyday when there is no crisis. Standards that are framed on the wall but not lived become advertisements that the rhetoric of management is hollow.

4 • JOURNALISTS HAVE FINAL SAY OVER NEWS

Like those who have drafted strict written rules, many other organizations involved in producing the news say that the clearest principle must be that the newsroom has final say over news. This is the rule at many of the best news organizations. At the *Washington Post*, executive editor Leonard Downie Jr. insists that advertorial products–those special sections labeled as advertising supplements–"are run by me, and we have vetoed them when we believe there is a problem. We also look to make sure they are properly labeled."

5 • COMMUNICATE CLEAR STANDARDS TO THE PUBLIC

The final key is to be clear with audiences—clearer than in the past—about how news organizations operate. In his address to the American Society of Newspaper Editors, Edward Seaton, the 1999 president of that group and editor of the *Manhattan Mercury* in Manhattan, Kansas, advised that the best way for newspapers to rebuild trust and credibility was to "explain yourself. . . . As editors, we have to lead. We have to state our values. When we have standards, we have something that we can explain to the public and our staffs, something that everyone can hear and understand. We must do much more and better than we have. Our emphasis has to be on serving citizens, not our bottom line or technology."[42]

Some television stations have taken similar approaches. When he was news director at KGUN-TV in Tucson, Forrest Carr created and repeatedly broadcast a "Viewers Bill of Rights" that outlined precisely what citizens in Tucson should expect from his station and his people.

The list of seven rights included such items as defining the public's right to know (the station "asks tough questions and conducts investigations"), the right to ethical news gathering (the station will live up to the ethics code of the Society of Professional Journalists), and the right to solution-oriented journalism (the station will attempt to find or spotlight solutions, not just focus on problems). The list also included a right to privacy with the explanation that "our journalistic duty and the public's right to know often require us to place people and organizations in the news who don't wish to be there. We will never do so in a cavalier or insensitive fashion and will always consider privacy concerns as we weigh the importance of a story. We will never stalk or hound the victims of crime."

Finally, the list included a "right to hold us accountable" and explained how viewers can do it—through the station's viewer representative investigating viewer complaints and by airing viewer feedback on the air.

The language of a bill of rights may strike some as corny. But focus groups conducted by the Project for Excellence in Journalism in Tucson around the time of the station's introduction of the program suggested that they connected with people. When the moderator asked citizens how they would raise the quality of local TV news, viewers pointed directly at what KGUN was doing. "It might go back to the station having some guidelines, something called ethics in reporting," said one man. "Define that . . . [and then] do it in a tasteful way. What they may need to do is pull a bunch of people like us in and ask what they would like to see happening." As it turns out, this is just what KGUN had done.

Some critics called the KGUN plan pandering, but the station's share of the Tucson television audience continued a steady climb. Carr, the news director, also said that the project had another benefit: making the values of the organization clear to those who work there. Nothing he has ever done, Carr said, has helped him more in improving the culture of his own newsroom. Obviously, KGUN's promises are only as good as the work behind them, but the station had given citizens a way to hold it accountable, which is why, of course, it is difficult.

Ironically, some news organizations are moving the other way. At the *Los Angeles Times,* one of the first things the Tribune Company did in 2005 as it faced hard times was gut the paper's budget for communicating with the public, from $12.7 million to $300,000. Editor John Carroll thought the paper should have been doing just the opposite. "The values of journalism are being reviled by marketing campaigns from competing organizations that belittle the very idea of mainstream media and by the likes of [Fox News President] Roger Ailes who comes out of attack politics," Carroll said. He believes the paper, and all mainstream news outlets, should be responding by spending more to promote the values that make traditional journalism important and distinctive. "Is the reduction of a newspaper's promotions budget from $12.7 million to $300,000 in a single year a logical response?" he asked. As much as anything that Tribune did, Carroll said, this signaled to him that they were in retreat and that it was time for him to leave.[43]

Whatever approach a news organization takes, the question of allegiance is pivotal and usually is ignored or misunderstood. The reason it is so important, however, is precisely that the press has become so unpopular. What is often missed in considering the decline in public trust of the press is that, at bottom, this credibility crisis is about motive. As citizens, we do not expect perfection of our journalists—or even a journalism with every word spelled correctly. The problem is more fundamental.

Journalists like to think of themselves as the people's surrogate, covering society's waterfront in the public interest. Increasingly, however, the public doesn't believe them. People see sensationalism and exploitation, and they sense that journalists are in it for a buck, or personal fame, or perhaps worse, a kind of perverse joy in unhappiness. When Bob Woodward's practice of interviewing administration officials for his books—and not letting much information be part of the immediate record—was revealed, readers challenged his allegiance. Was he an author working for himself or was he a *Washington Post* reporter working for the public? Some readers did not trust Woodward to decide whether something needed to be exposed immediately or could wait a year or two to make it into a book. "Does Woodward always decide for us which information he feels we need to know?" one reader asked *Post* editor Leonard Downie Jr. in a Q&A on the paper's website.[44]

To reconnect people with the news, and through the news to the larger world, journalism must reestablish the allegiance to citizens that the news industry has mistakenly helped to subvert. Yet even this, ultimately, will not be enough. Truth and loyalty to citizens are only the first two steps in making journalism work. The next step is just as important: the method that journalists use to approach the truth and convey that method to citizens.

ENDNOTES

1. Geneva Overholser, "Editor Inc.," *American Journalism Review* (December 1998), 58.
2. Ibid., 57. A Project on the State of the American Newspaper, a survey of 77 senior newspaper editors, found that 14 percent reported spending more than half their time on business matters, while another 35 percent spent between one-third and one-half of their time on business matters.
3. CCJ and the Pew Research Center for the People and the Press, "Striking the Balance: Audience Interests, Business Pressures and Journalists' Values," March 1999, 79; available at www.journalism.org.
4. Research findings by our academic partners, William Damon, Howard Gardner, and Mihaly Csikszentmihalyi; unpublished interviews for the book *Good Work: When Excellence and Ethics Meet* (New York: Basic Books, 2001).

5. Nick Clooney, interview by William Damon, Howard Gardner, and Mihaly Csik-szentmihalyi, ibid.

6. CNN.com, "Top New York Times Editors Quit," March 1, 2004; available at www.cnn.com/2003/US/Northeast/06/05/nytimes.resigns.

7. Don Van Natta Jr., Adam Liptak, and Clifford J. Levy, "The Miller Case: A Notebook, a Cause, a Jail Cell and a Deal," *New York Times*, October 16, 2005.

8. Alex Jones and Susan Tifft, *The Trust: The Private and Powerful Family Behind The New York Times* (Boston, New York, London: Little, Brown, 1999), 43.

9. *Washington Post DeskBook on Style*, 2nd edition (New York: McGraw Hill, 1989).

10. Tom Goldstein, "Wanted: More Outspoken Views," *Columbia Journalism Review* (November/December 2001).

11. Paul Alfred Pratte, *Gods Within the Machine: A History of the American Society of Newspaper Editors, 1923–1993* (Westport, CT: Praeger, 1995), 2.

12. "Dow Jones Code of Conduct," New York: Dow Jones, 2000; see ethics codes at www.journalism.org.

13. "Project for Excellence in Journalism, Local TV Project," focus groups, January 26, 1999, in Atlanta and January 28, 1999, in Tucson.

14. American Society of Newspaper Editors, "The Newspaper Journalists of the '90s," a study, 1997; available at www.asne.org.

15. Ibid. In 1988, 41 percent said they were less involved than others. In 1996, that number had risen to 55 percent.

16. Tom Rosenstiel, "The Beat Goes On: Clinton's First Year With the Media," Twentieth-Century Fund essay, 30. By 1993, a two-month examination of the front pages of the *New York Times, Los Angeles Times,* and *Washington Post* showed that only slightly more than half of the stories could be classified as straight news, while nearly 40 percent were analytical or interpretive treatments of news events or trends.

17. Daniel Hallin, "Sound Bite News: Television Coverage of Elections, 1968–1988," *Journal of Communications*, 42 (Spring 1992), 6.

18. Ibid., 11.

19. Joseph N. Cappella and Kathleen Hall Jamieson, *Spiral of Cynicism: The Press and the Public Good* (New York: Oxford University Press, 1997), 31.

20. Rosenstiel, "The Beat Goes On," 30.

21. Michael Kelly, "Farmer Al," *Washington Post*, March 24, 1999; available at www.washingtonpost.com.

22. Michael Kelly, "Gore: 'His Wife, His Public Life, It's All Been Too Perfect,'" *Baltimore Sun*, December 13, 1987; available at www.baltimoresun.com.

23. Philip J. Trounstein, at CCJ Forum, Washington, DC, March 27, 1998.

24. Lou Urenick, "Newspapers Arrive at Economic Crossroads," *Nieman Reports*, special issue (Summer 1999), 3–20.

25. Ibid., 6.

26. Ibid., 5. According to figures from the Inland Press Association, these percentages are for the five years ending 1992 and the five years ending 1997. Smaller newspapers were defined as papers of around 50,000 circulation. Larger were defined as papers of roughly 500,000 circulation. Newspaper payroll was cut 8 percent and 15 percent, respectively. Production costs were trimmed 21 percent and 12 percent,

respectively. Rather than investing more in product, the newspaper industry invested more in marketing and marketing technology, increased sales staff, and advertising presentations.

27. Based on interviews with television news executives, we believe the practice is equally common for broadcast.

28. Overholser, "Editor Inc.," 54.

29. Thomas Leonard, "The Wall: A Long History," *Columbia Journalism Review* (January 2000), 28.

30. Figures are reflected in the *Editor and Publisher International Yearbook*.

31. Numbers on staff cuts in 2001 come from the Project for Excellence in Journalism, "State of the News Media 2005," March 2005; available at www.journalism.org.

32. Pew Internet and American Life Project, "Online News: For Many Home Broadband Users, the Internet Is a Primary News Source," March 22, 2006; available at www.pewinternet.org.

33. Jay DeFoore, "More Than 2,000 Newspaper Jobs Lost in 2005," *Editor & Publisher*, November 17, 2005; available at www.editorandpublisher.com.

34. Peter Goldmark, "Setting the Testbed for Journalistic Values," Fourth Annual Aspen Institute Conference on Journalism and Society, August 23, 2000; available at www.aspeninstitute.org.

35. Joseph N. DiStefano, "Former Knight Ridder Journalists Plan to Nominate Board Candidates," *Philadelphia Inquirer*, November 18, 2005; available at www.philly.com.

36. "Pruitt's Code," sidebar to Susan Paterno's story, "Is McClatchy Different?" *American Journalism Review* (August/September 2003); available at www.ajr.org.

37. Ken Auletta, "The Inheritance," *The New Yorker*, December 19, 2005, 76.

38. Tom Johnson, "Excellence in the News: Who Really Decides," speech delivered at Paul White Award Dinner, October 2, 1999; Walter Cronkite Award acceptance speech, November 12, 1999.

39. Joe Strupp, "Where There's a Wall There's a Way," *Editor & Publisher*, December 11, 1999, 23.

40. Ibid., 22.

41. Ibid.

42. Edward Seaton, at the convention of the American Society of Newspaper Editors, April 13–16, 1999; retrieved from proceedings published on the ASNE website; available at www.asne.org.

43. Interview with John Carroll by the authors, October 11, 2005.

44. "Post Executive Editor Discusses Woodward," *Washington Post*, November 18, 2005; available at www.washingtonpost.com.

4

Journalism of Verification

As he sat down to write, the Greek correspondent wanted to convince his audience that it could trust him. He was not writing an official version of the war, he wanted people to know, nor a hasty one. He was striving for something more independent, more reliable, more lasting. He had been mindful in his reporting of the way memory, perspective, and politics blur recollection. He had double-checked his facts.

To convey all this, he decided to explain the methods of his reporting right at the beginning. This is the dedication to the methodology of truth that Thucydides drafted in the fifth century B.C., in the introduction to his account of the Peloponnesian War:

> With regard to my factual reporting of events . . . I have made it a principle not to write down the first story that came my way, and not even to be guided by my own general impressions; either I was present myself at the events which I have described or else heard of them from eyewitnesses whose reports I have checked with as much thoroughness as possible. Not that even so the truth was easy to discover: different

eyewitnesses gave different accounts of the same events, speaking out of partiality for one side or the other, or else from imperfect memories.[1]

Why does this passage seem so contemporary more than 2,000 years after it was written? Because it speaks to the heart of the task of nonfiction: How do you sift through the rumors, the gossip, the failed memories, the manipulative agendas, and try to capture something as accurately as possible, subject to revision in light of new information and perspective? How do you overcome your own limits of perception, your own experience, and come to an account that more people will recognize as reliable? Strip away all the debate about journalism, all the differences among media or between one age or another. Day to day, these are the real questions faced by those who try to gather news, understand it, and convey it to others.

While not following any standardized code, every journalist operates by relying on some often highly personal method of testing and providing information–his or her own individual discipline of verification. Practices such as seeking multiple witnesses to an event, disclosing as much as possible about sources, and asking many sides for comment are, in effect, tools in the discipline of verification. These methods may be intensely personal and idiosyncratic. Writer Rick Meyer at the *Los Angeles Times* would splice his facts and interviews into note-card-like snippets and organize them on his office floor. Or the methods may be institutionalized, like the fact-checking department of *The New Yorker*. But by whatever name, in whatever medium, these habits and methods underlie the third principle:

The essence of journalism is a discipline of verification.

In the end, the discipline of verification is what separates journalism from entertainment, propaganda, fiction, or art. Entertainment–and its cousin "infotainment"–focuses on what is most diverting. Propaganda selects facts or invents them to serve the real purpose: persuasion and manipulation. Fiction invents scenarios to get at a more personal impression of what it calls truth.

Journalism alone is focused on getting what happened down right.

This is true be it the work of a network TV news division or a lone citizen journalist blogging on the Internet, and it is the first criterion by which any work claimed as journalism would be judged for competence.

Journalists often fail to connect their deeply held feelings about craft to the larger philosophical questions about journalism's role. They know how to check a story even if they can't always articulate the role that checking a story plays in society. But verifying facts resides in the central function of journalism. As Walter Lippmann put it in 1920, "There can be no liberty for a community which lacks the information by which to detect lies."[2]

This is why journalists become so upset with Hollywood moviemakers when they stray into real-life accounts. *60 Minutes* correspondent Mike Wallace was livid in 1999 when the movie *The Insider* put invented words in his mouth and altered time frames to suggest that he was worried about his "legacy" when he caved in to the tobacco industry on a story. "Have you ever heard me invoke the word *legacy*? That is utter bullshit . . . and I'm offended."[3] The film's director, Michael Mann, countered that though things were changed to make the story more dramatic, the film was "basically accurate" to some larger definition of truthfulness, since Wallace had indeed caved. If words were invented or if Wallace's conscious motives were different, it didn't matter. In this sense utility becomes a higher value and literal truth is subordinated to necessary fictions.

The two men were talking different languages. Mann was saying that Wallace was hiding behind the facts to obscure the significance of what he did. Wallace was suggesting that the significance can never be detached from an accurate account of the details. In this case both arguments may be defensible. But the journalistic process of verification must take both of them into account.

From the moment news became a commodity that is instantly and continuously available in almost unlimited outlets, the process of verification—the beating heart of credible journalism in the public interest—came under new pressure. There are two principal sources of this pressure. The first is the temptation to publish immediately because something could always be corrected later. The second is the impulse to publish news simply because it's already "out there" in this new media system.

The problem was made more complex in the new reality created by a war against terrorism declared in the aftermath of September 11. This new reality conflicted with the popular notion of the "we media" culture, which suggested that since citizens could communicate with each other at will, they could be closer to real truth and more accurate information.

No doubt they can communicate more easily. Whether or not the end result sustains a journalism of verification depends on the degree of commitment to that goal by those who produce the information in competition with other powerful mediating institutions that produce information for persuasion or manipulation.

THE LOST MEANING OF OBJECTIVITY

Perhaps because the discipline of verification is so personal and so haphazardly communicated, it is also part of one of the great confusions of journalism—the concept of objectivity. The original meaning of this idea is now thoroughly misunderstood and by and large lost.

When critics, including many in journalism, reject the notion of objectivity they usually do so on the grounds that no person can ever be objective. As Dan Gillmor, author of *We the Media,* wrote in a much circulated 2005 essay called "The End of Objectivity," "we are human. We have biases and backgrounds and a variety of conflicts that we bring to our jobs every day."[4] Gillmor was advocating that journalists drop the word *objectivity* and replace it with thoroughness, accuracy, fairness, and transparency.

His is only the latest in nearly eight decades of skepticism about the notion of objectivity. What dominates the argument, however, is largely a confusion. When the concept of objectivity originally migrated to journalism, it was not meant to imply that journalists were free of bias. Quite the contrary.

The term began to appear as part of journalism early in the last century, particularly in the 1920s, out of a growing recognition that journalists were full of bias, often unconscious. The call for journalists to adopt objectivity was an appeal for them to develop a consistent method of testing information—a transparent approach to evidence—precisely so that personal and cultural biases would not undermine the accuracy of their work.

In the nineteenth century, journalists talked about something called realism rather than objectivity.[5] This was the idea that if reporters simply dug out the facts and ordered them together, the truth would reveal itself rather naturally. Realism emerged at a time when journalism was separating from political parties and becoming more accurate. It roughly coincided with the invention of what journalists call the inverted pyramid, in which a journalist lines the facts up from most important to least important, thinking it helps audiences understand things naturally.

At the beginning of the twentieth century, however, some journalists began to worry about the naivete of realism. In part, reporters and editors were becoming more aware of the rise of propaganda and the role of press agents. At a time when Freud was developing his theories of the unconscious and painters like Picasso were experimenting with Cubism, journalists were developing a greater recognition of human subjectivity. In 1919, Walter Lippmann and Charles Merz, an associate editor for the *New York World*, wrote an influential and scathing account of how cultural blinders had distorted the *New York Times*'s coverage of the Russian Revolution.[6] "In the large, the news about Russia is a case of seeing not what was, but what men wished to see," they wrote. Lippmann and others began to look for ways for the individual journalist "to remain clear and free of his irrational, his unexamined, his unacknowledged prejudgments in observing, understanding and presenting the news."[7]

Journalism, Lippmann declared, was being practiced by "untrained accidental witnesses." Good intentions, or what some might call "honest efforts," by journalists were not enough. Faith in the rugged individualism of the tough reporter—what Lippmann called the "cynicism of the trade"—was also not enough. Nor were some of the trends of the times, like bylines or columnists.[8]

The solution, Lippmann argued, was for journalists to acquire more of "the scientific spirit. . . . There is but one kind of unity possible in a world as diverse as ours. It is unity of method, rather than aim; the unity of disciplined experiment." Lippmann meant by this that journalism should aspire to "a common intellectual method and a common area of valid fact." To begin, Lippmann thought, the fledgling field of journalism education should be transformed from "trade schools designed to fit men for higher salaries in the existing structure." Instead, the field should make its cornerstone the study of evidence and verification.[9]

Although this was an era of faith in science, Lippmann had few illusions. "It does not matter that the news is not susceptible of mathematical statement. In fact, just because news is complex and slippery, good reporting requires the exercise of the highest scientific virtues."[10] In the original concept, in other words, the journalist is not objective, but his method can be. The key was in the discipline of the craft, not the aim.

The words seem ironic today. Much of the modern understanding of objectivity in journalism has inverted what Lippmann meant to be the problem he was trying to address. Most people think of objectivity in journalism as an aim, not as a method. And many citizens scoff at this intention, since they have little idea of the methods journalists might be employing. Yet the notion that the aim of objectivity is insufficient without a unity of method to put it into practice is as valid today as ever. Indeed, it comes close to what Gillmor has advocated as an alternative.

What's more, this original understanding of objectivity has some important implications that are absolutely contemporary to a twenty-first-century understanding of media. One is that the impartial voice employed by many news organizations—that familiar, supposedly neutral style of newswriting—is not a fundamental principle of journalism. Rather, it is an often helpful device news organizations use to highlight that they are trying to produce something obtained by objective methods. The second implication is that this neutral voice, without a discipline of verification, is a veneer atop something hollow. Journalists who select sources to express what is really their own point of view, and then use the neutral voice to make it seem objective, are engaged in deception. This damages the credibility of the whole profession by making it seem unprincipled, dishonest, and biased. This is an important caution in an age when the standards of the press are in doubt.

This idea is worth repeating for emphasis. In this original understanding of objectivity, neutrality is not a fundamental principle of journalism. It is merely a voice, or device, to persuade the audience of one's accuracy or fairness.

It is interesting, too, that those in the commercial press, Left and Right, who produce opinionated journalism often deny it and claim fairness instead. Fox News markets itself as "fair and balanced." Ann Coulter on the Right offers to expose the "lies" of the Left. Al Franken on the Left markets his book as "truth." They echo Hearst and Pulitzer and the yellow press of the nineteenth century, claiming that their sensationalized reporting is more accurate than their competitors'. Rarely do people in journalism even on the opinion end of the craft market themselves as better arguers, but instead as more accurate.

Another implication of the original meaning of objectivity as method is that it reconciles how various other forms of American journalism fall inside the broad principles of journalism. This includes the alternative press that typically came from the Left in the 1960s and 1970s, or the magazine journalism of opinion from all sides of the political spectrum. If journalism starts with accuracy, a professional method or discipline of verification, and some unity of method to this process of verifying facts, then it can encompass a range of presentations. (We will discuss this in greater detail in the next chapter, on the meaning of the concept of independence in journalism.)

Unity of method rather than aim, as Lippmann put it more than eighty years earlier, is the one unity that can be assessed in a diverse culture. And that method relates to the gathering of information, not the style of presentation. Lippmann was not alone in calling for a greater sense of professionalization, though his arguments are the most sophisticated. Joseph Pulitzer, the great populist journalistic innovator a generation earlier, had just created the Graduate School of Journalism at Columbia University for many of the same, though less clearly articulated, reasons. The Newspaper Guild was founded in large part to help professionalize journalism.

Over the years, however, this original and more sophisticated understanding of objectivity was utterly confused and its meaning lost. Writers such as Leo Rosten, who authored an influential sociological study of journalists, used the term to suggest that the journalist was objective. Not surprisingly, he found that idea wanting. So did various legal opinions, which declared objectivity impossible. Many journalists never really understood what Lippmann meant.[11] Over time, journalists began to reject the term *objectivity* as an illusion. They remained largely "accidental witnesses."

People in the alternative press often feel antagonistic toward so-called mainstream journalists for their faith in objectivity, when really what divides them are their positions about neutral voice, not how they go about gathering and verifying information. Newspaper people often move effortlessly to magazine work such as *The New Yorker* magazine, where they produce journalism in a voice not dissimilar to what the alternative press might be employing, or even in the more subjective forms of TV news.

In the meantime, reporters have gone on to refine the concept Lippmann had in mind, but usually only privately, and in the name of technique or reporting routines rather than journalism's larger purpose. The notion of an objective method of reporting exists in pieces, handed down by word of mouth from reporter to reporter. Developmental psychologist William Damon at Stanford University, for instance, has identified various "strategies" that journalists have developed to verify their reporting. Damon asked his interviewees where they learned these concepts. Overwhelmingly the answer was by trial and error, on my own, or from a friend. Rarely did journalists report learning them in journalism school or from their editors.[12] Many useful books have been written on the subject. The group calling itself Investigative Reporters and Editors, for instance, has tried to develop a methodology for how to use public records, read documents, and produce Freedom of Information Act requests.

By and large, however, these informal strategies have not been pulled together into the widely understood discipline that Lippmann and others imagined. There is nothing approaching any standard rules of evidence, as in the law, or an agreed-upon method of observation, as in the conduct of scientific experiments. Nor have the older conventions of verification been expanded to match the new forms of journalism. Although journalism may have developed various techniques and conventions for determining facts, it has done less to develop a system for testing the reliability of journalistic interpretation.

Most important, at the dawn of the twenty-first century, the notion that journalists or anyone else can arrive at a truthful account of things or follow an objective method of verification has been eroded in the public mind. This amounts to a threat not only to the notion of journalism but also to the possibility of civil society's confronting and solving its problems. The public sphere becomes an arena solely for polarized debate, not for compromise, consensus, and solution.

If journalists are to make a case for the values that have guided their work for 250 years, or even in the instincts of the first chroniclers since Thucydides, they must understand the principles and methods of first getting the facts right, then find some way to reveal that method to the public.

JOURNALISM OF ASSERTION VS. JOURNALISM OF VERIFICATION

In many ways, the modern press culture is weakening the methodology of verification that journalists have developed, if not adequately named or codified. Technology is part of it. "The Internet and Nexis [plus services developed over the last decade or so for sharing and disseminating video] afford journalists easy access to stories and quotes without doing their own investigating," journalist Geneva Overholser told us at one Committee of Concerned Journalists forum. Facts have become a commodity, easily acquired, repackaged, and repurposed. In the age of the 24-hour news cycle, journalists now spend more time looking for something to add to the existing news, usually interpretation, than trying to independently discover and verify new facts. "Once a story is hatched, it's as if all the herd behavior is true. The story is determined by one medium—one newspaper or TV account.... Partly because news organizations are being consolidated and partly because of electronic reporting, we all feed at the same trough," said Overholser.[13]

The case of presidential candidate Al Gore is only one example of how technology can weaken the process of double-checking. As Gore campaigned in the 2000 election, the press began to focus on his seeming propensity to exaggerate past accomplishments. One account referred to Gore's "Pinocchio problem," another called him a "liar," and a third "delusional."[14] A key bit of evidence was his supposed claim that he had discovered the Love Canal toxic waste site in upstate New York. The problem is, Gore had never made any such claim. He had told a group of

New Hampshire high school students that he first learned about hazardous waste dangers when a constituent told him about a polluted town in Tennessee called Toone, and Gore wanted to hold hearings. "I looked around the country for other sites like that," he told the students. "I found a little place in upstate New York called Love Canal. Had the first hearing on the issue, and Toone, Tennessee—that was the one that you didn't hear of. But that was the one that started it all."[15]

The next day, however, the *Washington Post* misquoted Gore completely as saying, "I was the one that started it all." In a press release, the Republican Party changed the quote to "I was the one who started it all." The *New York Times* printed the same misquote as the *Post.* Soon the press was off and running, relying on the faulty accounts ingrained in the Nexis database of the two papers. It didn't catch anyone's attention that the Associated Press had the quote correct. The matter was not cleared up until the high school students themselves complained.

As journalists spend more time trying to synthesize the ever-growing stream of data pouring in through the new portals of information, the risk is they can become more passive, more receivers than gatherers. To combat this, a better understanding of the original meaning of objectivity could help put the news on firmer footing. We are not the only ones to recognize this. "Journalism and science come from the same intellectual roots," said Phil Meyer, University of North Carolina journalism professor, "from the seventeenth- and eighteenth-century enlightenment. The same thinking that led to the First Amendment"—the idea that out of a diversity of views we are more likely to know the truth—also "led to the scientific method. . . . I think this connection between journalism and science ought to be restored to the extent that we can. . . . I think we ought to emphasize objectivity of method. That's what scientific method is—our humanity, our subjective impulses . . . directed toward deciding what to investigate by objective means."[16]

Seen in this light, fairness and balance take on new meaning. Rather than high principles, they are really techniques—devices—to help guide journalists in the development and verification of their accounts. They should never be pursued for their own sake or invoked as journalism's goal. Their value is in helping get us closer to more thorough verification and a reliable version of events.

Balance, for instance, can lead to distortion. If an overwhelming percentage of scientists, as an example, believe that global warming is a scientific fact, or that some medical treatment is clearly the safest, it is a disservice to citizens and truthfulness to create the impression that the scientific debate is equally split. Unfortunately, all too often journalistic balance is misconstrued to have this kind of almost mathematical meaning, as if a good story is one that has an equal number of quotes from two sides. As journalists know, often there are more than two sides to a story. And sometimes balancing them equally is not a true reflection of reality.

Fairness, in turn, can also be misunderstood if it is seen to be a goal unto itself. Fairness should mean that the journalist is being fair to the facts and to a citizen's understanding of the facts. It should not mean, "Am I being fair to my sources, so that none of them will be unhappy?" Nor should it mean that journalist asking, "Does my story seem fair?" These are subjective judgments that may steer the journalist away from the need to do more to verify his or her work. Fairness, in other words, is also an aim, not a method, and ultimately is subjective.

Clarifying such common misunderstandings and improving the discipline of verification may be the most important step journalists can take to improve the quality of news and public discussion. In the end, this discipline is what separates journalism from other fields and creates an economic reason for it to continue. A more conscious discipline of verification is the best antidote to being overrun by a new journalism of assertion, and it would provide citizens with a basis for relying on journalistic accounts.

A stronger, more unified, and more transparent method of verifying the news would also be the single most important step that those who practice journalism could take to address and, if necessary, correct the rising perception that the work of journalists is marred by bias. We will explain more about this below.

What would this journalism of objective *method*—rather than aim—look like? What should citizens expect from the press as a reasonable discipline of reporting? As we listened to and studied the thoughts of journalists, citizens, and others concerning the news, we began to see a core set of concepts that form the foundation of the discipline of verification. They are the intellectual principles of a science of reporting:

1. Never add anything that was not there.
2. Never deceive the audience.
3. Be as transparent as possible about your methods and motives.
4. Rely on your own original reporting.
5. Exercise humility.

Let's examine them one at a time.

An important parallel to the new journalism of assertion is the rise of fiction posing as nonfiction. It has had different names in different areas. On television, producers have called it docudrama. In the publishing world, some—such as author James Frey—have hijacked the memoir genre to pass fiction off as biographical truth. In 2006 Frey was exposed to have fictionalized much of his memoir *A Million Little Pieces*. But all of it is making stuff up. In some cases it is just lying.

Oddly, there are some in journalism who believe that narrative nonfiction—the use of literary style to tell nonfiction—needs to blend into the area of invention. A long list of some of the best narrative stylists in nonfiction also doesn't show the problem, but the problem is growing. Ironically, it is also unnecessary. Narrative nonfiction doesn't need to invent to succeed. While running a narrative nonfiction writing program at Boston University, Mark Kramer developed a clear set of rules that any deadline journalist or literary stylist could live with—for example, regarding interior monologues: "No attribution of thoughts to sources unless the sources have said they'd had those very thoughts." Newspaper columnist Steve Lopez, while working as a writer at Time Inc., concluded that the rules and devices may differ depending on the style of story, but the principle does not: if it isn't verified, don't use it. Perhaps John McPhee, a *New Yorker* writer noted for the strength of his narrative style, summarized the key imperatives best: "The nonfiction writer is communicating with the reader about real people in real places. So if those people talk, you say what those people said. You don't say what the writer decides they said. . . . You don't make up dialogue. You don't make a composite character. . . . And you don't get inside their [characters'] heads and think for them. You can't interview the dead.

Where writers abridge that, they hitchhike on the credibility of writers who don't."[17]

In 1980, John Hersey, the Pulitzer Prize–winning author of *Hiroshima*, the story of the effects of the first use of the atomic bomb in World War II, attempted to articulate a principle to help make journalism compelling without crossing the line between fact and fiction. In "The Legend on the License," Hersey advocated a strict standard: never invent. Journalism's implicit credo is "nothing here is made up."[18]

Today, we think Hersey's standard of "never invent" needs to be refined. In his book *Midnight in the Garden of Good and Evil*, John Berendt used composite characters and condensed several events into one for dramatic effect. Ronald Reagan biographer Edmund Morris believed he could make the former president's life more vivid if he, the biographer, were a character in it. But reconstructing dialogue, using composite characters, compressing events, and moving people in time are inventions.

Along with Roy Peter Clark, the senior scholar at the Poynter Institute in St. Petersburg, Florida, we developed an updated pair of ideas for journalists trying to navigate the shoals lying between fact and fiction.

DO NOT ADD

Do not add things that did not happen. This goes further than "never invent" or make things up, for it also encompasses rearranging events in time or place or conflating characters or events. If a siren rang out during the taping of a TV story, and for dramatic effect it is moved from one scene to another, it has been added to that second place. What was once a fact becomes a fiction.

Usually, when people do add or embellish, they hide it—a tip off in itself that it is not acceptable. This was the point of Hersey's original essay, which challenged among others the author Tom Wolfe. And when authors of nonfiction have invented and admitted it, critics and readers have generally reacted poorly. Biographer Edmund Morris discovered this when he wrote *Dutch*, his authorized biography of Ronald Reagan, in which he made himself a character in the book witnessing Reagan in his early life, before the author was actually born. Morris said he was trying to make a point about how Reagan himself created fictional reality. Yet this intermingling of fantasy and reality did little to illuminate and much to damage the credibility of the book. "Why would I want to read that?" former *Washington Post* editor Ben Bradlee exclaimed in reaction, at a panel at the State University of New York at Oswego in the fall of 2005.[19]

DO NOT DECEIVE

Never mislead the audience. Fooling people is a form of lying and it mocks the idea that journalism is committed to truthfulness. This principle is closely related to the first one. If you move the sound of the siren and do not tell the audience, you are deceiving them. If acknowledging what you've done would make it unpalatable to the audience, then it is self-evidently improper. This is a useful check. How would the audience feel if they knew you moved that sound to another point in the story to make it more dramatic? Most likely they would feel the move was cheesy.

Do not deceive means that if one is going to engage in any narrative or storytelling techniques that vary from the most literal form of eyewitness reporting, the audience should know. On the question of quoting people, a survey of journalists that we conducted found broad agreement. Except for word changes to correct grammar, the overwhelming majority of journalists believe some signal should be sent to audiences—such as ellipses or brackets—if words inside quotation marks are changed or phrases deleted for clarity.[20]

If a journalist reconstructs quotes or events he did not witness, do not deceive also suggests that the audience should know these specific quotes were reconstructed and how these secondhand quotes were verified. A vague author's note at the beginning or end of a book or story that tells audiences merely "some interviews involved reconstruction" doesn't come close to adequate. Which interviews? Reconstructed how? These kinds of vague disclosures are not disclosures at all. They really amount to evasions.

We believe these two notions—Do Not Add and Do Not Deceive—serve as guideposts for journalists navigating the line between fact and fiction. But how as citizens are we to identify which journalism to trust? Here some other concepts help.

TRANSPARENCY

If journalists are truth seekers, it must follow that they be honest and truthful with their audiences, too—that they be truth presenters. If nothing else, this responsibility requires that journalists be as open and honest with audiences as they can about what they know and what they don't. How can you claim to be seeking to convey the truth if you're not truthful with the audience in the first place?

The only way in practice to level with people about what you know is to reveal as much as possible about your sources and methods. How do you know what you know? Who are your sources? How direct is their knowledge? What biases might they have? Are there conflicting accounts? What don't we know?

Call it the spirit of transparency. We consider this idea the most important single element in creating a better discipline of verification.

Most of the limitations journalists face in trying to move from accuracy to truth are addressed, if not overcome, by being honest about the nature of their knowledge, why they trust it, and what efforts they make to learn more.

Transparency has a second important virtue: it signals the journalist's respect for the audience. It allows the audience to judge the validity of the information, the process by which it was secured, and the motives and biases of the journalist providing it. This makes transparency the best protection against errors and deception by sources. If the best information a journalist has comes from a potentially biased source, naming the source will reveal to the audience the possible bias of the information—and may inhibit the source from deceiving as well.

Transparency also helps establish that the journalist has a public-interest motive, the key to credibility. The willingness of the journalist to be transparent about what he or she has done is at the heart of establishing that the journalist is concerned with truth. The lie, or the mistake, is in pretending omniscience, or claiming greater knowledge than we have.

How does the Spirit of Transparency work? It starts at the top, where it may mean public meetings, speeches, or editors' columns, especially during controversy. At the *Washington Post*, editor Leonard

Downie wrote a column explaining the separation between news and editorial pages the day the paper made its presidential endorsement. It flows down to individual stories, where it may demand specificity. If a piece reports "experts say," how many experts did the reporter actually talk to? Perhaps the most valuable thing about the simple concept of transparency is that its natural ally is the new open architecture of the Internet. Two-way communication allows consumers of news to ask the most important question they can in order to screen the credibility of the information they are offered: "How do you know that?" Asking that question of their news provider can encourage a clear accounting of the original source of assertions, conclusions, labels, and facts.

This clear and detailed identifying of sources is the most effective form of transparency that journalists have at their disposal and it forms the basis of a more open relationship with the ultimate consumer. In 2002, the *Los Angeles Times* even answered the question through extensive footnotes detailing the sources of quotes, facts, scenes, and other information in "Enrique's Journey," a six-part Pulitzer Prize–winning series about a Honduran teenager journeying to the United States to find his mother. More than 7,000 words of footnotes kept the narrative clean of overattribution but also provided detailed information about sourcing to the reader.

Since the first edition of this book appeared in 2001, the concept of transparency has gained substantial momentum in journalism. The Web and its dedicated outlets for journalism debates, criticism, and gossip–such as the Poynter Institute's Romenesko blog–helped push organizations to be more candid in explaining their work. Newspapers such as the *Modesto Bee* or the *Austin American Statesman* have started blogs in which editors explain newsroom decisions, such as how and why they do what they do, how they decide what goes in the paper, and how they determine the front page stories.

Newspapers also use the Internet to supplement their printed version of a longer project with databases, original documents, methodologies, or audio and video of interviews with sources or the reporters on the story. Yet the execution of transparent journalism is just evolving.

One area where newspapers have tried to be more transparent, for instance, is in the explanation of anonymous sourcing. Yet the examples we see often strike us as insufficient, and sometimes even missing the point. A *New York Times* story from November 2005 on self-prescribed drugs attempted transparency when attributing a quote to a character who did such self-medicating. The paper described her simply as Katherine K. "'I acquire quite a few medications and then dispense them to my friends as needed. I usually know what I'm talking about,' said Katherine, who lives in Manhattan and who, like many other people interviewed for this article, did not want her last name used because of concerns that her behavior could get her in trouble with her employer, law enforcement authorities or at least her parents."[21]

Why Katherine wanted anonymity is obvious. Why the paper gave it to her is what is relevant to the audience. Was it because the paper was afraid she would get in trouble with her parents?

Or consider this Knight Ridder story about the 2006 State of the Union address. In his speech, President George W. Bush pledged to reduce America's imports of Middle Eastern oil by more than 75 percent by 2025. The day after the address, Bush cabinet members told reporters the example of the Middle East was not to be taken literally. Knight Ridder reported: "Asked why the president used the words 'the Middle East' when he didn't really mean them, one administration official said Bush wanted to dramatize the issue in a way that 'every American sitting out there listening to the speech understands.' The official spoke only on condition of anonymity because he feared that his remarks might get him in trouble."[22]

Again, we know why the Bush administration official wanted self-serving anonymity, but we don't know why Knight Ridder journalists agreed to protect him.

The key is this: the Spirit of Transparency first involves the journalist asking for each event, "What does my audience need to know to evaluate this information for itself?" This includes explaining as much as is practical about how the news organization got its information.

A second element of transparency involves answering the question, "Is there anything in our treatment of this that requires explanation, including any controversial decisions made about leaving something in or taking something out?" In an age of doubt about journalists, more explanation about decisions that might be misconstrued is critical. The question of motive and decision making is essential to rethinking the objectivity of the press.

A third element of the Spirit of Transparency involves something that runs contrary to what most journalists do. Journalists should acknowledge the questions their stories are not answering. Traditionally, journalists were taught never to raise a question the story could not answer. Make stories seem airtight, even omniscient. Never appear unknowing. Write around the hole in the story. In the twenty-first century, when journalists cannot control everything the public knows about public events, when they are no longer gatekeepers, that view is no longer sensible—if it ever was.

These ideas about transparency can solve myriad problems. Consider the case of Richard Jewell. The *Atlanta Journal-Constitution* broke the story that police briefly thought Jewell might be the bomber at the 1996 Olympics. The story came from law enforcement sources who wished to remain anonymous and said that Jewell, who was initially hailed as a hero for alerting police to the pipe bomb, had become a suspect in the investigation. The story also said Jewell fit the profile of a "lone bomber."

To make matters more complicated, the paper had to deal with its own rules, which prohibited the use of anonymous sources. So how did the *Journal-Constitution* handle the story? It used what the paper called a "Voice of God" approach, in which the journalists did not attribute this information but simply stated it as their own understanding of the facts.

The piece never mentioned all the things police did not know. This included the fact that they had no physical evidence linking Jewell to the crime. The police had also not interviewed Jewell as a suspect. Nor had they yet worked out a timeline to see if Jewell could have called in the tip to the police and still gotten to the place where he found the knapsack in the time allotted.

The paper insists it didn't get anything wrong. It simply reported what police were thinking. However, had the news organization noted all the things that police had not yet done to establish their unfounded suspicions of Jewell, the story might have been less explosive, but far more complete—and accurate. It also would have avoided what turned out to be years of litigation.[23]

The Spirit of Transparency is the same principle that governs the scientific method: explain how you learned something and why you believe it so the audience can do the same. In science, the reliability of an experiment, or its objectivity, is defined by whether someone else can replicate the experiment. In journalism, only by explaining how we know what we know can we approximate this idea of people being able, if they were of a mind to, to replicate the reporting. This is what is meant by objectivity of method in science, or in journalism.

Even as he began to develop doubts about whether journalists could really sort out the truth, Walter Lippmann recognized this.

> There is no defense, no extenuation, no excuse whatsoever, for stating six times that Lenin is dead when the only information the paper possesses is a report that he is dead from a source repeatedly shown to be unreliable. The news, in that instance, is not that "Lenin is Dead" but "Helsingfors Says Lenin is Dead." And a newspaper can be asked to take responsibility of not making Lenin more dead than the source of the news is reliable. If there is one subject on which editors are most responsible it is in their judgment of the reliability of the source.[24]

Unfortunately, too much journalism fails to say anything about methods, motives, and sources. Network television newscasts, as a matter of course, will say simply "sources said," a way of saving valuable time on the air, yet most of these sources are hardly confidential. In 2003, for instance, 43 percent of stories on the three commercial nightly newscasts contained sourcing that to the audience was anonymous; in 2004, anonymity was up to 53 percent.[25] It is a standing rule in most offices on Capitol Hill, similarly, that staffers be quoted anonymously at all times.

Withholding information from the public like this is a mistake. As citizens become more skeptical of both journalists and the political establishment, this is also a disservice to the public and brings journalism under greater suspicion.

MISLEADING SOURCES: A COROLLARY
TO TRANSPARENCY

The Spirit of Transparency also suggests something about the way journalists deal with their sources. Obviously journalists should not lie to or mislead their sources in the process of trying to tell the truth to their audiences.

Unfortunately, journalists, without having thought the principle through, all too often have failed to see this. Bluffing sources, failing to level with sources about the real point of the story, even simply lying to sources about the point of stories are all techniques some journalists have applied in the name of truth seeking. While at first glance candor may seem a handcuff on reporters, it won't be in most cases. Many reporters have come to find that it can win them enormous influence. "I've found it is always better to level with sources, tell them what I'm doing and where I'm going," then *Boston Globe* political correspondent Jill Zuckman told us. *Washington Post* reporter Jay Mathews makes a habit of showing sources drafts of stories. He believes it increases the accuracy and nuance of his pieces.[26]

At the same time, journalists should expect similar veracity from their sources. A growing number of journalists believe that if a source who has been granted anonymity is found to have misled the reporter, the source's identity should be revealed. Part of the bargain of anonymity is truthfulness.

There is a special category of journalists misleading sources. It is called masquerading. This occurs when journalists pose as someone else to get a story by misleading sources. The "undercover" reporting technique is nothing new. At the beginning of the twentieth century, muckrakers like Nellie Bly, who among other remarkable achievements posed as an inmate in an insane asylum to expose mistreatment of the mentally ill, used masquerade. Television today frequently uses masquerade and tiny hidden cameras to expose wrongdoing.

What does avoiding deception and being transparent with audiences and sources suggest about masquerade? These ideas do not preclude journalists' use of masquerade. Rather, they suggest that journalists should use a test similar to the concepts justifying civil disobedience in deciding whether to engage in the technique. Citizens should also apply this test in evaluating what they think of it. There are three steps to this test:

1. The information must be sufficiently vital to the public interest to justify deception.
2. Journalists should not engage in masquerade unless there is no other way to get the story.
3. Journalists should reveal to their audience whenever they mislead sources to get information, and should explain their reasons for doing so, including why the story justifies the deception and why this was the only way to get the facts.

With this approach, citizens can decide for themselves whether journalistic dishonesty was justified or not. And journalists, in turn, have been clear with the citizens to whom they owe their first loyalty.

We have dealt at length with this notion of a more transparent journalism because it will help over the long run to develop a more discerning public. This is a public that can readily see the difference between journalism of principle and careless or self-interested imitation. In this way, journalists can enlist the new power of the marketplace to become a force for quality journalism. This transparency means embedding in the news reports a sense of how the story came to be and why it was presented as it was.

During the reporting on the Clinton-Lewinsky scandal, the *New York Times* did just this in explaining to readers why a story about the allegations of a woman named Juanita Broaddrick was held for a time and then placed on page 16. Broaddrick was alleging that President Clinton had forced himself sexually on her roughly twenty-one years earlier in Arkansas, though she had not made the allegations at the time or even earlier in the Lewinsky scandal. Nor was she pressing the case legally.

Reporters Felicity Barringer and David Firestone interviewed their own managing editor, Bill Keller, and included his explanation in the story: the merits of Broaddrick's allegations are ultimately "probably unknowable ... legally it doesn't seem to go anywhere.... Congress isn't going to impeach him again ... and 'frankly we've all got a bit of scandal fatigue,'" Keller reasoned in the story. Some citizens might disagree, but at least they now had some explanation for the news they were receiving, not some false sense that news is an objective reality rather than the product of human judgment.[27]

Two elements are important here. First, the reporters felt it was important to let readers know how news decisions were made and just what standards are applied to those decisions. Second, the atmosphere inside the newsroom of the *New York Times* was such that the reporters felt comfortable questioning the managing editor's decision, pen in hand, with the intention of quoting his comments in the story.

ORIGINALITY

Beyond demanding more transparency from journalism, citizens and journalists can look for something else in judging the value of a news report. Journalist Michael Oreskes, when he was Washington bureau chief of the *New York Times,* offered this deceptively simple but powerful idea in the discipline for pursuing truth: do your own work.

Throughout the sex and legal scandal involving President Bill Clinton and White House intern Monica Lewinsky, news organizations found themselves in the uncomfortable position of what to do with often explosive exposés from other news organizations that they could not verify themselves. Usually, to make matters more complicated, these were based on anonymous sources, meaning that the news organization had to take even greater responsibility for the veracity of the story than if they were quoting someone. Based on such sourcing, three different news organizations reported that a third-party witness had seen the president and Lewinsky in an intimate encounter—stories that were later found to be inaccurate. Should a news organization report these exposés because they know others might, and that the story will be, in the popular phrase, "out there"?

Oreskes concluded that the answer was an adamant no. "The people who got it right were those who did their own work, who were careful about it, who followed the basic standards of sourcing and got their information from multiple sources. The people who worried about what was 'out there,' to use that horrible phrase that justifies so many journalistic sins, the people who worried about getting beaten, rather than just trying to do it as well as they could as quickly as they could, they messed up."[28]

Originality is deeply grounded in journalism. Some ancient axioms of the press say much the same thing: "When in doubt leave it out." The tradition of "matching" stories is rooted in the same idea. Rather than publishing another news outlet's scoop, journalists have tended to require one of their reporters to call a source to confirm it first. In part, this was a way of avoiding having to credit the other news organization. Yet it had another more important effect. Stories that couldn't be independently confirmed would not be repeated.

This concept of originality dovetails with the notion of transparency. There are levels of knowledge in reporting, and journalists should be aware of them and consider acknowledging them with their audience. Journalism is first concerned with the physical externality of events. A dump truck ran a stop light and crashed into a bus. The president said these words. This many people died. The document said this. The closer you are to the center, the easier it is to verify the information, and in these cases journalism is on pretty solid ground.

As reporting moves toward the interior world, trying to report on what someone believes, what motivates the person, journalism necessarily becomes more speculative. What was the truck driver thinking when he ran that light? Why did the president say these words? Why does Osama bin Laden hate America?

This may be something the journalist feels the audience should know, but the level of proof is almost always softer. There may be multiple interpretations and different levels of knowledge. This softer level of proof should be indicated to the audience. If the newsroom decided the best way to address motive and answer the "why" is through an expert, it should signal to the public why the expert was chosen and describe his expertise or involvement with the topic. Newsrooms should not hide behind experts to abdicate their responsibility for getting as close to truth as possible.

Why do we suggest this? Because the more honest the journalist is with the audience about what he or she knows and doesn't know, the more trustworthy the journalist is. Level with people. Make no claims to an omniscience you cannot justify. Acknowledging what is not known is a claim to more authority, not less.

HUMILITY

A fifth and final concept is that journalists should be humble about their own skills. In other words, not only should they be skeptical of what they see and hear from others, but just as important, they should be skeptical about their ability to know what it really means. Jack Fuller has suggested that journalists need to show "modesty in their judgments" about what they know and how they know it.[29] A key way to avoid misrepresenting events is a disciplined honesty about the limits of one's knowledge and the power of one's perceptions.

An incident unearthed in our forum on diversity helps illustrate the point. The event, described by then *New York Times* religion writer Laurie Goodstein, was a Pentecostal prayer revival on the steps of the U.S. Capitol. The gathering featured faith healings, calls for school prayer, condemnations of abortion and homosexuality—a fairly typical evangelical revival meeting. A reporter for a newspaper covering the event related all this, but added this sentence: "At times, the mood turned hostile toward the lawmakers in the stately white building behind the stage." Then the reporter quoted a Christian radio broadcaster speaking from the stage: "Let's pray that God will slay everyone in the Capitol."[30]

The reporter assumed the broadcaster meant slay as in "kill." But, Goodstein explained, "any Pentecostal knows that asking God to slay someone means to slay in spirit, slay in the sense of holy spirit, praying that they are overcome with love for God, for Jesus."

The problem was the reporter didn't know, didn't have any Pentecostals in the newsroom to ask, and was perhaps too anxious for a "holy shit" story to double-check with someone afterward whether the broadcaster was really advocating murder of the entire Congress. "It made for a very embarrassing correction," said Goodstein. It also makes a strong case for the need for humility.

Humility also means that you are open-minded enough to accept that the next person you talk to could change the entire meaning of your story or even convince you that you have no story.

. . .

Together, these five ideas amount to a core philosophy that frames the discipline of verification. They also establish a closer relationship between the journalist and the citizen, which is mutually beneficial. By employing the powerful tools of transparent, narrative storytelling, the journalist engages citizens with important information they might otherwise pass by and does so without sacrificing factual integrity. At the same time, by being more open about his or her work, the journalist is encouraged to be more thoughtful in acquiring, organizing, and presenting the news.

BIAS

The discipline of verification, and particularly the notion of transparency, is one of the most powerful steps journalists can take to address the problem of bias. By bias we don't mean simply political or ideological bias. We mean bias in a broader sense that covers all the journalist's judgments, decisions, and beliefs. Bias encompasses all kinds of predilections, both appropriate and troubling. This could include a bias for truth or facts or giving voice to the voiceless, as well as a bias toward one's own personal social, economic, or political leanings. The critics are right that we're all shaped by personal history and the biases of the culture in which we live. Looked at this way, it becomes impossible to communicate without engaging some of these biases, including those that make a story compelling.

Understood in this broader, and frankly more realistic sense, bias is not something that can or should be eliminated. Rather, the job of the journalist is to become more conscious of the biases at play in a given story and decide when they are appropriate and useful, and when they are inappropriate. The journalist needs to become, if you will, a manager of his or her own bias and the biases of the news organization.

There is some validity to the old saw that bias is in the eye of the beholder—or that a biased story is just one you disagree with. The problem with this interpretation is that it's an excuse to let everyone off the hook. You can't please everyone so why worry about it? Problem solved. Dismissing the issue this way, however, doesn't address the frustrations of the audience and it doesn't improve the reporting.

Managing bias involves several components that relate to the discipline of verification. The first task is to become more systematic and conscious about getting the facts right, using any number of the techniques described below. Adopting a method of verification, rather than simply having faith in one's good intentions, is the most effective thing journalists can do to overcome preconceptions about the news.

The second way in which bias is helped is by moving toward the Spirit of Transparency. This changes the relationship with the audience from one of talking down to one of sharing as equals. Journalists have told us that explaining their decisions often forces them to evaluate and sometimes reconsider what they are doing. They have also told us that more transparency has a remarkable impact in defusing assumptions that audiences would otherwise make about the motives of journalists.

TECHNIQUES OF VERIFICATION

Obviously, these concepts are not specific enough to constitute "a scientific method" of reporting–that is for individual journalists to refine. The key is that they are clear about it. But by way of illustration, we would like to offer some concrete methods from journalists around the country. While not encyclopedic, any journalist could fashion a superb method of gathering and presenting news from adapting the following few techniques.

EDIT WITH SKEPTICISM

Sandra Rowe, the editor of the *Oregonian* in Portland, Oregon, employs a system at her paper that she and executive editor Peter Bhatia call "prosecutorial editing." The term may be an unfortunate one. Reid MacCluggage, a former editor and publisher of *The Day* in New London, Connecticut, has suggested a better one, "skeptical editing."[31] Regardless, the concept is important for journalists and citizens to understand.

The approach involves adjudicating a story–in effect, line by line, statement by statement–editing the assertions in the stories as well as the facts. How do we know this? Why should the reader believe this? What is the assumption behind this sentence? If the story says that a certain event may raise questions in people's minds, who suggested that? The reporter? A source? A citizen?

Amanda Bennett, when working as an *Oregonian* managing editor, said the notion—which she learned at the *Wall Street Journal*—was designed for "rooting out not so much errors of fact but unconscious errors of assertion and narrative—to root out the things that people put in because 'they just know it's true.'"[32]

If a story says that most Americans now have a personal computer, the editor would ask for verification. If a story said "according to sources," the editor would ask, "Who are the sources? Is there more than one?" If there was only one, the story would have to say so. If a story said that candidate Smith's flip-flop on some tax bill proposal raises questions about his ideological consistency, the editor would ask, "What questions?" and "In whose mind?" If the answer is merely the reporter and his friends, the story would either have to say so or that line would come out.

Whenever practical, said editor Rowe, this kind of editing involves the editor and the reporter sitting side by side, and the reporter producing original material. "The more of it we did, the more we were sending true fear" through the newsroom, said Rowe.[33] Bennett began teaching it in the newsroom in front of groups of reporters and editors. "People didn't know it was okay to ask these questions," Bennett said. The purpose, in large part, is to "make that role of asking questions okay, and to make it conscious." Rather than including more in stories, more was taken out, unless it could be absolutely verified.[34]

The technique, Bennett and Rowe believe, makes editors and reporters better and more thorough. The objective of the *Oregonian*'s skeptical editing is to create an atmosphere in which people can question a story without questioning the integrity of the reporter. It becomes part of an atmosphere of open dialogue in a newsroom, which goes bottom-up as well as top-down.

KEEP AN ACCURACY CHECKLIST

Several newspapers use accuracy checklists to remind staffers of the importance of verification. Some of the checklists we collected are more conceptual and ask questions like:

- Is the lead of the story sufficiently supported?
- Is the background material required to understand the story complete?
- Are all the stakeholders in the story identified and have representatives from that side been contacted and given a chance to talk?
- Does the story pick sides or make subtle value judgments? Will some people like this story more than they should?
- Have you attributed and/or documented all the information in your story to make sure it is correct?
- Do those facts back up the premise of your story? Do you have multiple sources for controversial facts?
- Did you double-check the quotes to make sure they are accurate and in context?

Others we have seen are more factual and concrete:

- Did you double-check the quotes to make sure they are accurate and in context?
- Have you checked Web sites, phone numbers, and unusual names?
- Did you check that all first references in your story have a first and last name?
- Have you checked ages, addresses, and titles to make sure they are correct? If so, have you written "everything else cq" above your byline to signal those things are correct?
- Do time references in your story include day and date?

Some editors consider such checklists too mechanistic, and if handled badly, they can erode the confidence of reporters by seeming to squash the creative element of storytelling. But properly handled, such questions can bring reports and editors together to make their work more accurate and credible.

ASSUME NOTHING

David Protess, a professor at Northwestern University's Medill School of Journalism, used the cases of death-row inmates to teach journalism students the importance of verifying presumed facts. Among the lessons were: Don't rely on officials or news accounts. Get as close as you can to primary sources. Be systematic. Corroborate.

Each year Protess received thousands of letters from people on death row who claimed wrongful conviction. Each year he chose a handful that he assigned his students to examine. In 1999, the appeal of Anthony Porter was one of the cases Protess used to introduce his aspiring journalists to the value of skepticism.

"Maybe the best way to understand my method is what I do for the students when they come into my class," Protess explained in an interview when we sought him out. "I draw a set of concentric circles on the blackboard. In the outermost circle are secondary source documents, things like press accounts. . . . The next circle in is primary source documents—trial documents like testimony and statements. The third circle in is real people—witnesses. We interview them to see if everything matches what's in the documents. We ask them questions that may have come up looking at the documents. And at the inner circle are what I call the targets—the police, the lawyers, other suspects, and the prisoner. . . . You'd be surprised how much is in the early documents. There is a lot there, especially early suspects the police passed by."

At the inner circle of the Porter case, Protess and his students found Alstory Simon, a suspect the police quickly overlooked. Using Protess's systematic approach to cross-checking the documents and sources, Protess and his students found a nephew who had overheard Simon confess to the murder on the night of the killings. Simon was ultimately convicted of the crime for which Porter was about to die. On March 19, 1999, Anthony Porter became the fifth prisoner wrongfully convicted of murder in Illinois to be freed by the work of Protess and his students. Protess's work is an extraordinary demonstration of the power of methodical journalistic verification.

TOM FRENCH'S RED PENCIL

If Protess's method is exhaustive, Tom French's is wonderfully simple. French specializes in writing long, deep narrative nonfiction for the *St. Petersburg Times* in Florida. He won the 1998 Pulitzer Prize for feature writing. He also writes on deadline.

French has a test to verify any facts in his stories. Before he hands a piece in, he takes a printed copy and goes over the story line by line with a red pencil, putting a check mark by each fact and assertion to tell himself that he has double-checked that it is true.

BE CAREFUL WITH ANONYMOUS SOURCES

As citizens, we all rely on other sources of information for most of what we know. The journalists monitoring the world on our behalf also most often depend on others for the details of their reporting. One of the earliest techniques adopted by journalists to assure us of their reliability was the practice of providing the sources of their information. Mr. Jones said so and so, in such and such a speech at the Elks Lodge, in the annual report, etc. Such dependence on others for information has always required a skeptical turn of mind for journalists. They early on adopt the reminder: "If your mother says she loves you, check it out." If the source of the information is fully described, the audience can decide for itself whether the information is credible.

In recent years, as the number of news outlets has grown and news sources have become more sophisticated in the art of press manipulation, confidentiality has shifted from a tool journalists used to coax reluctant whistleblowers into confiding vital information to something quite different—a condition press-savvy sources imposed on journalists before they would even speak to them.

Consider the peculiar leak-investigation scandal involving sources in the White House during the George W. Bush administration. This scandal involved leaking the identity of an undercover Central Intelligence Agency operative named Valerie Plame to the press. In 2005, the case became a celebrated battle over the press's right to protect confidential sources. Judith Miller, a *New York Times* reporter, spent 85 days in jail refusing to testify, though she eventually changed her mind and came forward. Yet the source she was protecting—a man named I. Lewis "Scooter" Libby—was not a whistleblower revealing secrets the administration wanted hidden. He was chief of staff to the vice president, engaged in an authorized leak of the administration's position to counter what Plame's husband, a former U.S. ambassador, had written in the *New York Times*. Miller, it was discovered, agreed to not only keep

Libby's identity confidential, but also she willingly took steps to mislead people about it by agreeing to describe him as a "former Hill staffer" and not as a "senior administration official," as previously agreed upon. Miller did not end up publishing a story on the ambassador.[35] As the *Washington Post* columnist Al Kamen later described it, in Washington DC, where nearly everyone in politics once worked on the Hill, that is the equivalent of calling him "some guy."[36]

As dependence on anonymous sources for important public information has grown, journalists have begun trying to develop rules to assure themselves and their audience that they are maintaining independence from the anonymous sources of their news. Joe Lelyveld, when he was executive editor of the *New York Times*, required that reporters and editors ask themselves two questions before using an anonymous source:

1. How much direct knowledge does the anonymous source have of the event?
2. What, if any, motive might the source have for misleading us, gilding the lily, or hiding important facts that might alter our impression of the information?

Only after they were satisfied by the answers to these questions were they to use the source. And then, to the maximum degree possible, they have to share with the audience information to suggest how the source was in a position to know ("a source who has seen the document," for example) and what special interest that source may have ("a source inside the Independent Prosecutor's office," for example). This effort at more transparency was a crucial factor in the degree to which the audience could judge for themselves how much credence to give the report, but more important it signaled the standards of the organization serving up their news.

Deborah Howell, the Washington editor of the Newhouse newspapers, has two other rules for anonymous sources that reinforce Lelyveld's.

1. Never use an anonymous source to offer an opinion of another person.
2. Never use an anonymous source as the first quote in a story.

Glenn Guzzo, the former editor of the *Denver Post*, had another set of questions he wanted reporters and editors to be able to answer when they requested approval for keeping a source anonymous from their audience.

1. Is the information essential to the story?
2. Is the information fact, not opinion or judgment? (He would not allow anonymity for judgmental statements.)
3. Is the source in a position to truly know—is this an eyewitness?
4. What other indicators of reliability are there (multiple sources, independent corroboration, experience with the source)?
5. What descriptors can you use so the audience can decide what weight to assign this source?

The three versions or tests also offer practical instructions for how to write stories, even after you have decided to use what an anonymous source is offering.

The point is not that a journalist develop fidelity to any one of these tests, or that a citizen look for proof of one. We hope that anyone practicing journalism will borrow and create his or her own.

The more important idea is that the journalist has applied some conscious judgment to when to allow a source to remain confidential, and that he or she in turn shares some of that reasoning with the audience. Public opinion surveys reveal that the public does not like anonymous sourcing, though they do appreciate that use of the practice may have value.[37]

How would that work in print? An example might be as follows: ". . . according to an attorney with access to the details of the case. The *Post* granted anonymity to the attorney because of the importance to the public of having this information and our belief that identifying him would put him in legal jeopardy."

TRUTH'S MULTIPLE ROOTS

In the end, everyone in the journalistic process has a role to play in the journey toward truth. Publishers and owners must be willing to consistently air the work of public-interest journalism without fear or favor.

Editors must serve as the protectors against debasement of the currency of free expression—words—resisting effort by governments, corporations, litigants, lawyers, or any other newsmakers to mislead or manipulate by labeling lies as truth, war as peace.

Reporters must be dogged in their pursuit and disciplined in trying to overcome their own perspective. Longtime Chicago TV newscaster Carol Marin explained it this way at one committee forum: "When you sit down this Thanksgiving with your family and you have one of the classic family arguments—whether it's about politics or race or religion or sex—you remember that what you are seeing of that family dispute is seen from the position of your chair and your side of the table. And it will warp your view, because in those instances you are arguing your position. . . . A journalist is someone who steps away from the table and tries to see it all."[38]

And, if journalism is conversation, in the end that conversation includes discourse among citizens as well as with those who provide the news. The citizens, too, have a role. They must, of course, be attentive. They also must be assertive. If they have a question or a problem, they should ask it of the news organization: How do you know this? Why did you write this? What are your journalistic principles? These are fair questions to ask, and citizens deserve answers.

Thus journalists must be committed to truth as a first principle and must be loyal to citizens above all so that they are free to pursue it. And in order to engage citizens in that search, journalists must apply transparent and systematic methods of verification. The next step is to clarify their relationship to those they report on.

ENDNOTES

1. Thucydides, *History of the Peloponnesian War*, bks. 1 and 2, trans. C. F. Smith (Cambridge: Harvard University Press, 1991), 35–39.

2. Walter Lippmann, *Liberty and the News* (New Brunswick, NJ, and London: Transaction Publishers, 1995), 58.

3. Claudia Puig, "Getting Inside the Truth, Filmmakers Accused of Fiddling with Facts Cite Dramatic Accuracy," *USA Today*, November 3, 1999; available at www.usatoday.com.

4. Dan Gillmor, "The End of Objectivity," *Bayosphere*, January 20, 2005.

5. Michael Schudson, *Discovering the News* (New York: Basic Books, 1978), 6. Schudson's book has a particularly useful analysis of the move away from naïve

empiricism of the nineteenth century to the initially more sophisticated idea of objectivity.

6. Walter Lippmann and Charles Merz, "A Test of the News," *The New Republic* (August 4, 1920), published in *Killing the Messenger: 100 Years of Media Criticism*, edited by Tom Goldstein (New York: Columbia University Press, 1989), 91.

7. Walter Lippmann, "The Press and Public Opinion," *Political Science Quarterly*, 46 (June 1931), 170. The fact that Lippmann wrote this last passage in 1931, twelve years after his study of the Russian Revolution, is a sign of how the problem continued to dog him.

8. Lippmann, *Liberty and the News*, 74.

9. Ibid., 60.

10. Ibid., 74.

11. Schudson, *Discovering the News*, 155-56.

12. William Damon, to Committee of Concerned Journalists steering committee, February 12, 1999, private meeting.

13. Geneva Overholser, at CCJ Forum, Minneapolis, MN, October 22, 1998.

14. Robert Parry, "He's No Pinocchio," *Washington Monthly*, April 2000; available from www.washingtonmonthly.com.

15. Ibid.

16. Phil Meyer, at CCJ Forum, St. Petersburg, FL, February 26, 1998.

17. Norman Sims, ed., *The Literary Journalists* (New York: Ballantine Books, 1984), 15.

18. Tom Goldstein, ed., *Killing the Messenger* (New York: Columbia University Press, 1989), 247.

19. Co-author Rosenstiel was a member of the panel with Bradlee at this event. The panel was "Why Don't We Trust the News Media? How Can the News Media Recover Public Trust?" Oswego, NY, October 27, 2005.

20. CCJ and the Pew Research Center for the People and the Press, "Striking the Balance: Audience Interests, Business Pressures and Journalists' Values," March 1999; Amy Mitchell and Tom Rosenstiel, "Don't Touch That Quote," *Columbia Journalism Review* (January 2000), 34–36; available at www.journalism.org.

21. Amy Harmon, "Young, Assured, and Playing Pharmacist to Friends," *New York Times*, November 16, 2005; available at www.nytimes.com.

22. Kevin G. Hall, "Administration Backs off Bush's Vow to Reduce Mideast Oil Imports," Knight Ridder Newspapers, February 1, 2006; available at www.common dreams.org/headlines06/0202-05.htm.

23. The information is taken from Ron Ostrow's "Case Study: Richard Jewell and the Olympic Bombing," available on www.journalism.org, the website of the Project for Excellence in Journalism.

24. Walter Lippmann, *Public Opinion* (New York: Free Press, 1965), 226.

25. Project for Excellence in Journalism, "State of the News Media 2005," March 2005; available at www.journalism.org.

26. Jay Mathews, interview by Dante Chinni, September 12, 2000.

27. Felicity Barringer and David Firestone, "On Torturous Route, Sexual Assault Accusation against Clinton Resurfaces," *New York Times*, February 24, 1999; available at www.nytimes.com.

28. Michael Oreskes, at CCJ Forum, Washington, DC, October 20, 1998.

29. Jack Fuller, *News Values: Ideas from an Information Age* (Chicago and London: University of Chicago Press, 1996), 350.

30. Laurie Goodstein, at CCJ Forum, Detroit, MI, February 2, 1998.

31. MacCluggage, in an address to regional editors, argued, "Edit more skeptically. If skeptics aren't built into the process right from the start, stories will slide onto page one without the proper scrutiny." Associated Press, "APME President Urges Editors to Challenge Stories for Accuracy," October 15, 1998.

32. Amanda Bennett, interview by author Rosenstiel, April 13, 2000.

33. Sandra Rowe, interview by author Rosenstiel, April 13, 2000.

34. Bennett, interview by author Rosenstiel, April 13, 2000.

35. Don Van Natta Jr., Adam Liptak, and Clifford J. Levy, "The Miller Case: A Notebook, a Cause, a Jail Cell and a Deal," *New York Times*, October 16, 2005; available at www.nytimes.com.

36. Al Kamen, "In the Loop: Ambiguously Anonymous," *Washington Post,* October 19, 2005, A19; available at www.washingtonpost.com.

37. Pew Research Center for People and the Press, "Public More Critical of Press, But Goodwill Persists," June 26, 2005; available at http://people-press.org.

38. Carol Marin, at CCJ Forum, Chicago, IL, November 6, 1997.

5

Independence
from Faction

A few months after the historic confrontation between the *New York Times* and the federal government precipitated by the publication of the Pentagon Papers in 1971, William Safire, a speechwriter for President Nixon, was seated next to *Times* publisher Arthur "Punch" Sulzberger at a fundraising dinner. During their conversation Safire mentioned that he was planning to leave government service.

Safire's comment fell on receptive ears. Since the election of Nixon in 1968, Sulzberger had been under pressure to find a conservative voice to balance the *Times* op-ed pages. The pressure was coming from Scotty Reston, the paper's legendary Washington correspondent, former bureau chief, and executive editor, who worried about how the political world viewed the paper, as well as from members of the *Times* board of directors, who believed a greater balance of voices would ensure the success of a plan to launch a national edition. At the time, the op-ed pages were dominated by liberals, including Tom Wicker, Anthony Lewis, Flora Lewis, and more moderately, Reston himself.

Sulzberger had come to the conclusion that he agreed: a strong conservative voice was a genuine need.

Safire was an appealing choice. He was a New Yorker with many friends in the city. He was also a brilliant writer, whose clear and sometimes stinging prose included memorable criticisms of the press. The fact that Katharine Graham, the publisher of the *Washington Post*, whose judgment Sulzberger respected, had tried to hire Safire but couldn't agree on a salary made the idea even more attractive.

Eventually, a deal was struck. Yet if the addition of Safire eased the pressure on Sulzberger from one side, it lighted a firestorm of criticism from long-time readers on the other, as well as from many in the *Times* newsroom, who were dismayed that a presidential speechwriter would be allowed to pass himself off as a journalist.

By what criteria could a partisan ex-political activist suddenly call himself a journalist? Was it enough that he now had a column? Certainly something more was required in the minds of the journalists at the *Times*. When Safire finally arrived in 1973, three weeks before the Watergate scandal broke wide open, he recalled years later that he was thoroughly "ostracized by my Washington bureau colleagues as an unreconstructed Nixon flack. The only reporter who would even have lunch with me was Martin Tolchin, a long-before classmate at the Bronx High School of Science."[1]

Two unrelated events changed Safire's status. The first was personal. "At the annual bureau picnic, the three-year-old child of a reporter fell in a pool and started to drown; as the only adult standing nearby, I jumped in fully clothed to fish him out. The general opinion changed to 'he can't be all bad.'" The second was journalistic. *Times* reporter John Crewdson had broken a story that said secret wiretaps had been placed on sixteen reporters and one Nixon aide. The aide was Safire. "That was a seemingly unprecedented assault on press freedom and was later made illegal; however, since I was the aide wiretapped, that made me "one of them," in Nixonian terminology, and when I blew my stack about secret taps in a *Times* column, that was reported in *Time* magazine as "Safire Afire" and helped establish my independence. It was like getting a shower; I was no longer a pariah."

Thirty-two years later, Safire would retire from the *Times* with a Pulitzer Prize and the esteem not only of his colleagues in journalism but also of millions of readers. What earned him that acclaim? It certainly wasn't neutrality, or a tepid tone, or the desire to be evenhanded. Safire remained a dyed-in-the-wool conservative with decidedly libertarian highlights who could skewer adversaries, end careers, and be strident when moved to be. What was it, then, that separated Safire from a partisan, activist, or propagandist?

The question is increasingly pertinent to the delivery of news and information in the new century. As the media landscape broadens and evolves to meet the needs of a more inclusive and activist public created by the social movements of the 1960s and the recent democratization of the content production, what makes something journalism?

Truthfulness and a commitment to citizens are parts of it. So are playing a watchdog role and providing a forum for public debate. Yet where does the role of opinion journalism fit? Isn't neutrality one of the principles of journalism?

The answer cannot possibly be yes. If it were, columnists and editorial writers would be excluded from the profession. Pulitzer Prize-winning reporters like Paul Gigot of the *Wall Street Journal* and Thomas Friedman of the *New York Times* would somehow have forgone their standing as journalists when they became columnists. What would we make of David Broder of the *Washington Post*, or Ronald Brownstein of the *Los Angeles Times*–esteemed journalists who write columns and also work as reporters–or Tom Brokaw or Walter Cronkite, who as anchors occasionally offered commentaries?

Every year the Pulitzer Board awards a prize for commentary and places that award under the heading "Journalism." And many would argue that the American alternative press, a vibrant part of the journalistic landscape, is closer to the historical roots of journalism than the large corporate-owned papers that often profess that they provide a neutral news account.

It is worth restating the point to make it clear. Being impartial or neutral is not a core principle of journalism. As we explained in the previous chapter on verification, impartiality was never what was meant by objectivity. But if neutrality is not a cornerstone of journalism, what then makes something journalism, as opposed to, say, propaganda? Propagandists publish. Political activists publish. Jesse Jackson has a talk show from the Left. Rush Limbaugh has a talk show from the Right. Scores of supporters from both sides of the political aisle write partisan blogs. Are they journalists? Is anyone who publishes or broadcasts a journalist?

After he departed the *Times*, we asked Safire to ruminate on the qualities that guided his thinking and propelled that transformation from politician to journalist. A central issue has to do with allegiance.

> Where does loyalty lie—with your old personal friends and colleagues, with your political ideology or party, with your news medium, with the cold facts—or with The Truth?
>
> In real life, it's a fluctuating combination of all these. You don't burn a good long-term source to get a pretty-good story. You don't let your ideology turn you away from a good story. (You don't let a copy editor change "story" to "article" without a fight.) You don't let a series of hard facts lead you to a softly untruthful or misleading conclusion. You don't become a hero by joining a pack savaging your ideological soulmates. You don't quote from this paragraph selectively, reporting accurately but corrupting its whole meaning.

In other words, Safire held the same fidelity to accuracy and facts as does any other journalist, and that allegiance to hard facts and truthful conclusions now separated him from his old partisan team. He was his own man, still conservative, but now working for his readers.

Safire also believed his experience in politics helped inform his second career as journalist, not detract from it. But he believed just as clearly that this was a transformation one could not repeat. "Going back and forth every few years confuses the reader/viewer and must trouble the inveterate switcher as well," he said. Journalism is more, in other words, than just having a perch at a TV station or on an op-ed page. But Safire believes political experience is good training for becoming a reporter.

Having learned to skirt an issue or fuzz up a statement on the inside helps a journalist detect such manipulation of words when on the outside. When on the inside, you develop lifelong relationships with people you trust (and you remember those less trustworthy). After you have crossed the street, these friendships can lead to confidential sourcemanship: the art of getting information from insiders, or predecessors of insiders, that you as a journalist are not supposed to get. Nothing beats a confidential source with whom you have shared a political foxhole. You know what to expect from that person, who knows how far you will go to protect a confidence.

Safire even believes that opinion journalists have more liberty than other journalists, not less, to call it as they see it, without the weighted qualifiers of a straight reporter. They may even have more obligation. "I like to think I helped launch a field called 'opinionated reporting,'" Safire said. "This was not the sneaky business of slanting a purported news story; it was the digging for a fresh fact that illuminated, or at least called attention to, a candidly labeled op-ed opinion column."

There was one other matter that bothered his new colleagues at the *Times* that Safire chose not to clear up. "[There] was still the 'nattering nabobs of negativism' problem," Safire would recall, referring to a speech he had helped write that would become one of the most famous denunciations of the American media ever delivered by a major political figure. "I wrote that phrase in a 1970 speech given by Vice President Agnew in San Diego denouncing defeatists in general, not the press in particular; but because it followed a televised speech he made, written by Pat Buchanan, excoriating the media for 'instant analysis' and other sins, my alliterative phrase, generously credited to me by Agnew, was associated with his caustic attack on the press. (I never tried to straighten that out, because having a reputation of media critic didn't hurt me a bit with readers.)" This, too, is revealing. Safire was less concerned with how his new colleagues perceived him than with how the audience reacted.

Hard facts. Truthful conclusions. Not letting ideology turn you away from a story. Candid labeling. Honesty. These are the words

Safire uses. In short, he won his acclaim over time because readers found in his column the same things those colleagues at the *Times* did, which thawed that initial cold shoulder. They found someone independent, true to a set of ideas rather than a member of a team, someone who put his readers first. They found, in other words, someone whose character they thought they liked, who might just be the kind of guy who would jump into a pool to save a child, someone who was so much his own man that it made sense that his White House colleagues might want to wiretap him.

These qualities thus emerge as the fourth key principle of journalism:

Journalists must maintain an independence from those they cover.

This applies even to those who work in the realm of opinion, criticism, and commentary. It is this independence of spirit and mind, rather than neutrality, that journalists must keep in focus.

Editorialists and opinion journalists like Safire are not neutral. Their credibility is rooted instead in the same dedication to accuracy, verification, the larger public interest, and a desire to inform that all other journalists subscribe to. "Do you need to present both sides to be impartial?" Safire wondered. "Clearly no. Don't be afraid to call somebody a 'terrorist' who strikes terror into a populace by deliberately killing civilians. That killer is not a 'militant' or 'activist,' which are suitable terms for political demonstrators or firebrands, nor is he or she a 'gunman,' which is not only evasive but sexist. To be excessively evenhanded is to be, as the Brits say, kak-handed—clumsy."

Safire also felt phony evenhandedness was a disservice to his readers. "Playing it straight does not mean striking a balance of space or time. When one side of a controversy makes news—issues a survey or holds an event—it's not the reporter's job to dig up the people who will shoot it down and give them equal attention. Comment, yes; 'balance' by column inch or stopwatch, no."

In some ways, this fourth principle is rooted more in pragmatism than in theory. One might imagine that one could both report on events and be a participant in them, but the reality is that being a participant clouds all the other tasks a journalist must perform. It becomes difficult to see things from other perspectives. It becomes more difficult to win the trust of the sources and combatants on different sides. It becomes difficult if not impossible to then persuade your audience that you put their interests ahead of those of the team that you are also working for. In other words, you might be a secret adviser to those you are writing about or a speechwriter, or take money. But it is an act of arrogance, and probably naivete or delusion, to think it won't get in the way. Thus, as Safire acknowledged, he worried about confusing the readers/viewers, and tried to play it straight for them.

INDEPENDENCE OF MIND

As we talked to journalists around the country from different fields, probed their motives and their professional goals, it became clear that Safire had articulated key but subtle notions that are widely shared. On the other side of the ideological spectrum, for instance, Anthony Lewis, then a liberal opinion columnist for the *New York Times*, said that the difference is grounded not only in a commitment to truthfulness but also in a kind of faith that this commitment implies. "Journalists who end up writing columns of opinion have a point of view. . . . But they still prize facts above all. C. P. Scott, the great editor of *The Manchester* (Great Britain) *Guardian*, put it, 'Comment is free but facts are sacred.' I think we tend to go from the particular to the general; we find facts and from them draw a conclusion," Lewis continued. Media "provocateurs like Ann Coulter or John McLaughlin are the other way around. All they care about are opinions, preferably shouted. Facts, if any, are incidental. They follow the advice of the Queen of Hearts, 'Sentence first—verdict afterward.'"[2]

Independence of spirit even reaches into opinion writing that is nonideological—the work of art critics and reviewers. John Martin, once dance critic of the *New York Times*, said that as he moved to judgment and opinion he believed he retained a kind of journalistic independence. "I feel that my first responsibility is to tell what happened, and secondarily, to express my opinion, let's say, or an interpretation, or, as briefly as possible, to put this particular performance in its place in the scene. And I think that, in a way, is reporting, too."[3]

This discussion, we hope, clarifies another frequent confusion. It has become fashionable in recent years to wonder who is and isn't a journalist. We think this is the wrong question. The question people should ask is not whether someone is called a journalist. The important issue is whether or not this person is doing journalism. Does the work proceed from an adherence to the principles of truthfulness, an allegiance to citizens and community at large, and to informing rather than manipulating—concepts that set journalism apart from other forms of communication? In this connection, by way of one popular example, blogs are merely a platform. They may be journalism or they may be political activism. They may be lie-mongering or they may be incisive academic debate. The issue is not whether the information appears in a blog. The issue is in the nature of the work itself. People should not become focused on the wrong thing.

The important implication is this: the meanings of freedom of speech and freedom of the press are that they belong to everyone. But communication and journalism are not interchangeable terms. Anyone *can* be a journalist. Not everyone *is*.

The decisive factor is not whether they have a press pass or an audience. Phil Donahue suggested at one of our forums that the man who walked into the bar at Chernobyl and said "The thing blew" was a reporter at that moment. If he was reporting an event he had witnessed or had checked out, not passing along a rumor, he was doing journalism. "The House of Journalism has many rooms," Safire said. "For the objective reporter and for the thoughtful thumbsucker; for the stridently partisan editorialist and the TV shouting head; for the house organist and the spidery website weaver. And don't forget to set aside a roomy closet in the House for the clearly labeled reportorial opinionmonger."

It is one thing to understand the difference between an opinion journalist and a partisan propagandist intellectually. Living up to that distinction can be harder. Friendships, opportunities, and flattery all will conspire to seduce the opinion writer to cross the line.

The case of Maggie Gallagher is instructive. At one of our forums in 1997, Gallagher, then a columnist with the Universal Press Syndicate and the *New York Post*, was among the most articulate thinkers we encountered on the line between opinion journalism and activism and

·propaganda. "I think there are three criteria that I use and remind myself of in my ambition to remain a journalist—one with a point of view," Gallagher said at the time. "One is an ultimate commitment to the truth. . . . I don't relate anything to my readers that I don't believe is true."[4]

Next, she argued, "one can be partisan, an opinion journalist, and still believe that one has a high obligation to be fair to those with whom one disagrees. It's related to the sense of obligation to one's audience." That requires being "open with the readers, to make it clear to the audience what your views are and what your biases are. . . . That's the difference between a journalist and a propagandist. I don't seek to manipulate my audience. I seek to reveal, to convey to them the world as I see it," she says.

And to accomplish all this finally, Gallagher said, it becomes essential to maintain distance from faction:

> I think it's possible to be an honest journalist and be loyal to a cause. It's not really possible to be an honest journalist and be loyal to a person, a political party or a faction. Why do I say that? I think it relates to my basic belief that there is some relationship between journalism and one's perception of the truth. One can believe that certain things, ideas, proposals, would be good for America and can openly state that. But to be loyal to a political party, a person or faction means that you do not see your primary goal as commitment to speaking the truth to people who are your audience. There's a fundamental conflict of loyalty there.

In the first edition of this book, we were so struck by Gallagher's articulation of these distinctions that we spotlighted them in the opening of this chapter. In 2005, however, it came to light that Gallagher had violated the principles she herself had outlined.

Washington Post media writer Howard Kurtz revealed that Gallagher had a $21,500 contract to write for the Department of Health and Human Services. Gallagher's work, Kurtz wrote, was to promote President Bush's marriage initiative as a way of strengthening families. Her contract, which ran for ten months in 2002, included drafting a magazine article for a department official, writing brochures, and conducting a briefing. The story followed the disclosure that the Bush administration's Education Department was paying conservative commentator Armstrong Williams more than $240,000 to promote Bush's No Child Left Behind program. The revelations cost Williams his newspaper column.

Gallagher said she saw her own case as different from Williams's. "I'm a marriage expert. I get paid to write, edit, research and educate on marriage," she wrote. "If a scholar or expert gets paid to do some work for the government, should he or she disclose that if he writes a paper, essay or op-ed on the same or similar subject? If this is the ethical standard, it is an entirely new standard."[5]

Actually it is not a new standard. It is an old one, fundamental to both the academy and to journalism: if there is a potential conflict of interest, it should be revealed, and if the revelation casts one in a clearly compromised position, don't take the work. Indeed, Gallagher's failure to disclose suggests that she knew what she was doing and compromised the independence essential to her claim as a journalist. The controversy over her role proves the point, and it suggests just how difficult living up to the principle can be.

THE EVOLUTION OF INDEPENDENCE

Ancient Greek philosophers understood that humans are political by nature and that an organized community requires some sort of political activity. It was into this crucible of political affairs that the first periodicals were born, inviting the broad public to become involved in the political decisions that affected their lives.

As we outlined in Chapter 3, on loyalty to citizens, the history of journalism over the last three hundred years has been a move away from fealty to political party toward public interest. "Journalistically, the twentieth century can be defined as the struggle for democracy against propaganda, a struggle inevitably waged by an 'objective' and 'independent' press,'" the late James Carey of Columbia University has written.[6]

In essence, the press swapped partisan loyalty for a new compact—that journalism would harbor no hidden agenda. Editorials and political opinion, which before had mixed with and sometimes even constituted the news on the front page, were now set apart by space or label. From these simple decisions—things that seem obvious today—much of today's standard journalistic ethics was formed, especially those principles concerning political positioning by reporters.

Those ethics strengthened generally through the twentieth century as journalists aspired to greater professionalism and also as the number of competing newspapers in cities shrank, leaving the survivors to appeal to a more mass audience, something to which television news organizations also aspired.

In the twenty-first century, one of the questions is whether this notion of journalistic independence will weaken. As the century begins, it is being undermined in large part because new technology, and the new competition it has spawned, allows niche markets of national size to be developed that are sufficient for an attractive economic base. These trends will tend to weaken the economic possibilities of mass markets that encouraged nonpartisan journalism in the first place.

INDEPENDENCE IN PRACTICE

The rules have been modified and strengthened over time, to the point that today reporters and editors are often forbidden from participating in political action such as public rallies on politicized issues. In 1989, for instance, *New York Times* Supreme Court reporter Linda Greenhouse was criticized for participating in a "Freedom of Choice" demonstration in support of abortion rights. She called her participation anonymous activism and made note of the fact that she did not call attention to herself. "I was just another woman in blue jeans and a down jacket," she said afterward. But the *Times* said her marching jeopardized the appearance of her reporting and reprimanded her.[7]

The Greenhouse incident came at a time when journalism was becoming more sensitive to the charge of liberal bias. The nature of the political debate had been changing since the 1960s, stimulated in part by the creation of an active network of conservative think tanks injecting new ideas into the public debate. And, beginning with Vice President Spiro Agnew's characterization of Washington journalists as "nattering nabobs of negativism," Republican lawmakers were more vocal in asserting press bias.

By 1991, newspapers were enforcing strict rules against participation in partisan political activity. The *Morning News Tribune* in Tacoma, Washington, reassigned education reporter Sandy Nelson to the copy desk because she had helped organize a city referendum to ban discrimination on the basis of sexual preference. The *Daily Ledger* in Fairfield, Iowa, fired two editors after they founded an anti-abortion organization. The *Morning Tribune* in Lewiston, Idaho, and the *Daily Hampshire Gazette* in Northampton, Massachusetts, prohibited staff members from participating in demonstrations for or against the Gulf War.[8] Ten years later political activity was still frowned upon. In 2004 the *San Francisco Chronicle* pulled two women reporters off a gay marriage story after they were married at City Hall.

The new publishing platforms, such as blogs, are fueling a debate about what journalists can and cannot do or say in their private lives. In April 2004, Rachel Mosteller was fired from the *Durham Herald-Sun* for keeping a blog, "Sarcastic Journalist," in which she talked about newsroom life. Her blog did not identify the company or her co-workers. In January 2006, the weekly *Dover Post* fired a reporter because his personal blog contained, among other things, disparaging references to people who sought coverage from the newspaper.

INDEPENDENCE REEVALUATED

Even as the rules of independence became stricter in the past decades, there were always those who challenged—or evaded—them.

In the March 2003 lead up to the Iraq War, conservative columnist George Will wrote a column dismissing the idea that America should wait for approval from its allies before invading the Middle Eastern country. To support his view that waiting for permission is foolish, Will quoted at length from a speech by British House of Lords member and newspaper owner Conrad Black. In his speech, Black said that America had the most successful foreign policy because its objective was not to be threatened and when threatened it removed the threat.

What Will did not write in his column is that for years he had been paid by Black to be on an international advisory board of Black's newspaper company, Hollinger International. The *New York Times* said that for every meeting Will attended, he received $25,000; Will said he did not remember how many meetings he was present at. The Washington Post Writers Group, which syndicates Will, was also not aware of this conflict. Asked by the *Times* if he should have told readers about receiving money from Black, Will replied: "My business is my business. Got it?"[9]

The Conrad Black episode was not the first for Will. In 1980, then a strong backer of then-Republican presidential candidate Ronald Reagan, Will coached Reagan in preparation for the candidate's debate with President Jimmy Carter. Will then took to the airwaves after the debate as an ABC commentator and hailed Reagan's performance, saying Reagan was a "thoroughbred" under pressure.

Such secret counsel to politicians has plenty of precedent. Among others, Walter Lippmann wrote speeches for various presidents, including Lyndon Johnson. But the rules of conduct changed over time, and the belated discovery of the secret advice tarnished Lippman's reputation.

What was new in the Will case was that the columnist continues to say he doesn't care. When news of the coaching of Reagan eventually surfaced, Will basically called criticisms of his coaching nitpicking. "Journalism (like public service, with its 'conflict of interest' phonetics) is now infested with persons who are 'little moral thermometers' dashing about taking other persons' temperatures, spreading, as confused moralists will, a silly scrupulosity and other confusions."[10]

Will was not making an ideological argument. Rather, he was implying something else, something that others, regardless of ideology, would echo: that the morality or ethics of journalism was subjective and invalid.

There was only one problem with Will's argument, the same one that reveals why the concept of independence is grounded in practical matters rather than theory. Will had kept his coaching of Reagan secret. He did not want to tell his readers that he had helped produce the performance by President Reagan that he then glowingly reviewed.

Will's pattern is an old one, but it continually undermines the credibility of the journalist as activist. In the presidential election of 2000, William Kristol, editor of *The Weekly Standard*, appeared often as a guest commentator on television, offering his assessment of the candidates' positions, strategies, and chances. Throughout the primary season, he presented himself as unaligned. In reality, he was an informal adviser and supporter of John McCain. Like Will, he tried to present himself as something else.

In 2005, the Bush administration similarly consulted with various journalists on drafts of the president's second inaugural speech, among them Kristol and syndicated columnist Charles Krauthammer. Both journalists confirmed that they met with officials before the inaugural address, but said these were informal discussions regarding various administration policies, not speech preparations. Both were unapologetic about offering their views and told the *Washington Post* that this was proper behavior for commentators.[11] Both Kristol and Krauthammer praised the speech after it was delivered.

There is another problem worth noting about this defense. While those who allow themselves to act as insiders see little problem, they may be deluding themselves as to what was really going on here. As a rule, politicians of any stripe, we would wager, are far less interested in what any journalist might actually contribute to a speech, which probably already has more authors than it needs, and far more interested in making the journalist imagine that his rhetorical and intellectual powers are so magical that they just had to be consulted. Often these negotiations, in other words, are generally far more likely attempts at seducing journalists to ensure good press than genuine efforts at wanting whatever they have to contribute.

Others have made several stronger challenges to the concept of independence of spirit and mind in journalism. They are worth examining one at a time.

One concern is the worry that journalistic independence has wandered into a kind of self-imposed solitary confinement from society at large. As Elliot Diringer, a former reporter with the *San Francisco Chronicle* who later joined the Clinton White House, told our academic research partners, "There is this notion that you should be disinterested to the point . . . that you should withdraw from civic affairs if you are a journalist. And I find that somewhat troubling. I don't know why being a concerned citizen should be antagonistic with being a journalist."[12]

There have been two major reactions to this sense that the newsroom has become distant and alienated. One, as we indicated in the chapter on loyalty to citizens, was the movement called public journalism, which says that journalism should not just point out problems but also examine possible answers. Proponents of the movement do not see this approach, when carefully pursued, as a rejection of the journalistic principle of independence. Critics argue that it puts journalists in a position where they are seen as advocates because they identify with outcomes. That divide, in the end, is a matter of careful execution.

The other reaction has been to try to exploit public disaffection toward journalism by abandoning the principle of independence and to reach the audience by arguing from one side or the other. In this new incarnation, partisans function as "media people"—talk show hosts, commentators, or guests on TV or radio. Usually they purport to be independent experts—they are identified as former federal prosecutors, legal scholars, or other disinterested professionals—when in fact they are party surrogates. They might better be described as "media activists." As we will explain more in Chapter 7 on the forum function of journalism, these people increasingly are far less expert than they pretend, and often they have little regard for accuracy. Yet rather than addressing the public anger toward the press, the partisan approach tries to take advantage of it. Berkley psychology professor Philip Tetlock surveyed more than 250 people who make a living from sharing their expertise and comments. His twenty-year study tried to assess the probability that various outcomes the experts predicted would or would not happen. The results showed the experts to be poor forecasters. They fared worse than they would have if they had given all possible outcomes equal weight.[13]

Perhaps the best example of this phenomenon comes from the political Right, where conservative media mogul Rupert Murdoch has created an entire news network, Fox News, focused heavily on argument and ideology. Privately, journalists inside Fox argue that they are creating balance by giving airtime to conservatives. Here there is a case to be made.

But publicly, Fox has made a more subtle and arguably less intellectually honest argument. Under the guidance of Roger Ailes, the former political operative and ad maker for such clients as Richard Nixon and George Bush, Fox is careful to wrap its programming in the mantle of independence. Its first marketing campaign featured the slogan, for instance, "We report, you decide," which it later dropped in favor of "Fair and Balanced." This is much the same way as Hearst and Pulitzer claimed to advertise themselves not as they are but as they wanted people to imagine them, as accurate and fair, not as simply as a source one was likely to agree with. It is an appeal to each audience member's sense of one as reasonable. If you like us, that is because we are more accurate, more complete, not because you agree with us.

Still, this represents a moving away from the market appeal that came to characterize American journalism starting in the mid-nineteenth century and that grew in the twentieth century. That appeal was built on independence as the source of journalism's trustworthiness. It adopted a neutral voice, taking no sides and claiming to cast a skeptical eye on all sources of power on behalf of the public.

The appeal of the new American partisan press rests instead on reinforcing the preconceptions of the audience, not on being a watchdog of the powerful. It might be called the Journalism of Affirmation. This is different from the old American partisan press of the colonial age and early nineteenth century, which was controlled by a party and existed to advance a political agenda, to persuade and even educate. The new Journalism of Affirmation exists as a corporate strategy: politics is a means to an end.

It is also important to make a distinction between journalism of opinion—the commentary of William Safire and Anthony Lewis, *The Weekly Standard* and *The Nation*—and the work of partisans delivering news, such as some programming on Fox. Partisan delivery also includes bloggers, most of whom resemble the early journalists, which spoke to like-minded people and aimed to proselytize the undecided. One is clear in its intent and remains committed to all the principles of other journalists. The other purports to be one thing—neutral—while using the language and form of balance to create something else, a kind of propaganda.

This distinction has an important implication. Open in its intent, journalism of opinion is also open in its allegiance to a set of intellectual principles, which it holds above faction or party. George Will calls himself an American Tory, William Safire a conservative libertarian, Anthony Lewis a liberal, and Victor Navasky a progressive. When a powerful institution or figure moves away from those ideals, journalists of opinion are usually quick to criticize even those they often otherwise align with. The Journalism of Affirmation, claiming fairness, balance, and neutrality, lacks that agility or that candor.

There is another difference as well. Journalism of opinion, be it in the columnizing of a conservative or liberal columnist, is not fundamentally about reporting the news, but about making sense of it. It assumes the reporting occurs elsewhere. While the journalism of opinion may involve reporting, there is no claim that this is occurring outside the realm of the opinion and interpretation that is its primary concern.

The Journalism of Affirmation stakes its claim on reporting. The success of Fox, or the rhetoric of people like Rush Limbaugh, has had an impact on the rest of the press. It has opened the door to political operatives and celebrities and, on some occasions, to both. In 1997, CBS News experimented with former New York congresswoman Susan Molinari to host one of its morning news shows. ABC News hired former Clinton official George Stephanopoulos as a commentator, assigning him to cover presidential politics, where he reported on people, including Vice President Al Gore, with whom he had served in the White House. Later Stephanopoulos became host of a Sunday morning news talk show.

The outright bias of these hosts does not damage the notion of accuracy, precisely because the Rashomon bias (that there is no accuracy or truth) is so easy it becomes an excuse. The notion that the only authentic approach to information is through opinion is appealing to some people because it requires no professional discipline or technique or even idealism. There is a purity to it, like a faith in pure markets or the idea that any emotion is valid if it is strongly felt.

This blurring of journalistic identities has taken on another dimension. It has changed attitudes about personal relationships between journalists and those they cover. The *New York Times*, for instance, allowed Todd Purdum to cover the Clinton administration even after he had a relationship with former White House press secretary Dee Dee Myers, whom he eventually married. The situation, which probably would not have been allowed a few years earlier at the *Times*, did not even engender much comment. A generation earlier *Times* reporter Laura Foreman was found to have been romantically involved with a corrupt politician on whom she was reporting. When, after Foreman had been hired by the *Times*, the affair was discovered, *Times* executive editor Abe Rosenthal famously declared, "I don't care if you sleep with elephants, as long as you don't cover the circus." The Myers-Purdum relationship was so open, by contrast, that it was replayed as a charming and apparently acceptable subplot on *The West Wing*, a TV drama about the White House. And why not, when CNN's premier foreign correspondent, Christiane Amanpour, while covering the war in Kosovo in the late nineties, was engaged to (and later married) James Rubin, then spokesman for the U.S. State Department.

Unlike the Foreman case, situations like Myers and Purdum or Amanpour and Rubin are arguably considered more acceptable in a contemporary media culture because they are open. But is that really good enough? Can anyone reasonably be expected to cover those to whom they have personal, even intimate, loyalties? How can this be squared with the obligation that the first professional loyalty be to the citizen?

Disclosure is important. As citizens, we deserve to know if a reporter is actively involved with the issues or people he or she is covering. But after listening to journalists and worried citizens, we conclude that disclosure is not sufficient. As Safire, Lewis, and others who write with a point of view understand, it is vital to maintain some personal distance in order to see things clearly and make independent judgments.

Certainly, as well, such conflicts are also more common today in the age of women in the workplace and more two-career families. That may also have made them something that people were not so quick to denounce, seeing a value in women's coming to have more full acceptance in all roles in society. Yet the principle does not change because it is challenged more often.

Nor is the remedy nearly as onerous as those who would be inconvenienced by it would imagine. Purdum could have a different beat,

Rubin or Amanpour a different post. Indeed, at a time when more of the public doubts the professionalism of journalists, such support for this principle of independence would demonstrate to a skeptical public how seriously news organizations take their responsibilities and how they are willing to live up to them to their own inconvenience, embarrassment, and occasionally sacrifice and unpleasantness in their own management.

INDEPENDENCE FROM CLASS OR ECONOMIC STATUS

The question of independence is not limited to ideology. It may, indeed, be easier to deal with here than in other areas. The solution to bias, as we outlined in Chapter 4 on verification, is to develop a clearer method of reporting. Yet to fully understand the role of journalists, it is important to look at other kinds of conflicts and interdependencies.

As journalists have become more highly trained, better educated, and in certain quarters better paid, another complication to the concept of independence has set in. As Juan Gonzalez, then a columnist for the *New York Daily News*, told us at one Committee of Concerned Journalists forum, "[T]he biggest problem . . . is that the American people feel there is a class divide between those who produce the news and information and those who receive it. That the class divide manifests a class bias toward most Americans whether they are conservative or center or liberal: if they're working class and they're poor, they're considered less important in the society. I think that's the principal bias."[14]

The late Richard Harwood, the former *Washington Post* ombudsman, agreed at the same forum that, "Journalists, as members of [the] cognitive elite, derive their worldviews, mind-sets, and biases from their peers. Their work is shaped to suit the tastes and needs of this new upper class. I must say there's a lot of evidence that the mainstream press is staking its future on this class because it's increasingly going upscale . . . and rejecting or losing working people, lower-income people."[15]

Tom Minnery, a former journalist who was later vice president of Focus on the Family, an evangelical Christian organization based in Colorado Springs, Colorado, told us at another forum that the class bias has helped accelerate commercialization of the news. "The direction of coverage . . . is a distortion of the way life is lived in the United States by a vast, broad middle of the country's population," Minnery has argued. "In the United States, 1 percent of the population owns thirty-five percent of all the commonly traded stock. You would think from watching the evening news or reading newspapers that we are all at home watching the streaming ticker across the bottom of CNBC." Or, he continued, watch the morning network shows "and see extensive, lovingly detailed coverage of the latest gizmos and googaws available at the Comdex show, when in fact only 12.5 percent of all households in the United States have a computer with a modem. The confluence of commerce and news coverage is now so deep and profound that we can't even see the edges of it anymore."[16]

This potential class isolation is reinforced by strategic targeting of elite demographics, a policy many news companies have adopted. The result was and continues to be a threat to all journalism. People increasingly see the press as part of an establishment from which they feel alienated, rather than as a public surrogate acting on their behalf.

The solution to this isolation is not to repudiate the concept of independence, however. The solution is to recruit more people from a diversity of classes and backgrounds and interests in the newsroom to combat insularity. The journalism that people with different perspectives produce together is better than that which any of them could produce alone.

Perhaps, some journalists have suggested, there should even be a system to recruit people who have had other kinds of life experiences. "If you're going to change the composition of the journalistic workforce there has to be some kind of a program that takes people that are already in other careers . . . [and] offers them an opportunity to help diversify in a class way," Gonzalez suggested.[17]

INDEPENDENCE FROM RACE, ETHNICITY, RELIGION, AND GENDER

The last thirty years of the twentieth century saw a growing awareness of the need for reflecting the diversity of American society in newsrooms. Trade groups such as the American Society of Newspaper Editors created industrywide diversity goals for newspapers. Various news organizations revamped their style books to root out racist language. To date, however, the newspaper industry has failed to meet the goals. As we will outline in discussing the principle of personal conscience, there are problems with the concept of diversity if it is narrowed simply to mean ethnic, gender, or other numerical targets. Those are a necessary means, but they should not be the goal of diversity.

Yet there is another issue within the question of diversity that must be wrestled with first. It is the question of the degree to which ethnicity and gender can be equated with identity or expertise. Do we think that only African Americans can capably cover African Americans, or Asian Americans alone capably cover Asian Americans, and so on? Shouldn't a good journalist be able to cover anything?

"The argument for diversity based on representation ... at its core, presupposes that persons of the same race and gender think alike because of their shared experiences of racism and sexism," African-American business executive Peter Bell has argued. "The argument, I believe, ignores and/or minimizes the influence of class, education, region, family, personal psychology and religion in shaping our personal ideas and beliefs. ... Observable traits such as race and gender ... serve as a proxy, and I would argue a crude proxy, for ideas. ... What is the black position on any given issue? The answer, of course, is there isn't one."[18]

Many journalists, even those in minority groups, have similar doubts. "To simply say ... that you're going to have an Asian and a black and a person in a wheelchair in your newsroom, and that this is somehow going to give you some license to say that you're diverse, is to fall into the same category of determining your content on the basis of demographics," award-winning TV and radio correspondent John Hockenberry, who is disabled, has argued. "You can determine revenue on the basis of demographics, but you can never determine content. ... Far from hiring in the newsroom being an indicator of where diversity comes from, it's knowing your audience, and to be truly interested in your audience from the top to the bottom, from the left to the right, and from all economic levels."[19]

The criticisms touch a serious point: to what extent does background influence a journalist's work? If an editor determines who covers what simply by ethnic heritage or skin color, isn't that just another kind of racial and ethnic stereotyping? It implies that there is such a thing as a single black perspective or a single Asian perspective.

Somewhere between rigid newsroom quotas and the fears of a new "politically correct" orthodoxy lies a richer area. There is already ample evidence that newsrooms lacking diversity are unable to do their jobs properly. They miss news. Their coverage has holes. The *Chicago Tribune*'s Clarence Page has recalled: "One editor in northern Illinois tried to beg off [of minority coverage] saying that he really didn't have much of a minority population in his town, even though I knew for a fact that his town has a 17 percent Latino population–17 percent. . . . A rural Wisconsin editor told me that he really didn't have any minorities in his area, even though his newspaper was just down the road from a major Indian reservation."[20]

The myopia of traditional definitions of news is proof enough that personal perspective colors journalism. Media companies, recognizing this problem, enlisted the help of organizations like the Maynard Institute, which developed a workshop that helped media outlets better understand the concerns of the full range of their audiences and helps expand the news organization's sources of information.

But if one accepts that things like race do matter, how do we reconcile the undeniable influence of personal perspective with the goal of maintaining something called journalistic independence?

Independence from faction suggests there is a way to be a journalist without either denying the influence of personal experience or being hostage to it. The key is whether one maintains allegiance to the core journalistic principles that build toward truthfulness and informing the public. Just as it should be with political ideology, the question is not neutrality, but purpose. This journalistic calling to independence from faction should sit atop all the culture and personal history journalists bring to their job. Whatever adjective attaches itself to them as journalists–Buddhist, African American, disabled, gay, Hispanic, Jewish, WASP, or even liberal or conservative–it becomes descriptive but not limiting. They are journalists who are also Buddhist, African American, conservative–not Buddhist first and journalist second. When that happens, racial, ethnic, religious, class, and ideological backgrounds inform their work, but do not dictate it.

Journalist Hockenberry's skepticism about the influence of his own disability proves how this can work. Hockenberry once avoided doing "stories on disability" but later came to understand what he could bring to such pieces. "When I arrived at *Dateline*, a producer came to me and said, We want to do a story, a hidden-camera story, about the disabled in employment and in hiring. . . . Even though my motives had something to do with this issue of not being pigeonholed as the disability reporter, what I said was [that] in my experience in encountering discrimination, it's inconclusive. I see people who sort of look at me wrong or maybe they make some sort of decision and I never really quite understand . . . how it affected me."

"This young man [the producer], a Korean-American named Joe Rhee, said, 'John, discrimination doesn't happen while you're there. It happens the moment you leave. That's why we have the hidden cameras.'"[21] The result was a story that showed how companies in every case passed over a paraplegic man to hire a nondisabled applicant. "It was the combination of our collaboration in that newsroom that brought together a story that actually did something that mattered," Hockenberry said.

Hockenberry's experience shows that the goal of a newsroom is not simply to create numerical diversity—in this case, the disability story would not have been done if the disabled reporter was working alone. The ultimate goal of newsroom diversity is to create an intellectually mixed environment where everyone holds firm to the idea of journalistic independence. Together their various experiences blend to create a reporting richer than what they would create alone. And in the end that leads to a richer, fuller view of the world for the public.

The journalist is committed to society. The model is not disinterested. It is not cynical. It is not disengaged. The journalist's role is predicated on a special kind of engagement—being dedicated to informing the public, but not to playing a direct role as an activist. It might be called "engaged independence."

Gil Thelen, executive editor of the *Tampa Tribune*, has thought hard about this role. Thelen has been intrigued with the idea of civic journalism designed to reconnect journalists with community, but he has also fought the publishers to protect the principle of journalistic independence. He ultimately left a newspaper in the Knight Ridder organization over the separation of news and business interests.

Thelen has described the journalist's role as that of a "committed observer." What he means by that, Thelen explains, is that the journalist is not removed from community. Journalists are "interdependent" with the needs of their fellow citizens. If there is a key issue in town that needs resolution and is being explored by local institutions, "we have a commitment to reporting on this process over the long term, as an observer." It would be irresponsible to cover the issue haphazardly— or ignore it because it seems dull. The journalist should be committed to helping resolve the issue, Thelen argues, and the way he or she does that is by playing the role of the responsible reporter.

Thelen's ideas are echoed in the words of other journalists, who talk about the press creating a common language, a common under- standing, or being part of the glue that defines and holds a community together. This is the proper understanding that many journalists have about the role of engaged independence.

Florida's *Sarasota Herald-Tribune* even developed an inventive pro- gram called "Reader Advocate," trying to ensure that its reporters remain independent without becoming isolated. Every journalist at the news organization works as the reader representative for a week, taking the phone calls from readers, passing them on to the right reporter or editor, and logging in each call with a note of the complaint or suggestion.

It took three years to get through the entire staff, but the paper's executive editor at the time, Janet Weaver, believed it was worth it. Her staff said that simply listening to how citizens react to the newspaper has made them more aware of their relationship with the people in their community. "There are some people whom I have been very afraid about when their name comes up. I know how they treat me, so I can only wonder how they will treat the public," said Weaver. But there is a person sitting across the table who observes the reader repre- sentative, and there are information materials given to the four journal- ists who will have the task each month.

Other journalists have also developed methods for testing that they are managing to maintain their intellectual independence. Paul

Taylor, former chief political correspondent at the *Philadelphia Inquirer* and *Washington Post*, used a before-and-after method. When he was assigned to a story that involved substantial reporting, Taylor used to write the lead at the outset, before he had done any reporting. Then he would test that lead against the one he had crafted at the end of the reporting. If the two leads were too similar, he would know he hadn't learned very much, that he may not have done enough reporting, and that he may have been simply rewriting his own preconceptions.

In the end, no rigid prohibition against any kind of personal or intellectual engagement will serve to guarantee that a journalist remains independent from factions, political or otherwise. In the end it is good judgment, and an abiding commitment to the principle of first allegiance to citizens, that separates the journalist from the partisan. Having an opinion is not only allowable, not only natural, but it is also valuable to the natural skepticism with which any good reporter approaches a story. But a journalist must be smart enough and honest enough to recognize that opinion must be based on something more substantial than personal beliefs if it is to be of journalistic use. It is not about believing in people or groups of people. It is a craft based on reporting, learning, understanding, and educating. Creating barriers to this process of discovery is, in the end, being disloyal to the public.

The importance of this independence becomes even more obvious when we consider the next special obligation of journalism, its role as watchdog.

ENDNOTES

1. William Safire, in a note to author Kovach, April 18, 2006. Subsequent quotes attributed to Safire are from the same note.
2. Anthony Lewis, in a note to the authors, October 10, 1999.
3. John Martin, in William L. Rivers, *Writing Opinion: Review* (Ames, IA: Iowa State University Press, 1988), 118.
4. Maggie Gallagher, at CCJ Forum, New York City, December 4, 1997.
5. Maggie Gallagher provided this defense in one of her columns titled "A Question of Disclosure," January 25, 2005; available at www.uexpress.com.
6. James Carey, *James Carey: A Critical Reader*, ed. Eve Stryker Munson and Catherine A. Warren (Minneapolis and London: University of Minnesota Press, 1997), 233.
7. Carol Emert, "Abortion Rights Dilemma: Why I Didn't March—A Reporter's

Struggle with Job and Conscience," *Washington Post*, April 12, 1992; available at www.washingtonpost.com.

8. Cassandra Tate, "Outside Activities: When Does a Journalist's Personal Opinion Become a Public Issue?," *Columbia Journalism Review* (March/April 1991), 13–15.

9. Jacques Steinberg and Geraldine Fabrikant, "Friendship and Business Blur in the World of a Media Baron," *New York Times*, December 22, 2003; available at www.nytimes.com.

10. Mary McGrory, "Casualty: George Will Finds Being a 'Stablemate to Statesmen' Can Cost," *Washington Post*, July 12, 1983.

11. Howard Kurtz, "Journalists Say Their White House Advice Crossed No Line," *Washington Post*, January 29, 2005; available at www.washingtonpost.com.

12. Elliot Diringer, interview by William Damon, Howard Gardner, and Mihaly Csikszentmihalyi.

13. Louis Menand, "Everybody's an Expert," *The New Yorker*, December 5, 2005, 98–101.

14. Juan Gonzalez, at CCJ Forum, New York City, December 4, 1997.

15. Richard Harwood, at CCJ Forum, New York City, December 4, 1997.

16. Tom Minnery, at CCJ Forum, Ann Arbor, MI, February 2, 1998.

17. Gonzalez, at CCJ Forum, New York City, December 4, 1997.

18. Peter Bell, at CCJ Forum, Ann Arbor, MI, February 2, 1998.

19. John Hockenberry, at CCJ Forum, Ann Arbor, MI, February 2, 1998.

20. Clarence Page, at CCJ Forum, Ann Arbor, MI, February 2, 1998.

21. Hockenberry, at CCJ Forum, Ann Arbor, MI, February 2, 1998.

6

Monitor Power
and Offer Voice
to the Voiceless

n 1964, the Pulitzer Prize, the most coveted award
in the newspaper business, went to the *Philadelphia
Bulletin* in a new reporting category. The award
honored the *Bulletin* for exposing police officers in that city who were
involved in running a numbers racket, a kind of illegal lotto game, out
of their stationhouse. The story presaged what would become a new
wave of scrutiny about police corruption in American cities. The award
had one other significance as well. It marked formal recognition by the
print establishment of a new era in American journalism.

The new Pulitzer category was called "Investigative Reporting."
The newspaper executives from around the country who run the
Pulitzer under the auspices of Columbia University had added it in
place of an older designation that they decided no longer required special recognition, "Local Reporting." They were putting new emphasis
on the role of the press as activist, reformer, and exposer.

In doing so, the journalism establishment was acknowledging a kind
of work increasingly done in recent years by a new generation of journalists. Reporters like Wallace Turner and William Lambert in Portland

and George Bliss in Chicago were reviving a tradition of pursuing and exposing corruption that had largely been absent from reporting during World War II and the years immediately following. The war years featured storytellers like Ernie Pyle of the Scripps Howard wire service, who evoked the heroic spirit of the Allies at war, the sturdy British people, or the simple but gutsy American GI. After 1964, that began to change. Eight years later, when Bob Woodward and Carl Bernstein of the *Washington Post* helped uncover the Watergate scandal inside the Nixon White House, investigative reporting would suddenly gain celebrity and sex appeal and would redefine the image of the profession.

All of journalism was changed, especially Washington journalism. A. M. Rosenthal, then executive editor of the *New York Times,* was so disturbed by the way the *Washington Post* dominated the Watergate story that he ordered a reorganization of his newspaper's Washington bureau to create a formal team of investigative reporters. So long as Rosenthal was executive editor, the job of Washington bureau chief would be only as secure as the strength of the bureau's investigative reportage. CBS News launched its own investigative news show, *60 Minutes,* which became the most successful news program network TV ever produced. Local television news, not to be left out, was soon awash in investigative teams – or "I-Teams" – of its own.

Some old-timers began to grumble. Investigative reporting, they harrumphed, was little more than a two-dollar word for good reporting. In the end, all reporting is investigative. While that is an oversimplification–investigative reporting is qualitatively different from other kinds of work in various ways–the critics were correct in one sense. What the Pulitzer Prize board formally recognized in 1964 had been, in fact, more than two hundred years in development.

Investigative reporting's roots were firmly established in the very first periodicals, in the earliest notions of the meaning of a free press and the First Amendment, and in the motivation of journalists throughout the profession's history. These roots are so strong, they form a fundamental principle:

Journalists must serve as an independent monitor of power.

This principle is often misunderstood, even by journalists, to mean "afflict the comfortable." Moreover, the watchdog principle is being threatened in contemporary journalism by overuse and by a faux watchdogism aimed more at pandering to audiences than doing public service. Perhaps even more serious, the watchdog role is threatened by a new kind of corporate conglomeration, which effectively may destroy the independence required of the press to perform their monitoring role.

When print periodicals first emerged in Europe in the early seventeenth century, they saw their role as investigatory. During the English civil war, when press freedom in England seemed to flicker alive, periodicals immediately began to promise that they would investigate what was going on and tell their readers. The *Parliament Scout*, which began publication in 1643, "suggested something new in journalism—the necessity of making an effort to search out and discover the news."[1] The next year a publication calling itself *The Spie* promised readers that it planned on "discovering the usuall cheats in the great game of the Kingdome. For that we would have to go undercover."

These early efforts at investigative work became part of the reason the press was granted its constitutional freedom. Periodicals like *Scout* and *Spie* were, for the first time, making the affairs of government more transparent. They marked the ambition of the press to be what would later be known as the Fourth Estate, and stated publicly that the affairs of government should be known to all, not just to the privileged. Until the journals appeared, the internal workings of government were primarily the knowledge of the privileged—those with business before the state or those directly involved in the administration of government. The general public's information on their rulers largely came from uninformed gossip or through official government messages. But unlike the proclamations and town criers who provided the information those in power wanted distributed, these new periodicals aspired to tell people what the government actually did. Though government often clamped down on these early printers, as it would so often throughout the world, they established investigative reporting as one of the earliest principles that would set journalism apart from other means of communication with the public. It was the watchdog role that made journalism, in James

Madison's phrase, "a bulwark of liberty," just as truth, in the case of John Peter Zenger, became the ultimate defense of the press.

These early efforts were often frustrated. The British government forbade note-taking of Parliamentary debate. People had to remember what was said and then run outside to recall or paraphrase the event before the paper went to press. These early journalists were dismissed as "newsmongers," and historians look back on that early parliamentary press as often dishonest and corrupt. Yet the instinct toward transparency and serving as watchdog that they represented, however crudely, proved enduring and ultimately would triumph.[2]

In the years to come, as conflict between a protected press and government institutions increased, it was this watchdog role that the Supreme Court fell back on time and again to reaffirm the press's central role in American society. Beginning with the case of *Near v. Minnesota,* which forbade the government from restraining publication of any journal except when the story threatened "grave and immediate danger to the security of the United States," the Court has methodically built a secure place within the law where journalists are protected so that they may aggressively serve the public's need for important information concerning matters of public welfare.[3] A full two hundred years after the revolution, Supreme Court Justice Hugo Black continued to focus on the press's watchdog responsibilities when he wrote, "The press was protected so that it could bare the secrets of government and inform the people. Only a free and unrestrained press can effectively expose deception in government."[4] With support from state and federal legislatures during the 1960s and 1970s, the press gained greater access through the Freedom of Information Act and so-called sunshine laws, which provided public access to many documents and activities of the government. Beginning in the twenty-first century— especially during the administration of George W. Bush—unprecedented efforts were launched to withhold government information from the public and even to criminalize the efforts by the press to publish. One question is how the courts will react to these efforts.

The watchdog principle means more than simply monitoring government, and extends to all the powerful institutions in society. And that was true early on. Just as *Spie* went "undercover" in order to discover the "cheats in the great game of the Kingdome," nineteenth-century journalist Henry Mayhew stayed out in the open to document the plights of that same kingdom's unknowns. Mayhew roamed the streets of Victorian London reporting on the lives of street people for the London *Morning Chronicle*.[5] By so doing he gave the watercress girl and the chimney sweep individual faces, voices, and aspirations. He revealed their humanity to a population that regularly passed them unnoticed.

Combining the search for voices that went unheeded and cheats undiscovered, the earliest journalists firmly established as a core principle their responsibility to examine the unseen corners of society. The world they chronicled captured the imagination of a largely uninformed society, creating an immediate and enthusiastic popular following.

Today journalists continue to see the watchdog role as central to their work. Nearly nine out of ten journalists believe the press "keeps political leaders from doing things they shouldn't do," and the watchdog role was second, after informing the public, among the answers journalists volunteered as to what distinguished their profession from other types of communication.[6]

As firmly as journalists believe in it, the watchdog principle is often misunderstood. At the turn of the century, Chicago journalist and humorist Finley Peter Dunne translated the watchdog principle to mean "comfort the afflicted and afflict the comfortable."[7] Dunne was half kidding, but the maxim has stuck. On the day the *St. Paul Pioneer Press* won the Pulitzer Prize in 2000 for uncovering a cheating scandal on the University of Minnesota basketball team, the paper's sports editor in a speech cited his boss's fondness for repeating the phrase.[8]

Unfortunately, the notion that the press is there to afflict the comfortable and comfort the afflicted misconstrues the meaning of the watchdog and gives it a liberal or progressive cast. The concept is deeper and more nuanced than the literal sense of *afflicting* or *comforting* would suggest. As history showed us, it more properly means watching over the powerful few in society on behalf of the many to guard against tyranny.

The purpose of the watchdog role also extends beyond simply making the management and execution of power transparent, to making known and understood the effects of that power. This logically implies that the press should recognize where powerful institutions are working effectively, as well as where they are not. How can the press purport to monitor the powerful if it does not illustrate successes as well as failures? Endless criticisms lose meaning, and the public has no basis for judging good from bad.

Like a theme in a Bach fugue, investigative reporting has swelled and subsided through the history of journalism but never disappeared. It has defined some of the most memorable and important eras in U.S. history:

- The press in colonial America found its purpose as tribune of a people chaffing under a distant government that interfered with the energy of its development. James Franklin's *New England Courant* established a role as watchdog over both governmental and religious institutions and the colonies had their own *Spie*–Isaiah Thomas's *Massachusetts Spy* exposed those who trafficked with the enemy.

- The revolutionary press gave way to a nation-building press in which the issues of the shape and character of the new government were reported. Federalists and anti-federalists each created their own newspapers to inform and encourage the public debate over the fundamental principles upon which the new country would be built. One of the most important roles of this partisan press was to serve as a watchdog over the opposition party, a process of discovery and disclosure that at times became so virulent that the government with limited success tried to legislate against the practice.[9]

- At the dawn of the twentieth century, a new generation of journalists dubbed "muckrakers" gave voice to reform at the local, state, and federal levels. Their detailed investigation and exposure of corrupt power, ranging from child labor abuses to urban political machines and railroad and oil trusts, led to a progressive movement in national politics.

As the practice of investigative journalism has matured, several forms have emerged. Today three main forms can be identified: original investigative reporting, interpretative investigative reporting, and reporting on investigations. Each bears some examination.

ORIGINAL INVESTIGATIVE REPORTING

Original investigative reporting involves reporters themselves uncovering and documenting activities that have been previously unknown to the public. This is the kind of investigative reporting that often results in official public investigations about the subject or activity exposed, a classic example of the press pushing public institutions on behalf of the public. It may involve tactics similar to police work, such as basic shoe-leather reporting, public records searches, use of informants, and even, in special circumstances, undercover work or surreptitious monitoring of activities.

Original investigative reporting would include the work of muck-rakers like Lincoln Steffens, whose *Shame of the Cities* series in 1904 led to wide-ranging reforms in local government; or Rachel Carson, whose revelations of the effects of pesticide poisoning in her 1962 book *Silent Spring* launched an international movement to protect the environment.

It would also include the reporting of Marcus Stern and Jerry Kammer, whose Pulitzer Prize–winning investigation in 2005 and 2006 for the *San Diego Union-Tribune* led to the resignation from office and eventual criminal conviction on corruption charges of Congressman Randy "Duke" Cunningham.[10] Using his own unique system that he called a "lifestyle audit," Stern became suspicious of relationships between some of the congressman's travel and his style of living. Digging into campaign contributions from defense contractors, Stern uncovered other suspicious financial exchanges. He enlisted Kammer's help, and the two eventually pulled on these strings to unravel what was later described by the U.S. Attorney's office in San Diego as "the most audacious bribery scheme" in congressional history.

In modern original investigative reporting, the power of computer analysis often replaces the personal observation of the reporter. The *Atlanta Journal-Constitution*'s 1989 Pulitzer Prize–winning series, "The Color of Money," by Bill Dedman, is an early example. It exposed racial discrimination by lending institutions in Atlanta and led to significant reforms in lending policies in banks throughout the country. A book on investigative reporting said of the series, "The most incontrovertible evidence of racially biased mortgage lending in Atlanta was the computer-based analysis of the documents that lenders were required to file with regulators."[11] If properly employed, the computer has the potential to alter the depth of investigative journalism, for the reporting can transcend traditional interviews and anecdotes and amass overwhelming documentary evidence.

INTERPRETATIVE INVESTIGATIVE REPORTING

The second form of investigative reporting is interpretative reporting, which often involves the same original enterprise skills but takes the interpretation to a different level. The fundamental difference between the two is that original investigative reporting uncovers information not before gathered by others in order to inform the public of events or circumstances that might affect their lives. Interpretative reporting develops as the result of careful thought and analysis of an idea as well as dogged pursuit of facts to bring together information in a new, more complete context that provides deeper public understanding. It usually involves more complex issues or sets of facts than a classic exposé. It reveals a new way of looking at something as well as new information about it.

One early example is the *New York Times*'s publication of the Pentagon Papers in 1971. The Papers themselves were a secret study of American involvement in Vietnam written by the government. Reporter Neil Sheehan went to great lengths to track down a copy. Then a team of *New York Times* reporters and editors expert in foreign policy and the Vietnam War interpreted and organized the documents into a dramatic account of public deception. Without this synthesis and interpretation, the Pentagon Papers would have meant little to most of the public.

A more recent example is a ten-part series on social class that the *New York Times* published in 2005. Using available demographic and socioeconomic data, a team of reporters explored "ways that class— defined as a combination of income, education, wealth and occupation— influences destiny in a society that likes to think of itself as a land of unbounded opportunity."[12]

Some reporting now pushes the boundaries of interpretative investigative work. Donald Barlett and James Steele became famous at the *Philadelphia Inquirer* and later *Time* magazine for ambitiously exploring elaborate issues in projects such as "America: What Went Wrong" and "America: Who Stole the Dream?" Both probed how the U.S. economic-political system had failed lower-income citizens. Both were the result of years of reporting, an intense examination of economic data, and hundreds of interviews. Both series operated under the premise that the country was leaving its poor behind.

The pieces were so interpretative, some journalists condemned them as polemics rather than journalism—for their authors had abandoned the role of engaged independent observer to become activists. *Newsweek*'s Bob Samuelson called "America: Who Stole the Dream?" "junk journalism" because it "does not seek a balanced picture of the economy—strengths as well as shortcomings."[13]

The critics are right that these pieces were not balanced in the sense of giving both sides their equal space. The reporters were attempting to expose an aspect of economic trends that had gone largely unnoticed and unreported by others, who were recording the impact on those at the top of the economic ladder who were active players in the economic boom. Even some journalists who praise the work believe the first series, "What Went Wrong," had more documentary evidence than the second. Evidence that the disclosures in the first series were a revelation to many people was the lines in the *Inquirer* lobby of people waiting for reprints, and that the paper received some 90,000 calls in the first week. "We've never seen anything like it," said then *Inquirer* executive Arlene Morgan. People were more critical of the second series, and *Inquirer* editor Maxwell King turned the editorial pages into a public forum for critics on all sides. While the first series was better than the second because of the level of documentation, in the end both succeeded in stirring public conversation about enormously important subjects. The criticisms about them, however, point out how important it is that the reporters engaged in this level of interpretation to provide sufficient outlet for alternative views.[14]

REPORTING ON INVESTIGATIONS

The third investigative category is reporting on investigations. It is a more recent development and has become increasingly common. In this case the reporting develops from the discovery or leak of information from an official investigation already under way or in preparation by others, usually government agencies. It is a staple of journalism in Washington, a city where the government often talks to itself through the press. But reporting on investigations is found wherever official investigators are at work. Government investigators actively cooperate with reporters in these cases for many reasons: to affect budget appropriations, to influence potential witnesses, or to shape public opinion. Most of the reporting on President Clinton's affair with Monica Lewinsky was actually reporting on the investigation of Independent Prosecutor Kenneth Starr's office, augmented by counterinformation leaked by the White House or lawyers for those going before the grand jury. Another example was the reporting that Richard Jewell had planted the bomb at the 1996 Atlanta Olympics, which was based on anonymous leaks from police and FBI sources and proved to be mistaken. In contrast, most of the work on Watergate, especially in the early critical months, was original investigative work in which the journalists were talking directly with principal sources about what had happened, not with investigators about what they theorized had happened.

Reporting on investigations has proliferated since the 1970s. In part, this is because the number of investigations has grown; in part, it is because after Watergate, federal and state governments passed new ethics laws and created special offices to monitor government behavior. But it also has spread because over time journalists have come to depend on unidentified sources to the point where the practice has become a concern both among journalists and a suspicious public.

In an article about the secretive National Security Agency (NSA), the primary collector of electronic intelligence for the U.S. government, reporter Seymour Hersh, writing in *The New Yorker,* quoted anonymous intelligence officers about how the deteriorating quality of the NSA's work left it unable to meet the threats of sophisticated terrorist groups and rogue states. Whitfield Diffie, an encryption expert at Sun Microsystems, was quick to seize on the vulnerability of Hersh's anonymous methods: "What bothers me is that you are saying what the agency wants us to believe–[that] they used to be great, but these days they have trouble reading the newspaper, the Internet is too complicated for them, there is too much traffic and they can't find what they want. It may be true, but it is what they have been 'saying' for years. It's convenient for NSA to have its targets believe it is in trouble. That doesn't mean it isn't in trouble, but it is a reason to view what spooky inside informants say with skepticism."[15]

The risks of this reporting, as Diffie points out, is that its value is largely dependent on the rigor and skepticism of the reporter involved. The reporter is granting the interview subject a powerful forum in which to air an allegation or float a suggestion without public accountability. This does not mean that reporting on investigations is inherently wrong. But it is fraught with usually unacknowledged risks. The reporters here usually are privy to only part of the investigation, rather than in charge of it.

The *New York Times* learned that lesson when it broke a story on nuclear espionage drawn from a secret congressional report. The *Times* story picked up the alarming language of the report and said that China was catching up with American nuclear technology because it obtained data on building warheads from a Chinese-American scientist, Wen Ho Lee. The *Times* did not name Lee, but it did allow authorities to characterize the scandal as the biggest in recent history. The story led investigators to rush into getting an indictment against Lee, who was eventually jailed for one year. Out of the fifty-nine counts brought against him, he pleaded guilty to one: illegally gathering and retaining national security information. He was sentenced to time served by a judge who issued a profound apology from the bench. The *Times* also printed a lengthy correction apologizing for taking so much of the report for granted and not giving Lee the benefit of the doubt.[16]

The chance of being used by investigatory sources is high. Rather than a watchdog of powerful institutions, the press is vulnerable to being their tool. Reporting on investigations requires enormous due diligence. Paradoxically, news outlets often think just the opposite—that they can more freely report the suspicions or allegations because they are quoting official sources rather than carrying out the investigation themselves.

Tom Patterson, Benjamin C. Bradlee Professor at the John F. Kennedy School of Government at Harvard, documented the shifting standards that gave rise to this new category of investigative journalism. "What we see in the studies," he told us at a Committee of Concerned Journalists Forum, "is that by the late 1970s we find a substitute for careful, deep investigative reporting—allegations that surface in the news based on claims by sources that are not combined with factual digging on the reporters' part. That tendency increased in the 1980s, increased again in the 1990s, and the mix began to change. The use of unnamed and anonymous sources becomes a larger proportion of the total, and of course that tendency emerged full blown in the Lewinsky story."[17]

Investigative reporter and author Jim Risen has argued that most investigative reporting usually involves elements of all three forms. Woodward and Bernstein, for instance, regularly checked in with government investigators as they worked on their own inquiry. Yet there are distinctions between whether a reporter's work is fundamentally original, interpretative, or about someone else's investigation. Each type of reporting carries its own distinct responsibilities and risks. Too often, though, journalists have not been sufficiently mindful or careful of the differences.

THE WATCHDOG ROLE WEAKENED

In the ebb and flow of the watchdog role over the last two centuries, we are reaching a moment of diminution by dilution. The celebrity of Woodward and Bernstein was followed by the success of *60 Minutes,* in which correspondents Mike Wallace, Morley Safer, Harry Reasoner, and Ed Bradley became stars in their own reports. People tuned in to see who Mike, Morley, Harry, and Ed would catch this week. Investigative journalism, particularly on television, thus became a means both for public good and for commercial ratings. In the nearly thirty years since, the proliferation of outlets for news and information has been accompanied by a torrent of investigative reportage. With most local news stations in America now featuring an "I-team" and prime-time newsmagazines offering the promise of nightly exposés, we have created a permanent infrastructure of news devoted to exposure.

Much of this reportage has the earmarks of watchdog reporting, but there is a difference. Most of these programs do not monitor the powerful elite and guard against the potential for tyrannical abuse. Rather, they tend to concern risks to personal safety or one's pocketbook. Among some popular topics of prime-time newsmagazines are: crooked car mechanics, poor swimming pool lifeguarding, sex slave rings, house-cleaning scams, and dangerous teenage drivers.

A study of prime-time newsmagazines in 1997, for instance, reveals a genre of investigative reporting that ignores most of the matters typically associated with the watchdog role of the press. Fewer than one in ten stories on these programs concerned the combined topics of education, economics, foreign affairs, the military, national security, politics, or social welfare—or any of the areas where most public money is spent. More than half the stories, rather, focused on lifestyle, behavior, consumerism, health, or celebrity entertainment.[18] Victor Neufeld, then executive producer of ABC's *20/20*, told the committee, "Our obligation is not to deliver the news. Our obligation is to do good programming."[19]

Safety can often be an important target for intense and critical watchdog reporting. Yet too much of the new "investigative" reporting is tabloid treatment of everyday circumstances. Local television news often employs its I-teams in such stories as "dangerous doors"—reporting on the hazards of opening and closing doors; or "inside your washing machine"—a look at how dirt and bacteria on the clothes consumers put in their washers get on other clothes. Consider the Los Angeles TV station that rented a house for two months and wired it with a raft of hidden cameras to expose that you really can't get all the carpeting in your house cleaned for $7.95. Or the series of reports, popular in the mid-1990s, about a bra whose metal wires could poke the owner.

While this reporting appears to be original investigative work, it often is not. First, much of it is what TV reporter Liz Leamy has called "just add water" investigative reports. These come from TV news consultants who literally offer stations the scripts, the shots, the experts to interview, or the interviews themselves already on tape, and are specifically designed for sweeps periods to generate ratings. Some TV news producers call such exposés "stunting," an acknowledgment that they are playing tricks with viewers' appreciation of investigative work without actually delivering it. The second problem is that exposing what is readily understood or simply common sense belittles investigative journalism. The press becomes the boy who cried wolf. It is squandering its ability to demand the public's attention because it has done so too many times about trivial matters. It is turning watchdogism into a form of amusement.

The significance of this shift should not be underestimated. On television, the primary medium for news, the prime-time magazine and I-team segments have effectively replaced the documentary or any other long-form investigative reportage. As a consequence, some journalists are beginning to question the expanded role of investigative journalism. Patty Calhoun, editor of *Westword,* an alternative newspaper in Denver, Colorado, wondered about the impact on a public that had no way of discerning between gossip and fact when she observed: "talk radio . . . puts out rumors and now thinks they're doing investigative reporting which is novel, but unfortunately, their listeners can't tell any better than the radio DJs that they're not."[20]

Even the broad public support for watchdog reporting is beginning to suffer, though it is difficult to pinpoint trivial exposés as the cause. Public concern seems to focus on the standards and techniques used by some investigative reporters. For years, the survey work of Andrew Kohut for the Pew Research Center for the People and the Press found public support of the watchdog role remaining stable while the press in general began to become unpopular in the 1990s. But by the end of the decade, even that began to change. By 1997, Kohut found the public objecting to techniques such as having reporters not identify themselves as reporters, paying informers for information, or using hidden cameras or microphones.[21]

Over the last two decades, the public has also had more doubts about press criticism of the military. The number of people who believe such reportage weakens the nation's defenses rose from 28 percent in 1985 to 47 percent in 2005. Yet the public's view of the watchdog role remains nuanced. As questions arose about the government's handling of the war in Iraq, public support for watchdog journalism over political leaders began to rise. By 2005, 60 percent of Americans thought news organizations kept political leaders from doing things they shouldn't, up from 54 percent in 2003.[22]

INVESTIGATIVE REPORTING AS PROSECUTION

Though all reporting involves investigation, what we have come to understand as investigative journalism adds a moral dimension. It engages the public to come to judgment about the disclosure and implies that the news organization considers it important—worthy of special effort. In that sense, investigative reporting involves not simply casting light on a subject but also usually making a more prosecutorial case that something is wrong. Here journalists should be careful that they have enough evidence to do so, especially since often pieces can be structured as either exposés or news stories. When questions arose about a state medical examiner's failing to investigate thoroughly the conduct of President Clinton's mother in a wrongful-death case (she was a nurse), the *Los Angeles Times* wrote the story as an exposé. The story suggested that Clinton as governor "refused for several years to dismiss a state medical examiner whose controversial decrees included a ruling that helped Clinton's mother . . . avoid scrutiny in the death of a patient." The problem was the story was inherently confusing, technical, and difficult to decide conclusively. Clinton, for instance, having been defeated for reelection as governor, was out of office at the time of the incident involving his mother. A good many reporters at the *Times,* even some involved in reporting it, were strongly divided over the piece's fairness and argued that it be written as a feature, not an exposé. The whole controversy could have been simply avoided if the paper had written the story another way. The *Times* failed to understand that an exposé is in effect a prosecutor's brief and the case it sets forth must be unambiguous; if the story does not meet this test, it should be written as something else.

The incident points out an important issue that arises with the investigative model: the news outlet is taking an implied stance on the issue that some wrongdoing has occurred. That is why investigative journalism has been called advocacy reporting, or as reporter Les Whitten called it, "reporting with a sense of outrage," and why the acronym for the professional association called Investigative Reporters and Editors spells out the word *ire.* Because what the investigative journalist discloses may lead to loss of reputation or change the flow of public events, it carries a greater weight of responsibility, not only in verification of fact but also in sharing information about the nature of the sources of that information.

To fulfill the watchdog principle responsibly, Bob Woodward says, he tries to keep an open mind. "You might start a story thinking you are going to look at how the city health department administers vaccines, but ... find that the story's really about the city's mismanagement in general. ... Look at as much as you can in every direction." To do so, "Some of the things I do are build a chronology, try to talk to everybody and interview them repeatedly."

Pulitzer Prize winner Loretta Tofani relied on the power of talking to potential sources face-to-face and spending a lot of time with them. In a story about a pattern of widespread rape inside a Maryland jail, which she wrote while at the *Washington Post,* she uncovered crimes that were occurring literally under the nose of law officers—crimes widely known to the police and judges. To get it, she spent months of her own time in the evenings after work doggedly knocking on doors in order to engage some of the most reluctant possible witnesses to talk to her, and she was able to produce a series of stories that documented the prevalence of rape inside the Prince George's Detention Center in Maryland. In the end, Tofani produced what her editors thought impossible: a story documenting the crimes by quoting, by name and on the record, the perpetrators, the victims, and responsible officials who should have acted to prevent the crimes from ever taking place.

As Tofani said, when the articles were published, all the needed documentation was "given to the government basically on a silver platter. ... It had everything. It had medical records. It had the victims' names. It had the rapists' names."[23] Public disclosure of the information forced the government to change the system that allowed the rapes to occur. In the end, the government convicted all the rapists.

In addition, another investigative reporter, Susan Kelleher, then with the *Orange County Register* in California, has said she discusses at length with her sources beforehand everything that is involved in an investigative report. This way, they know she is honest and also what they're getting into. "Before anybody participates with me in a story in the sense of a source," she said, "I tell them how I work. I tell them they have to go on the record. I tell them I am going to be asking other people about them, that even though I find them really nice people, I am going to have to check them out. . . . I say to them, 'Once you agree to talk to me, that's it. You don't really have control, but you do have control to the degree you want to participate. And once you are on the record, if there's something you don't want me to know, then don't tell me because it's going to be on the record.'"[24]

This level of honesty with sources has allowed Kelleher to uncover some remarkable stories. One exposed abuses at an infertility clinic where some doctors were secretly, and illegally, taking extra eggs from their patients and selling them to other patients. As with Tofani's story on jailhouse rape, Kelleher's story was meticulously documented with medical records and on-the-record information by people involved in the process. Also, like Tofani's report, this one won a Pulitzer Prize.

Michael Hiltzik, a Pulitzer Prize–winning investigative business reporter for the *Los Angeles Times,* has said that the single most important technique in his career is "get[ting] the documents." The rest of it is fine, he says, the confidential sources, secret meetings, "all the decor of investigative reporting you see in Hollywood. But the whole aim is you must have everything documented. The whole point of dealing with sources is to get them to point you to things you can get in black and white." Hiltzik and his partner, Chuck Phillips, won the Pulitzer in part for a story exposing that the Grammy Awards, which are supposedly for charity, generate huge income but little charitable proceeds. The Grammy organizers threatened the reporters with legal action and more. "They couldn't lay a hand on us because everything was written down in documents. When it is documented, all the 'bloviating' and threats are for naught. You are on solid ground."[25]

As the twenty-first century advances, the revolution in technology and the economic organization it has spawned are creating new opportunities but are also threatening an independent watchdog press. Digital communications allow information to move more easily and quickly, but they are also leading to the creation of international communications corporations that challenge the concept of the nation-state itself. As we have outlined earlier, in many cases these new international conglomerates, such as General Electric or Walt Disney or AOL–Time Warner Inc., have subsumed journalism inside their larger corporate cultures. The interdependencies inside a company like AOL–Time Warner are myriad so that any claim by its journalists to independence will soon no longer be realistic. It becomes more difficult for a *Time* reporter to cover not only AOL but also all of the Web, e-commerce, entertainment, cable, and telecommunications. Over time, as news executives nurtured in this new environment rise to positions of leadership, experience suggests that it may no longer seem worth the cost to play watchdog over your own corporate parent.

The theory of a free press that evolved out of the Enlightenment—that there would be an independent voice that could monitor the influence of powerful institutions in society—is put into question. "[These] mergers in the media business matter in ways that other takeovers don't," Rifka Rosenwein wrote in an article examining media mergers in *Brill's Content.* "Having five or six major widget companies may be enough to safeguard the price and product competition with which traditional economic theory and antitrust law have been concerned. But concentrating much of the power to create and distribute news and ideas in five or six media conglomerates with a vast array of interests raises all kinds of other issues. There is, after all, a virtue in diversity, lots of it, when it comes to expression that transcends widget economic theory."[26]

History promises that a market economy in an open society has the capacity to renew itself from the grassroots. And there are signs of a market response to concerns about the loss of independence in American journalism. The decade of the 1990s saw a noticeable upgrading in content, depth, and critical nature of the work of not-for-profit publications that monitor the press, including the *Nieman Reports,* the *Columbia Journalism Review,* and the *American Journalism Review.* In 1998, journalistic entrepreneur Steven Brill perceived a market for a publication to monitor the media, including the press, that would operate at a profit.[27]

Although Brill's venture failed as a commercial enterprise, it served as a harbinger of an incipient new role for citizen investigators. As individual bloggers proliferated on the Internet, many of them focused on monitoring the press itself, including its investigative reporting efforts. Instant communities of interest developed online in the late 1990s to effectively raise questions about press disclosures. In one of the most celebrated cases a blogger who described himself as "Buckhead," after the name of the community in Atlanta where he lived, challenged a 2004 report on CBS's Wednesday edition of *60 Minutes* alleging political favoritism toward George W. Bush by the Texas National Guard during the Vietnam War years. Buckhead's challenge questioned the authenticity of documents used by Dan Rather to support his allegations. Although he provided no real evidence to support his challenge, within hours his Internet audience exploded and the doubts and bits of supporting data that followed soon forced CBS to investigate the validity of its claims. In the end, Rather publicly called the story "a mistake" and apologized. Four CBS staff members were removed from their jobs, including the senior producer of the Bush story.[28] Rather himself would later step down as anchor of *CBS Evening News* and not long after, CBS News president Andrew Heyward would be replaced as well.[29]

Maybe more important than the new vigilance of these media monitors is the fact that the tools provided by new communications technology have created the possibility for virtually anyone to monitor or even to compete with the established press. Though few bloggers appear to be moving this way—producing citizen news gathering in a reportorial or investigative sense—some professional journalists have taken up the challenge to operate outside organized press institutions and organizations.

An example of this possibility is the Center for Public Integrity in Washington, which was founded in 1990 by Charles Lewis, a thirty-four-year-old producer from CBS's *60 Minutes.* Frustrated by the pressures to produce "more entertaining" stories and not to pursue stories that would require greater time and effort, Lewis resigned his job to found a new kind of news organization that did "not have to worry about overnight Nielsen ratings or the latest subscription numbers."[30] With financial support from philanthropic organizations, Lewis organized a workshop of like-minded journalists to harness the power of the computer and the reach of the World Wide Web. By 1999, forty of the center's major reports had been readily picked up and distributed by traditional news organizations that no longer supported the staff to do similar work.

Although the center Lewis founded has become the best known of the independent journalism initiatives, there are others: The Fund for

Investigative Journalism, Inc., provides grants to freelance reporters working "outside the protection and backing of major news organizations."[31] The Alicia Patterson Foundation makes supporting financial grants to reporters and editors working in traditional news organizations.[32] The Soros Foundation's Open Society Institute has recently begun a similar fellowship for reporting on criminal justice matters. Journalist David Burnham, using nonprofit funding and help from universities, has created software to allow journalists to do computer-assisted investigative reporting of government records. During the 2000 presidential primaries, journalist Morton Mintz, a longtime investigative reporter for the *Washington Post*, consistently reported on issues that were not raised on the campaign trail for TomPaine.com, a nonprofit website that features analyses on topics that the mainstream media often overlooks.

As interesting as these new efforts are, they have to be considered fragile and embryonic, certainly compared with mainstream journalism. The support of private philanthropy can disappear as quickly as it can be given, and their ability to draw an audience depends on getting the attention of for-profit media outlets to air their research.

The independent journalism centers show how the new technology could reorganize the way news is produced and communicated. Potentially, at least, this offers a challenge to the traditional organization of news, and it suggests that if the old media abandon the watchdog role in any serious sense, others might take it up. Even a lone hacker rummaging through the databases and chat rooms now has the ability to shape or even dictate the flow of news, as Matt Drudge has demonstrated.

Beyond the utopian vision about the technology, however, there are more practical economic questions still unanswered. Can any one of these new outlets focus the attention of a significant amount of the public around what they might have to say? And if they can, will they be purchased and pulled inside a large corporate culture their founders wanted to escape? At the moment, the answer is unclear. But there are reasons to be doubtful. Network television news divisions offer the clearest model we have of the new economic organization of news. They were the first of the major journalism institutions to be subsumed inside large nonjournalism corporations. Yet as they began to suffer a structural loss of audience to new technology, they moved away from a serious watchdog function and toward a model of news, even investigative news, as entertainment. That model, the only evidence we have at the moment of the effect of global conglomeration of news, raises substantial doubts that investigative journalism will continue on the level that we have come to know in the last half-century.

The watchdog is unlike any other role. For all that it is similar to all other journalism, it requires special skills, a special temperament, a special hunger. It also requires a serious commitment of resources, a desire to cover serious concerns, and a press independent of any interest except that of the ultimate consumer of the news. For all the lip service paid to it, the watchdog principle, like the others outlined here, faces more challenge today than ever. Yet, as we will see next, the expanding nature of journalism as a public forum has spawned a new wave of journalism as assertion, which makes the need for a vibrant and serious watchdog journalism all the more critical. In this new century, the press must watchdog not only government but also an expanding nonprofit world, a corporate world, and the expanding public debate that new technology is creating.

This raises the possibility of a new approach to journalism. As the example earlier of a blogger's doubts about the accuracy of a national news report demonstrates, the emergence of an engaged and active citizen monitoring of the press moves watchdog journalism into a new direction. Adapting the elements of journalism to the techniques of the citizen blogger could not only produce a powerful new tool for watchdog reporting but also engender a recognition of the need for a new journalism based on cooperation between the press and the public.

ENDNOTES

1. John C. Sommerville, *The News Revolution in England: Cultural Dynamics of Daily Information* (New York: Oxford University Press, 1996), 65.
2. Mitchell Stephens, *A History of News* (Fort Worth, TX: Harcourt Brace College Publishers, 1996), 226–27.
3. *Near v. Minnesota*, 283 US 697 (1931).
4. *New York Times Co. v. United States*, 403 US 713 (1971).
5. For a detailed account of Henry Mayhew's work, see Anne Humphreys, *Travels*

into the Poor Man's Country: The Work of Henry Mayhew (Athens, GA: University of Georgia Press, 1977).

6. CCJ and the Pew Research Center for the People and the Press, "Striking the Balance: Audience Interests, Business Pressures and Journalists' Values," March 1999, 79; available at www.journalism.org.

7. Finley Peter Dunne, in *Bartlett's Familiar Quotations.* Dunne actually put the quote into the mouth of a fictional wag of his creation named Mr. Dooley. The full quote shows Dunne's satirical tone: "The newspaper does everything for us. It runs the police force and the banks, commands the militia, controls the legislature, baptizes the young, marries the foolish, comforts the afflicted and afflicts the comfortable, buries the dead, and roasts them afterward."

8. Emilio Garcia-Ruiz, sports editor of the *St. Paul Pioneer Press,* quoted his executive editor, Walker Lundy, at the annual Premack Journalism Award presentation, Minneapolis, MN, April 10, 2000.

9. Signed in 1798, the Act for the Punishment of Certain Crimes, as the sedition act was known, made it illegal to "write, print, utter or publish . . . any false, scandalous, and malicious writing or writings against the government of the United States, or the President of the United States." The law was basically a partisan measure aimed at silencing the opposition to the Federalist Party in the 1800 elections—it had a built-in sunset of 1801. In total there were twenty-five arrests, twelve trials, and eleven convictions under the act.

10. The story that began the *Union-Tribune*/Copley News Service investigation, "Cunningham Defends Deal with Defense Firm's Owner," ran June 12, 2005. It was written by Marcus Stern.

11. James S. Ettema and Theodore L. Glasser, *Custodians of Conscience: Investigative Journalism and Public Virtue* (New York: Columbia University Press, 1998), 36, 42.

12. *New York Times,* "Class Matters—Social Class in the United States of America," May–June 2005.

13. Robert Samuelson, "Confederacy of Dunces," *Newsweek,* September 23, 1996. Jack Fuller makes a virtually identical argument against "America: What Went Wrong" in *News Values: Ideas for an Information Age* (Chicago: University of Chicago Press, 1996).

14. Arlene Morgan, interview by author Rosenstiel, March 2000.

15. Seymour Hersh, "The Intelligence Gap," *The New Yorker*, December 6, 1999, 76.

16. Kirsten Lundberg, "The Anatomy of an Investigation: The Difficult Case(s) of Wen Ho Lee" (1641.0), President and Fellows of Harvard College, 2001.

17. Thomas Patterson, at CCJ Forum, Washington, DC, March 27, 1998.

18. Project for Excellence in Journalism, "Changing Definitions of News: A Look at the Mainstream Press over 20 Years," March 6, 1998, 3; available at www.journalism.org.

19. Marc Gunther, "The Transformation of Network News: How Profitability Has Moved Networks Out of Hard News," *Nieman Reports,* special issue (Summer 1999), 27.

20. Patty Calhoun, at CCJ Forum, Chicago, November 6, 1997.

21. Pew Research Center for the People and the Press, "Press 'Unfair, Inaccurate and Pushy': Fewer Favor Media Scrutiny of Political Leaders," March 21, 1997; available at http://people-press.org.

22. Pew Research Center for the People and the Press, "Public More Critical of Press, But Goodwill Persists," June 26, 2005.

23. "Watchdog Conference: Reporters Wrestle with How to Use Sources," *Nieman Reports* (Fall 1999), 7.

24. Ibid., 8.

25. Michael Hiltzik, interview by author Rosenstiel, May 2000.

26. Rifka Rosenwein, "Why Media Mergers Matter," *Brill's Content,* December 1999–January 2000, 93.

27. Bill Kovach was publisher of *Nieman Reports* from 1990 until June 30, 2000, and independent ombudsman for *Brill's Content* from its inception until August 2000.

28. CBC.ca, "Rather Boasts about 'Total, Absolute' Control over Cable News Show," July 12, 2006; available at www.cbc.ca/story/arts/national/2006/07/12/rather-hdnet-news.html.

29. Poynter online, "McManus Replaces Heyward as CBS News President," October 26, 2005; available at www.Poynter.org/column.asp?id=45&aid=91148.

30. Center for Public Integrity brochure, Washington, DC, 1999.

31. These journalists have investigated corruption, malfeasance, incompetence, societal ills, and media criticism. Fund-supported journalists have provided major news stories in recent years on such subjects as prisoner abuse; racial bias in reporting in American newspapers; the role of U.S. intelligence in the American media; effects of welfare legislation on American Indians; environmental abuses in Mexican forests by U.S. companies (a radio series); environmental pollution and abnormal rates of cancer in a New Jersey community; and whether Kenneth Starr had been using journalists to extend his investigatory powers.

32. This program offers the parent news organization the simultaneous right to publish the work and has included such areas as the new immigration laws; youth and gang violence in America; the world of work in an age of downsizing and deregulation; managed health care; coping with illiteracy; foster care and the politics of poverty; and corruption of the law.

7

Journalism As a
Public Forum

ody Shearer had just returned from a trip to Europe when he sat down one Tuesday night to watch television. The Washington freelance journalist cruised across channels, stopping on CNBC, and watched a few minutes of the talk show *Hardball* with host Chris Matthews.

Matthews's guest was Kathleen Willey, a woman who claimed President Clinton had groped her in the White House. Matthews was trying to talk about whether someone had tried to silence Willey by threatening her. But it soon became clear that the topic of the interview was not the president or Willey's allegation—it was Shearer himself.

CHRIS MATTHEWS: When this man came up to you in—at dawn that morning, in Richmond five years after this incident, who was that guy? I'm gonna ask you again, because I think you know who it was.

KATHLEEN WILLEY: I do know. I think I know.

MATTHEWS: Why don't you tell me who it was? This is an important part of the story here, why would you want—come out and—on this program tonight on live television and not tell us who you think that person was? . . . [L]et me ask you a more careful way. Were you ever led to believe who it might be, and who led you to believe it and what did they lead you to believe?

WILLEY: I was shown a picture and–

MATTHEWS: And who was in the picture?

WILLEY: I can't tell you. I'm not trying to be coy–

MATTHEWS: Would I recognize the picture?

WILLEY: Yes.

MATTHEWS: Is it someone in the president's family, friends? Is it somebody related to Strobe Talbott? Is it a Shearer?

WILLEY: I've been asked not to dis–

MATTHEWS: You've been asked not to admit that?

WILLEY: Yes, by–

MATTHEWS: OK.

With a sinking stomach, Shearer knew what Matthews was getting at. A rumor had been floating around Washington that it was Shearer who had approached Willey while she was jogging and threatened her if she didn't drop her case against the president. The rumor was unsubstantiated. It was also untrue. Shearer had been in California when the encounter had supposedly taken place, but no one had bothered to check out that part of the story. Now he could only watch as Matthews made the false rumor public knowledge and sound like fact.

MATTHEWS: Let's go back to the jogger, one of the most colorful and frightening aspects of this story. You were confronted as you were out walking. You couldn't sleep, your neck was hurting–this guy came upon you you never met before–. You never met him before.

WILLEY: No.

MATTHEWS: And tell me about that–what he said, finish up that whole story.

WILLEY: Well, he mentioned my children by name. He asked how they were and, at the–at this point, I started asking him who he was and what he wanted. And he just looked me right in the eye and he said, "You're just not getting the message, are you?" And I turned around and—and ran. I had no business running, and probably ran about 100 yards, I was so frightened, and I turned around and he was gone.

MATTHEWS: Who showed you the picture of the person you think might have been him?

WILLEY: Jackie Judd.

MATTHEWS: From ABC?

WILLEY: Yes.

MATTHEWS: And did you identify it positively?

WILLEY: Yes.

MATTHEWS: So it's Cody Shearer.

WILLEY: I can't tell you.

MATTHEWS: OK. But you identified it pos–. Let's talk about a couple of other things just to tie up the loose ends here.[1]

The show had been over for only a few minutes when the first call came. It was an anonymous deep voice threatening Shearer's life. Shearer was unnerved, but he figured it was only a crank who had gotten charged up by the *Hardball* show. Then, however, came a second call. And a third. Shearer began to grow concerned.

The next day conservative talk radio host Rush Limbaugh broadcast the rumor: "She says Ken Starr asked her not to reveal the identity of the man who she says threatened her two days before her testimony in the Paula Jones case. . . . Here's who it is: It's Cody Shearer, S-H-E-A-R-E-R."[2]

Limbaugh had an even greater impact. Call after call came in that day to Shearer's house, nearly a hundred, nearly all of them threatening death or physical harm. Though the story was demonstrably untrue, that night on *Hardball* Matthews reprised some of the Willey interview and played a clip of his "scoop" for *Newsweek*'s Michael Isikoff, *U.S. News and World Report*'s Michael Barone, and National Organization for Women president Patricia Ireland.

Shearer left town for a few days and tried to forget the incident. Washington is a town with attention deficit disorder, he figured. In a few days, no one would care about this. But he was wrong. Sunday morning, back in Washington, Shearer was taking a shower when a houseguest ran into his bathroom and said there was a man in his yard with a gun claiming he had come to kill Shearer. Shearer thought it was a joke, until he came out and saw the man, with a gun aimed directly at another friend and demanding to see him.

Suddenly, inexplicably, the gunman ran to his car and fled. Shearer and his friends copied down the license plate number and called the police. An hour later the police delivered the weird incident's even weirder denouement. The crazed gunman was Hank Buchanan, the brother of Patrick Buchanan, the former talk show host and GOP and Reform Party presidential candidate. Hank Buchanan had a history of mental illness.

Shearer was mostly appalled by Chris Matthews. "If I made a mistake like that, I would have sat down and written a letter explaining I was on a tight deadline and apologizing," Shearer said. "But I got nothing, not even from the producer. . . . And the most amazing thing is that nothing happened to him. He was back on the air the next night."[3]

The two had met on a train a few days after the broadcast, but before the Buchanan incident. They argued heatedly, according to Shearer, and he thought Matthews was unapologetic. After receiving letters from Shearer's attorney, Matthews made an on-air apology that included the attorney's assertion that Shearer "had nothing whatever to do with the events described by Ms. Willey."

"I now regret having spoken—not spoken—beforehand with him [Shearer] before I mentioned his name on the air. I should have never brought his name up till we had vetted it," Matthews said on his program.

This was something less than a correction. More importantly, the story was untrue. The case of Chris Matthews and Cody Shearer offers a caution for understanding the next element of journalism. From its origins in the Greek marketplace to the colonial American taverns, journalism has always been a forum for public discourse. The Hutchins Commission in 1947 placed this mission as an essential obligation of the craft, second only to telling the truth. "[T]he great agencies of mass communication should regard themselves as common carriers of public discussion," the commission wrote.[4]

This is the sixth principle or duty of the press:

Journalism must provide a forum for public criticism and compromise.

New technology has made the forum more robust and journalism less paternal. But the Shearer incident suggests also that the forum's greater speed and velocity have also increased its power to distort, mislead, and overwhelm the other functions of a free press. And this is only increasing with the dawning of the potential of citizen journalism, blogs, and even the blending of journalism and conversation.

In Chapter 2, on truth, we already examined the natural forum the first periodicals provided and its relationship to the creation of public opinion. This forum-creating capacity is so pervasive that it informs almost every aspect of the journalist's work, beginning with the initial report by which the journalist alerts the public to an event or condition in the community. These reports may contain analysis that suggests potential impacts. Context may be provided for comparison or contrast, and accompanying editorials may evaluate the information. Columnists may provide personal comments on the matter.

All the forms that journalists use every day can serve the forum-creating function by alerting the public to issues in a way that encourages judgment. The natural curiosity of humankind means that by reporting details of scheduled events, disclosing wrongdoing, or outlining a developing trend, journalism sets people to wondering. As the public begins to react to these disclosures, the community becomes filled with the public voice—on radio call-in shows, television talk shows, personal opinions on op-ed pages, in blogs, chat rooms, and in public opinion polling and elsewhere. As these voices are heard by those in positions of power, they make it their business to understand the nature of the public opinion developing around the subject. It is this process that daily re-creates in modern society the ancient forums in which the world's earliest democracies were formed.

This forum function of the press would make it possible to create a democracy even in a large, diverse country by encouraging what James

Madison and others considered the basis upon which democracy would stand—compromise, compromise, compromise.

None of this today is lost on the advocacy groups and political parties. Every year millions of dollars are spent trying to sway public opinion, often by employing half-truths and sometimes outright lies. As a result, it is crucial that the news media play the role of honest broker and referee as it carries the common discussion. In the new age of media, it is more incumbent on those providing us with journalism that they decipher the spin and lies of commercialized argument, lobbying, and political propaganda. The editorial pages of the newspaper, the opinion columnist, the talk show, and the point-of-view magazine essay, bloggers, and anyone else have every right to be opinionated. That is their mission. But if their authors want to call themselves journalists, then it follows that they should not misrepresent the facts—that they should hold to the same standards of truthfulness or allegiance to public interest as any other part of the profession.

So journalism must provide a forum for public criticism and compromise. Yet in a new age, it is more important, not less, that this public discussion be built on the same principles as the rest of journalism, starting with truthfulness, facts, and verification. For a forum without regard for facts fails to inform. A debate steeped in prejudice and supposition only inflames.

Just as important, this forum must be for all parts of the community, not just the affluent or demographically attractive.

Finally, there is another element to understand about the public forum the media carry: a debate focused only on the extremes of argument does not serve the public but instead leaves most citizens out. Even as the news media give air to the wide variation of opinions that reflect so pluralist a society, they must not lose sight of the fact that democracies are, in the end, built on compromise. The public forum must include the broad areas of agreement, where most of the public resides and where the solutions to society's problems are found.

Some people might consider this argument for stewardship anachronistic—and more than a little elitist—a leftover from an era when only a few outlets controlled public access to information. In a new century, with its new communications technologies, isn't it enough for Matthews to let Willey speak and then let Shearer respond? Now we can let the journalist mediator get out of the way, and let the debate occur in the genuine public square, not the artificial one defined by NBC or CBS News. This is where the technology-versus-journalism debate comes to its clearest philosophical divide.

It is true that we have the potential for a more open debate. And it is appealing, on some level, to think that technology will free those who produce the news from having to exercise judgment and responsibility. The proliferation of debate created by the machines will minimize human fallibility and raise us all. We can rely on the marketplace of facts and ideas, not on journalists, to sort out the truth.

The blogosphere makes this philosophy even purer. The protocol holds, at least in the first decade of the new century, that if a blogger posts an opinion he or she also includes a link to whatever it is she is reacting or referring to. The knotty issue of flawed humans misrepresenting or deliberately distorting the facts is eliminated.

The problem is this: By what criteria is Matthews or anyone else freed of any obligation to engage in the discipline of verification or to have concern for the larger public interest? More channels? Interactivity? The prospect of infinite links? While this might seem correct from a purely technological perspective, in the real-world marketplace of communication and political culture, it is creating a public square with a diminished regard for fact, fairness, and responsibility. Spin replaces verification. Right becomes a matter of who has the greatest might, wattage, or rhetorical skill.

On much of television and radio, for instance—particularly on cable news and morning news—electronic journalism has gone a significant distance toward abdicating its responsibility to verify as it presents a public forum. The reason is that these platforms now rely on live interviews as their primary method of news gathering. The live interview format, as any newsmaker will happily acknowledge, cedes power to the interviewee. The guest controls what they say, with broad power to filibuster, mislead, or even lie. The journalist host, for all intents and purposes, has a limited ability to check or correct all but the most obvious deceptions. Although electronic journalists may not realize it, they have structured their programs in such a way that facts are effectively replaced by whatever the guests on these programs feel they can sell. TV news has thus added to the atmosphere in which facts are devalued in favor of spin.

In practice, unfortunately, the technological argument is the digital equivalent of tyranny, not freedom. Rather than liberated, we become captive to the technology. The job of journalists becomes simply to make sure the technology is functioning. It is the nightmare of the HAL 9000 computer in *2001: A Space Odyssey*.

One of the great supporters of the citizens' watching over citizen-produced content phenomenon is Wikipedia, a user-edited online encyclopedia. Wikipedia is based on a technology called wiki, which allows articles to be created and modified by multiple people; the wiki stores a history of the article along with edits made by each individual. The philosophy of Wikipedia is that factual errors inserted by one user will be caught and changed by another. Wikipedia is not journalism, although wiki-based news sites do exist.

In May 2005, a Nashville man posted a biography of retired journalist John L. Seigenthaler Sr. on Wikipedia. The originally anonymous posting included several fabricated statements, including that Seigenthaler was once thought to be involved in the assassination of John F. Kennedy and Robert Kennedy, and that he had lived in the Soviet Union for thirteen years.

In fact, the brief bio contained only one factual sentence—Seigenthaler was the administrative assistant to Robert Kennedy in the early 1960s. Despite the inaccuracies, the entry was not detected until September, when Seigenthaler learned of it and had it taken down.

Seigenthaler outlined what happened to him in an account in *USA Today*, sparking a discussion in both traditional media and on the Internet about the rules and virtues of Wikipedia, and, by extension, the notions of fact and accuracy in the online community. Some suggested an expansion of libel laws to cover the Internet, while others criticized Seigenthaler for not simply modifying his bio—which Wikipedia allowed anyone to do—rather than have it removed.

This is not meant to suggest that traditional sources of reference and information are automatically more reliable. A study published by the journal *Nature* in December 2005 said that Wikipedia "comes close" to *Encyclopedia Britannica* in terms of accuracy. The study analyzed forty-two entries in both encyclopedias and counted 123 errors in *Britannica* and 162 in Wikipedia. *Britannica* released a lengthy rebuttal calling the *Nature* study flawed, inaccurate, and misleading because of the way it selected the entries. *Nature* responded by saying it believed "the comparison was fair" and refused to retract what it had published.[5]

There is certain to be more study of Wikipedia and others. But as of 2006, there is certainly no evidence to support the claims of technologists that the open architecture of the Internet is somehow superior to the efforts of a more limited number of professionals trying to verify facts and information.

The Internet provides more people with a voice than ever before. And participation is good. But journalists and citizens should be mindful of the risks incurred anytime a new format gains leverage. As this new and more robust public forum gains momentum, the strength of what is replaced–the professional effort of verification–diminishes. So as we justly celebrate public conversation becoming more integral to media dialogue, we must remember what we stand to lose. Rather than consider the issue of verification settled, as facts are discounted as mere commodity and more value and time is given to argument, we should be more mindful, not less, that we have the facts right.

Public discourse lies at the heart of and actually predates formal American journalism. Before the printing press, as we have said, "news" was something exchanged over a pint of ale in publick houses. News accounts weren't static printed words, and they didn't exist in a void; they were part of conversation. And though conversations obviously involved the exchange of information, much of the point was the exchange of ideas and opinions.

With the arrival of the printing press, this tradition did not disappear, but carried forward into the essays that filled the earliest newspapers. Noah Webster (whose dictionary first defined the term *editorial*) described this function in an "ADDRESS to the PUBLIC," published in the inaugural issue of his *American Minerva* (December 9, 1793): "[N]ewspapers are not only the vehicles of what is called news; they are the common instruments of social intercourse, by which the Citizens of this vast Republic constantly discourse and debate with each other on subjects of public concern."[6]

In the eras that followed, journalism worked to keep alive the idea of an open forum with the public. When newspapers finally had "news" to deliver, the editorial page became a place for community discussion through published letters to the editor and later the page opposite the editorials, usually written by readers. Publishers also kept the forum concept alive in more elementary ways. By 1840 the *Houston Star* was among the first to make its lobby more than an entryway into the newsroom; it became an open salon for the public. Residents were encouraged not only to come by but also to help themselves to "a good glass, an interesting paper and a pleasant cigar." In many cities, the tradition of the newspaper lobby as an inviting public reading room and salon continued for more than another hundred years. The newspaper was not only part of the community but also in a very concrete way was a place for the community to gather and talk.[7]

Tom Winship thought his newspaper failed in this role after he reassessed its coverage of the school busing crisis in Boston, for which the *Boston Globe* won the 1975 Pulitzer Prize for distinguished public service. Winship, then the paper's editor, decided he had made a mistake in asking his columnists to refrain for two weeks from discussing the controversy. In retrospect, he said, the *Globe*'s columnists might have made constructive suggestions regarding details of the implementation of the plan. "Why didn't we question more vigorously the details of the busing plan?" he asked rhetorically. "I think we became overwhelmed by the street demonstrations and the opposition assaults on the paper. . . . I have been plagued by my censorship of the paper's columnists."[8]

The difficulty is that today the concept of media as a public forum has taken on extraordinary dimensions. In the 1990s, the media helped develop what linguist and author Deborah Tannen described as the "Argument Culture." It was led by television programs such as *Crossfire* on CNN, *The McLaughlin Group* on commercial television, and talk radio, but it reflected something deeper and more cultural about what was occurring in politics. By 1998, programs such as the following, drawn from the cable program *Crossfire* on CNN, were not unusual.

In the exchange that follows, Larry Klayman, chairman and general counsel of Judicial Watch, a conservative legal group dedicated to challenging Democratic officeholders, is arguing that President Bill Clinton should be impeached for a second time because he failed to turn over to the Justice Department missing White House e-mails relating to the "Filegate" controversy and because he released personal correspondence with Kathleen Willey.[9] Klayman is on the program with *Crossfire* co-hosts Bill Press, a liberal Democrat, and Robert Novak, a conservative.

KLAYMAN: This is the first time in American history that a president has been held guilty of a crime, and I would suggest, Bill, let me finish here. . . . [I]t's time for another impeachment proceeding.

PRESS: I think we have a chance to, first of all, appeal a ruling. And number two, I would like to point out that your guy, . . . [Supreme Court Justice] Antonin Scalia in 1975 ruled that the Privacy Act does not apply.

KLAYMAN: He didn't rule. He did not rule. He did not rule.

PRESS: In fact, that was his opinion at the time, and it's been followed by Republican and Democratic administrations ever since.

KLAYMAN: Bill, the talking points that the White House gave you tonight were defective.

PRESS: Not—not.

KLAYMAN: They didn't tell you that there are internal memoranda in the White House which admit—the Clinton White House—that the Privacy Act applies. There's absolutely no dispute.

PRESS: Absolutely, absolutely IN dispute!

KLAYMAN: The plain language of the statute says it applies to the executive office of the president.

PRESS: Let me move on to the letters themselves. I've got a stack of these letters upstairs. These are personal letters, copies of them, . . . handwritten letters by Kathleen Willey. . . .

KLAYMAN: How did you get them, Bill?

PRESS: None of your damned business.

KLAYMAN: Why?

PRESS: "Dear Mr. President—"

NOVAK: You may get a subpoena, Press.

PRESS: "—on November thirteenth, 1996. Dear—"

NOVAK: I see a subpoena in your future.

PRESS: May I read this, Bob, if you would stop interrupting me?

By 2000, in an average television day, there were 178 hours of news and public affairs programming in a 24-hour period, of which about 40 percent was talk shows.[10] The moment might well have been the peak of the Argument Culture, culminating in the impeachment of Bill Clinton. But its rise reflected several factors.

One of the driving forces behind the Argument Culture was not purely that audiences wanted it but rather that, quite literally, talk is cheap. The cost of producing a talk show is only a fraction of the cost of building a reporting infrastructure and delivering news. As a consequence, what we have elsewhere called the new Mixed Media Culture of radio and TV talk shows, websites, chat rooms, blogs, bulletin boards, and more that now dominate the communications systems has seen the urge to comment replace the need to verify, sometimes even the need to report. The communications revolution is often more about delivering news than gathering it. Consider that by 2006, we knew of only one talk show in all of cable news that made any attempt to check its facts and correct them during the program. That show was *Pardon the Interruption*, a talk show about sports on ESPN.

Second, as we first discussed in our earlier book *Warp Speed*, the Argument Culture tended to devalue expertise. Desperate to expand its shrinking audience base on television, or create a new one on the Web, the Argument Culture tends to put a premium instead on newness. Listen to Bill Shine, executive producer of Fox News's prime-time programming, talk in 2000 about why he hired Heather Nauert, now a correspondent for ABC, one of a growing class of loosely credentialed, often young, pseudo-expert commentators who populate the new media culture: "When I first saw her, I thought Heather was our demographic, that she could bring in younger people," Shine told the *Washington Post*.[11] What's more, younger pundits, "exude more energy. Older men and women tend to . . . sit back and relax. If you've got a debate show, you want that energy."

Even though the then twenty-nine-year-old Nauert had no experience in politics, television, or print journalism and had never worked for the Republican Party, Fox usually falsely identified her as a "GOP consultant" or "a GOP strategist." "They need the label, I guess," Nauert explained. Unfortunately, often the new pundit class is untethered to any professional responsibility, or knowledge, other than the desire to continue to be on TV. Thus the new combatants are dedicated most of all to providing television producers the energy, attitude, and extremism the programs desire. Rather than deciphering or mediating the spin—exaggeration and innuendo, in other words—the media often are lusting for it. By creating "experts," the media are not reflecting real public debate; they are creating their own artificial made-for-TV debate.

A third feature of the new larger media forum was that it doesn't necessarily expand the scope of public discussion. The most significant media forums—the cable talk shows, radio programs, and major Internet sites—tend to focus on a surprisingly narrow range of blockbuster stories. Without any reporting infrastructure, chat venues have to rely on these long-running, simple stories that audiences can easily dip in and out of. This media diet offers everything from soap-opera dramas, to turning unknown people into celebrities, to relating the latest scare in the war on terror.

The social consequences are obvious. Missing from the larger public square are many of the important concerns facing the nation. These are consigned to a series of smaller media ghettos. The reluctance of TV networks to broadcast key moments of public life such as political conventions, leaving that job to cable television, is only one sign. The result is that the mass media no longer help identify a common set of issues. One of the most distinguishing features of American culture—the potential of the nation to summon itself to face great challenges as we did facing fascism or communism or the Depression—now becomes doubtful.

Finally, there was the nature of the discussion itself. The media's penchant for talk increasingly grew into a penchant for polarization. In the more commercial venues of radio and television, the "discussions" too often have little or nothing to do with journalism's mission of enlightening. On the theory that everyone likes a good fight, instead, all problems begin to seem unsolvable. Compromise is not presented as a legitimate option. It is what author Michael Crichton as early as 1993 called "the Crossfire Syndrome," in homage to the CNN program. The irony is that though it does build a small but passionate following, the shouting matches over time tend to alienate the larger public that increasingly fails to see itself in the debate.

Crichton deconstructed the nature of the Argument Culture discourse: "Are you a protectionist? . . . Do you think your Mideast trip was a waste of time? . . . The structure of the questions dictates the answer." More important, "such questions assume a simplified either/or version of reality to which no one really subscribes."[12]

"We are all assumed these days to reside at one extreme of the opinion spectrum or another. We are pro–abortion, anti–abortion. We are free traders or protectionist. We are pro–private sector or pro–big government. We are feminists or chauvinists. But in the real world, few of us hold these extreme views. There is instead a spectrum of opinion."

The problem with these features of the Argument Culture–the diminished level of reporting, the devaluing of experts, the emphasis on a narrow range of blockbuster stories, and the emphasis on an oversimplified, polarized debate–is that they tend to disenfranchise people from the public discussion that the media not only are supposed to support but need for their own survival. Making politics into a shouting match drives people away from the media.

"Democracy is based on a fundamental compromise between the majority and the minority," Robert Berdahl, the chancellor of the University of California at Berkeley, told a gathering of journalists in 1998.[13] "Compromise, however, becomes impossible if every issue is raised to the level of a moral imperative," simplified to fit a set of stereotypical preconceptions, or "framed in a way to produce ultimate shock value." This is what, however, the press typically does.

"I don't think for a moment that the media and newspapers are the sole source of cynicism in our society," Berdahl added. "But a wave of cynicism is upon us and it is very damaging to the institutions of civil society. . . . For the kind of corrosive cynicism we are witnessing leads to apathy and indifference. It leads to withdrawal. It leads to the focus on the individual at the expense of concern for the larger community. . . .

Cynicism, I believe, is corroding the quality of civil discourse in America and threatening the basis for democratic institutions."

The press, Berdahl argued, needs to understand that though it is independent, it is not detached. Journalists are not, as he put it, "observers with no stake in the issue at hand." They are independent, but very much have a stake.

None of which is to say that holding a forum with the public can't also mean being engaging; it just means the exchange should be more thoughtful, more focused on discussion, and drive at something—a resolution.

"I'm very much inspired by this culture of people who believe that journalism should be about raising hell in an intelligent way," media critic Jon Katz told our academic research partners.[14] "But I don't mean throwing a brick at someone's head and saying 'Yeah, yeah, you're a jerk.' You should really be provoking people to think—challenging them to justify and defend their ideas, just as I have to justify and defend mine."

In short, the public debate should not be a shouting match—political pie throwing or argument as entertainment. The press has a stake in that discussion being inclusive and nuanced, and an accurate reflection of where the debate in society actually exists, as well as where the points of agreement are.

By 2006, the Argument Culture had changed into something new. That change was probably most dramatically demonstrated on October 15, 2004, with the appearance of comedian Jon Stewart on *Crossfire*, the iconic example of the culture, and a program that by then had been on the air for more than a decade.

Stewart, host of the *Daily Show* on Comedy Central, which had become wildly popular especially with the young audiences coveted by advertisers, had become a critic of *Crossfire* and the argumentative way it dealt with political figures, particularly Democratic presidential candidate Senator John Kerry. Stewart was invited to the show by co-hosts Paul Begala, representing the political Left, and Tucker Carlson, representing the Right of the political spectrum.[15]

"Well, he's been called the most trusted name in fake news," Carlson said with a broad smile that suggested the relish with which he looked forward to the conversation with Stewart and "his one-of-a-kind take on politics, the press and America." But it became obvious from a reading of the transcript almost immediately, to the audience at least, that Stewart had not come onto the show to trade jokes with his hosts.

STEWART: Why do you argue, the two of you? I hate to see it.

CARLSON: We enjoy it.

STEWART: Let me ask you a question.

CARLSON: Well, let me ask you a question first.

STEWART: All right.

CARLSON: Is John Kerry—is John Kerry really the best? I mean, John Kerry has . . .

STEWART: Is he the best? I thought Lincoln was good.

CARLSON: Is he the best the Democrats can do?

STEWART: Is he the best the Democrats can do?

CARLSON: Yes, this year of the whole field.

STEWART: I had always thought, in a democracy—and again, I don't know—I've only lived in this country—that there's a process. They call them primaries.

CARLSON: Right.

STEWART: And they don't always go with the best, but they go with whoever won. So is he the best? According to the process.

CARLSON: Right. But of the nine guys running, who do you think was the best? Do you think he was the best, the most impressive?

STEWART: The most impressive?

CARLSON: Yes.

STEWART: I thought Al Sharpton was very impressive. I enjoyed his way of speaking. I think, oftentimes, the person that knows they can't win is allowed to speak the most freely, because, otherwise shows with titles, such as *Crossfire* . . .

BEGALA: *Crossfire.*

STEWART: Or *Hardball* or "I'm Going to Kick Your Ass," or . . . will jump on it. In many ways, it's funny. And I made a special effort to come on the show today, because I have privately, amongst my friends and also in occasional newspaper and television shows, mentioned this show as being bad.

BEGALA: We've noticed.

STEWART: And I wanted to . . . I felt that that wasn't fair and I should
come here and tell you that I don't—it's not so much that it's bad, as
it's hurting America. But I wanted to come here today and say . . .
Stop, stop, stop, stop hurting America.

Clearly by now the hosts realized what the audience had earlier
noticed—that the show was not the comedy banter expected—and
Carlson tried to turn the tables on Stewart by challenging the way he
interviewed John Kerry on his own show.

CARLSON: Don't you feel like . . . you got the chance to interview the guy.
Why not ask him a real question, instead of just suck up to him?
STEWART: Yes. "How are you holding up?" is a real suck-up. And I'm
actually giving him a hot stone massage as we are doing it.
CARLSON: It sounded that way. It did.
STEWART: You know, it's interesting to hear you talk about my
responsibility.
CARLSON: I felt the sparks between you.
STEWART: I didn't realize that . . . and maybe this explains quite a bit.
CARLSON: No, the opportunity to . . .
STEWART: . . . is that the news organizations look to Comedy Central
for their cues on integrity . . .
STEWART: So what I would suggest is, when you talk about you're
holding politicians' feet to the fire, I think that's disingenuous.
I think you're . . .

[Crosstalk]

STEWART: But my point is this. If your idea of confronting me is that
I don't ask hard-hitting enough news questions, we're in bad
shape, fellows.

After more crosstalk, Stewart drives home his point to the complete
dismay of Carlson, who struggles to get the show back under control.

STEWART: You know, the interesting thing I have is, you have a
responsibility to the public discourse, and you fail miserably.

CARLSON: You need to get a job at a journalism school, I think.

STEWART: You need to go to one. The thing that I want to say is, when you have people on for just knee-jerk, reactionary talk . . .

CARLSON: Wait. I thought you were going to be funny. Come on. Be funny.

STEWART: No. No. I'm not going to be your monkey.

BEGALA: Go ahead. Go ahead.

STEWART: I watch your show every day. And it kills me.

CARLSON: I can tell you love it.

STEWART: It's so . . . oh, it's so painful to watch. You know, because we need what you do. This is such a great opportunity you have here to actually get politicians off their marketing and strategy.

CARLSON: Is this really Jon Stewart? What is this, anyway?

STEWART: Yes, it's someone who watches your show and cannot take it anymore. I just can't.

CARLSON: What's it like to have dinner with you? It must be excoriating. Do you, like, lecture people like this or do you come over to their house and sit and lecture them: they're not doing the right thing, that they're missing their opportunities, evading their responsibilities?

STEWART: If I think they are.

CARLSON: I wouldn't want to eat with you, man. That's horrible.

STEWART: I know. And you won't . . . Why can't we just talk . . . please, I beg of you guys, please.

CARLSON: I think you watch too much *Crossfire*. We're going to take a quick break.

STEWART: No, no, no. Please.

CARLSON: No, no, hold on. We've got commercials.

STEWART: Please, please stop.

In the speeded up culture of the twenty-first century, Stewart's appearance became something of an instant classic, replayed and rehashed across the media landscape. CNN, *Crossfire*, and Carlson in particular took a beating on Internet blogs and chat rooms for days after. By January 2005, CNN President Jonathan Klein announced he was canceling the show. Announcing its demise, he told the press "I guess I come down more firmly in the Jon Stewart camp."

By then, Klein was hardly alone. The Argument Culture wasn't over. But it was morphing into something else. The programs that were dotting the media culture now were not so much open arguments, without winners or losers, as programs that were more one-sided and offered audiences more of a sense of having the answer—a style of program epitomized by Rush Limbaugh on radio or Bill O'Reilly on cable.

O'Reilly, Limbaugh, MSNBC's Keith Olbermann on the Left, or Air America on radio, and even their cousins in the blogosphere, are not offering debate. They are promising answers. Even programs that appear to be debates, such as *Hannity and Colmes* on Fox, fall into this new camp. Colmes is a liberal straw man, nearly always unpersuasive. In an era when information seems in oversupply, the new Argument Culture is offering the comfort of easy answers that seem to hold the promise of helping people make sense of things, of putting them in order. Many of the most popular blogs by 2006 fell into this category as well.

Beyond the feeling that opinion helps people make sense of information, another appeal of the new version of the Argument Culture is the belief that argument with a point of view is a more authentic, more honest form of discourse in an age when the notion of an independent account of events is in doubt. In the Argument Culture, I know where you stand.

For those engaged in more commercial media, a related factor is that media companies see argument as a way to reconnect with community at a time when those connections have weakened. The irony in this is that an open mike alone is an inadequate and even self-defeating response to the problem.

The reasons are succinctly stated by Jack Fuller, president of the Tribune Publishing Company. He is discussing print, but the concepts apply across media: "Here is the tension," Fuller told us at a forum of the Committee of Concerned Journalists. "A newspaper that fails to reflect its community deeply will not succeed. But a newspaper that does not challenge its community's values and preconceptions will lose respect for failing to provide the honesty and leadership that newspapers are expected to offer."[16] To be at once the enabler and the goad of community action is a great challenge, but it is one journalism has always claimed as its own. It is a challenge that can be met by accepting the obligation to provide the members of the community not only with the knowledge and insights they need but with the forum within which to engage in building a community.

The need for a press that strives to be responsible is enhanced, not lessened, by the existence of the Internet, where bulletin boards, chat rooms, blogs, and other forums have made what was once private conversation part of public discourse.

The posting on the Daily Kos blog on February 11, 2006, was titled "WaPo's Jim Brady Is Still a Wanker." The posting, which had more than 200 comments, referred to Jim Brady, the executive editor of WashingtonPost.com, who for days had been dodging shots from left-leaning bloggers over his decision to shut down comments on a *Post* blog in response to reader reactions Brady deemed obscene. The more than 1,000 comments on post.blog in mid-January 2006 referred to the *Post*'s ombudsman, Deborah Howell, who incorrectly implied that disgraced lobbyist Jack Abramoff had given money directly to Democrats— in addition to Republicans.[17]

The Daily Kos and other liberal-leaning blogs had been flogging Howell, and then Brady, after he wrote an op-ed describing the reasons for his decision first to remove the comments (some were later restored) and then shut them off completely (they were later re-opened with a new policy about when they would be used). Brady's column did not convince Daily Kos or its readers, and they reacted on February 11.[18]

One responder using the alias Tamifah offered this:

I want to zero in on a part of Mr. Brady's article and answer his own two questions for him. Why are people so angry? Very good question, Mr. Brady. There are a lot of reasons why people are so angry. Here are a few examples:

- *We are less safe than we were five years ago.*
- *We've been lied into a war.*
- *None of us has any job security and some of us are working 2 and 3 menial jobs to make up for the jobs we've lost in the glowing economy.*

- We've arguably had two elections stolen from us at the federal level and God only knows what at other levels.
- We've had fundy hypocritical pious bullshit hate shoved down our throats practically every time we've turned around (gay marriage hate, right of conscience hate, AFA hate, hatred for Terri Schiavo's right to expire in dignity per her wishes, hatred for the weak, the poor, and the old).

And why are we angry with you in particular, Mr. Brady? Because every time someone like Deborah Howell tells a deliberate lie on behalf of the usurpers and thieves in control of our nation, and every time someone like you backs her up, you make yourself a part of the problem and part of the oppressive regime. . . . We don't go to the mat to defend Republican lies like you and Deborah Howell. We don't withold information like, oh, say, the FREAKING GOVERNMENT IS SPYING ON AMERICANS right before an election like the New York Times does. We don't hide locations where the U.S. Government is holding people indefinitely to torture and God knows what like the Washington Post. We don't lie about our associations with the Plame case and try to manipulate the story like your own Bob Woodward. We are taking on responsibilities of the free press which you have abdicated, Jim Brady.

This was followed by someone calling himself Jurassic Pork, who suggested:

[Brady's] a GOP gasbag and stooge who's merely a clone of Bill Keller of the NY Times, who's also well-known for his hostility toward bloggers. . . .

Gasbag? Stooge? Liar? This is language not found in the vernacular of mainstream media discourse. Yet bloggers often erupt with such proclamations, replete with a deep sense of betrayal, outrage, and an overriding suspicion of corruption and hypocrisy on the part of the establishment politicians and the press. How should journalists react to this kind of vocabulary and innuendo? On one level it is vicious and personal. On another, however, it touches a chord of public sentiment that is authentic, possibly widespread, and missing in the mainstream public discourse.

Vitriol, however, is not the only thing that characterizes the new Argument Culture in the blogosphere. Nor is an obsession with the perceived failures of the MSM, the mainstream media.

The same blog on the same day, responding to the same root posting, also contained comments that were not attacks on Brady at all but focused rather on Abramoff and the lobbying scandal itself. This exchange was public discourse of a different sort—a detailed debate over complex minutiae of the scandal—and it was so detailed many citizens might have had difficulty following it. Someone calling himself Viceroy was arguing with another citizen on the site, named Thomas William, about whether Abramoff had directed Indian tribes to give money to Democrats. It is difficult to imagine an argument this steeped in the subtleties of semantics to appear anywhere in the traditional press.

VICEROY: *You [William] have established nothing concerning the use of the word "directed" and when we try to discuss the word "directed" you accuse [me] of being "semantic." You've failed with fiduciary, client, employer or master relationships. You fail to deal with the fact that the tribal organizations have free will. Claiming that you have won arguments when you haven't is really ridiculous—you really have barely even tried to discuss the issue.*

Thomas William responds in kind, with discussion of the meaning of the word *directed* and the free will of Indian tribes.

THOMAS WILLIAM: *If you're arguing the meaning of "directed," I will admit that you can define that in such a way that Abramoff didn't "direct" anything, including contributions to either party. But, that's a pretty lame way to reach the conclusion you desire, which is that Abramoff didn't direct any contributions to Democrats. If you want that, you have to admit he didn't direct any tribal contributions to Republicans, either. . . . If we have to agree to disagree, I disagree and find your suggested construction of the word "directed" in this context to reach a somewhat absurd result, in that it would basically ignore the entire relationship between Abramoff and the tribes, whatever you want to label it as, and say that their donation patterns are completely the result of their "free will," all in order to protect Democrats. Sorry, I'm not a Democrat, I'm an independent, and I don't have a preconceived opinion about Abramoffgate.*

One blog on one day, on one subject, and there is a range here that is dazzling. There is dripping personal attack brinking on slander toward journalists. There is a detailed public debate of a major news event. There is citizen engagement. There is, above all, passion.

Where does journalism in any style reside in relation to this new version of the Argument Culture? The blogosphere and other new corridors of the Internet may inspire a range of emotions. They clearly, too, are adding something to the public dialogue that the traditional press may not be able to offer. But the character of Internet discussion groups is not the issue. Technology did not create the attitudes of those who participate. Machines do not change human nature.

The issue is what happens to the rest of the media landscape. As rich and empty as the new forums may be, depending on the posting, they cannot supplant the search for fact and context that the traditional journalism of verification supplies. If those who gather and then deliver the news no longer spend the time and money to report and verify and synthesize—if they fear that applying judgment is an act of elitism, or that the technology now frees them of these old burdens—then cyberspace chatter is all we are left with.

Who will exist to find out which of the assertions in any chat room are actually true? Who will explore the backgrounds and motives of the various factions? Who will answer the questions even these most angry polemicists want answered?

In the future, we may well rely more on citizens to be sentinels for one another. No doubt this will expand the public forum and enrich the range of voices. But unless the forum is based on a foundation of fact and context, the questions citizens ask will become simply rhetorical. The debate will cease to educate; it will only reinforce the prejudgments people arrive with. The public will be less able to participate in solutions. Public discourse will not be something we can learn from. It will dissolve into noise, which the majority of the public will tune out. The worry is not the wondrous addition of citizen media, but the decline of full-time, professional monitoring of powerful institutions.

So, first, the journalistic forum should adhere to all the other journalistic principles, and, second, it relates directly to Madison's recognition of the central role of compromise in democratic society. But if the primary role of the forum, then, is to illuminate rather than agitate, how is it that journalists engage an audience? This is the next element of journalism.

ENDNOTES

1. *Hardball with Chris Matthews*, CNBC News, transcript, May 11, 1999.
2. Gene Lyons, "Long-Running Farce Plays On," *Arkansas Democrat-Gazette*, May 26, 1999, B9; available in LexisNexis.
3. Cody Shearer, interview by Dante Chinni, June 2000.
4. Robert D. Leigh, *A Free and Responsible Press* (Chicago: University of Chicago Press, 1947), 23.
5. The dispute began with an article by Jim Giles, "Internet Encyclopaedias Go Head to Head," *Nature*, December 22, 2005; available at www.nature.com/news/2005/051212/full/438900a.html. *Britannica* posted a lengthy response on its website in March 2006 headlined "Fatally Flawed"; available at http://corporate.britannica.com/britannica_nature_response.pdf. A few days later *Nature* posted its response.
6. Warren G. Bovée, *Discovering Journalism* (Westport, CT: Greenwood Press, 1999), 154–55.
7. Tom Leonard, *News for All* (New York: Oxford University Press, 1995), 152.
8. Tom Winship, "Obvious Lessons in Hindsight," *Media Studies Journal* (Spring/Summer 1998), 4.
9. *Crossfire*, CNN, transcript, March 30, 2000.
10. These estimates are based on television in Washington, DC, July 10, 2000. The percentage of chat was based on the fact that, on broadcast TV, there were 39.5 hours of news, 27 hours of talk, 3 hours of pseudo-news (*Access Hollywood, Inside Edition*), plus 108 hours of cable news, which was a mix of both talk and news.
11. Paul Farhi, "The New Face of the Talking Head," *Washington Post*, May 25, 2000; available at www.washingtonpost.com.
12. Michael Crichton, "Mediasaurus," speech delivered to National Press Club, Washington, DC, April 7, 1993.
13. Robert Berdahl, speech delivered to American Society of Newspaper Editors Credibility Think Tank, San Francisco, CA, October 8, 1998.
14. Jon Katz, interview by William Damon, Howard Gardner, and Mihaly Csikszentmihalyi, 1998.
15. *Crossfire*, CNN, transcript, October 15, 2004.
16. Jack Fuller, at CCJ Forum, Chicago, November 6, 1997.
17. Jim Brady, "Blog Rage," *Washington Post*, February 11, 2006; available at www.washingtonpost.com.
18. Daily Kos, "WaPo's Jim Brady Is Still a Wanker," February 11, 2006; available at www.dailykos.com/storyonly/2006/2/11/23938/9747.

8

Engagement and Relevance

P roviding end-of-life medical care to children is one of those subjects journalists know to be important, but most find impossible to approach. A family's struggle to save a child with a terminal illness is a tough story, if only for the possibility that it will read as yet another account of media breaking and entering the souls of grieving folks. And when the tragedy of a child's death is compounded by the medical dilemma of prolonging life through invasive procedures at the expense of less painful final moments, the story can become intangible to most reporters.

But not to Diana Sugg. Sugg, a Pulitzer Prize–winning health reporter at the *Baltimore Sun*, waited all her life for such a story, the kind of story she was wired for: "emotional, raw and unspoken."[1] She circled the subject for two years. She often had to remind herself that one common flaw among journalists is that they give up too soon. She had secured documents, identified experts, and interviewed a few families, but she felt this wouldn't do the story justice.

"The story I wanted to tell in the beginning was how hard it was for a sick child in America to die," Sugg said. "What grabbed my attention is that children are suffering unnecessarily, children are being scared, children are not being told they're dying even though they know it on some level."[2]

Pain was at the core of the story: parents and doctors did everything out of hope and love, but the ironic result was that children were suffering. Yes, Sugg had gathered tons of information, but she knew that the words of experts and medical personnel could never show the complete picture. For this she wanted more than the underlying meaning, the dilemmas of a medical field named "pediatric palliative care." She wanted the literal meaning. She found it in R. J. Voigt, a twelve-year-old whom she followed for the last four weeks of his life.

R.J. illustrated the force of a child's personal story, one that readers could not ignore. Nobody could forget a weakened boy with swollen eyelids struggling to whisper to his mom: "The angels. The angels are coming."

"I knew that this story could change the emotional destiny of other families," Sugg wrote. "Maybe a mom could ask, 'Are you scared?' Maybe a dying boy could say, 'I don't want this anymore.'" It took almost three years for Sugg to get the story she wanted. To write it, she used medical records, R.J.'s personal journals, and scores of interviews with family, friends, physicians, and others. In addition, Sugg and *Baltimore Sun* photographer Monica Lopossay spent more than twenty days in R.J.'s hospital room and were present for most of the events they described, with the exception of his death. The result was a four-part series that drew enormous response from both parents who lost their children and professionals in the medical community.

The story was a balancing act between R.J. and the larger issue, and both had to be complete. "Too often we tell the tale of a person just because it's a great tale. We need to not just go seize on following a kid with cancer just to see how it goes, but because there are larger issues. It's anchored in some news that people need to know," Sugg said. What Sugg did with the tragic story of R.J.'s death translates into the seventh principle:

Journalists must make the significant interesting and relevant.

Unhelpfully, when people talk about making the news engaging and relevant, the discussion becomes a dialectic—engaging versus relevant. Should we emphasize news that is fun and fascinating, and plays on our sensations? Or should we stick to the news that is the most important? Should journalists give people what they need or what they want?

This classic way of posing the question of engagement—as information versus storytelling, or what people need versus what people want—is a distortion. This is not how journalism is practiced, journalists told us. Nor is it, we believe, how people come to the news. The evidence suggests that most people want both: they read the sports and the business pages, *The New Yorker* and cartoons, the book review and the crossword puzzle. The *New York Times* supports some twenty-five foreign bureaus and its eighty-plus-person Washington bureau, and covers the City Council meetings, but it also has a bridge column, restaurant reviews, and home and food sections. The *New York Daily News* excels in sports reporting, entertaining photographs, and gossip columns, but competes fiercely to inform its readers of miscarriages of justice or government programs and failures.

Storytelling and information are not contradictory. They are better understood as two points on a continuum of communicating. At one end, perhaps, is the bedtime story you make up to tell your children, which may have no point other than intimate and comforting time spent together. On the other end is raw data—the sports agate, community bulletin boards, or stock tables—that contain no narrative at all. Most journalism, like most communication, exists somewhere in the middle. Writing coaches Roy Peter Clark and Chip Scanlan say that effective newswriting can be found at the intersection of civic clarity, the information citizens need to function, and literary grace, which is the reporter's storytelling skill set.

Understood this way, the best work—that which rises above its subject matter—pushes a story further toward the middle of that continuum than the audience would expect. It does so through superior reporting, thinking, narrative, or other treatment. It is the Hollywood profile that says something deeper about filmmaking; the investigative exposé that also reveals the human condition; the treatment of demographic data that brings a neighborhood to life. Thus the journalist's task is to find the way to make the significant interesting in each story and finding the right mix of the serious and the less serious that offers an account of the day.

Perhaps it is best understood this way: journalism is storytelling with a purpose. That purpose is to provide people with information they need to understand the world. The first challenge is finding the information that people need to live their lives. The second is to make it meaningful, relevant, and engaging.

Engagement really falls under the journalist's commitment to the citizenry. As one reporter interviewed by the team of our academic research partners put it, "If you are the kind of person who, once you have found out something, find that you are not satisfied about knowing it until you figure out a way to tell somebody else, then you're a journalist."[3]

Part of a journalist's responsibility, in other words, is not just providing information but also providing it in such a way that people will be inclined to listen. "Our most important challenges revolve around choosing what will keep readers' attention—many readers, many different kinds of readers," says Howard Rheingold, author and former executive editor of the online magazine *HotWired*. "At one end of the spectrum it is what is most important—is there going to be war or peace, are taxes going up, are they going down? The other end of the spectrum is just what's purely interesting. . . . And most stories are something of a mix of the two."[4]

So how does the question of engagement get so distorted, as if there were no mixing? If journalism can be both significant and engaging, if people do not basically want it one way or the other, why does the news so often fall short?

A litany of problems stand in the way of news being delivered compellingly: haste, ignorance, laziness, formula, bias, cultural blinders. Writing a story well, outside of the inverted pyramid in print or the intro/sound bite/bridge/sound bite/close in TV, takes time. It is, in the end, a strategic exercise that involves more than just plugging facts into short, declarative sentences. And time is a luxury that journalists today feel they have less and less of.

Unfortunately at a time when the public has ever more exciting and interesting alternatives to the news and are more skeptical of journalism, cutbacks in traditional newsrooms create smaller staffs and the focus is often more on the quantity of stories than the quality. There is also the time it takes to develop an understanding of the topic. Good journalistic presentation is always the result of solid, deep reporting that adds the detail and context that hold a piece together. Not every story needs the three years Sugg spent, but good work involves more than attending an event and then sitting down at a keyboard or an Avid video editing machine.

Even if reporters are given the time to report and write, there is the question of space in the paper or time on the newscast. With news organizations convinced that ever-shortening attention spans require ever-shorter stories, it is difficult for a reporter to get the space and time necessary to tell a story right.

Yet getting the audience's attention right now becomes even more important because the Internet makes the limitation of space obsolete. Online, the length of the video package, the text narrative, the number of background elements, explanatory boxes, charts, or graphs are all potentially infinite. Audiences will increasingly demand that journalists make the best choices about how much information to provide and not provide, given that arbitrary space limits are not an issue. Time will become the only scarcity.

Ironically, the evidence suggests that some of the conventional wisdom about attention spans is misguided and has hurt journalism, not helped. A multiyear study of local television news by the Project for Excellence in Journalism, for instance, has found that stations that do more very short stories—under 45 seconds—tend to lose audience. Stations that do more stories over two minutes, on the other hand, tend to gain audience. [5]

Ira Glass, host of the radio program *This American Life*, which broadcasts "stories that are like movies for radio," says the average listener is tuned in for 48 out of the 60 minutes of the show. *This American Life* reaches around 1.7 million people a week and usually runs three stories per episode, ranging from extended reports, to essays, to found audio material. [6]

Yet this is hardly the only example of how conventional wisdom about what citizens want or expect from journalism is leading us down a self-destructive path.

THE LURE OF INFOTAINMENT

ABC News personality Barbara Walters peered at the young woman with a studied sympathy.

"He kissed you?" she asked.

"Yes," Monica Lewinsky answered.

"What did you think?" Walters said with a look suggesting a caring aunt who couldn't entirely hide her titillation.

"He's a good kisser."

"You are a very sensual young woman?"

"Mm-hmm."

"Passionate?"

"Yes."

"Is Bill Clinton a passionate man?" Walters leaned in.

Lewinsky blushed a moment, and Walters teased her. Then Lewinsky answered.

"I think he's a very sensual man who has a lot of sensual feelings. And I think he also has a very strong religious upbringing. I think he struggles with his sensuality because I don't think he thinks it's okay. And then I think he tries to hold himself back and then can't anymore."

"That first encounter," the network newscaster of thirty-seven years, continued, "the president took a phone call from a congressman while you were very closely together. How did you feel about that?"

"It's an intimate topic," the twenty-five-year-old Lewinsky began. "There was a level of excitement about that. Excitement and maybe a little bit of danger that was involved in this relationship, and to pretend that there wasn't wouldn't be truthful."

ABC News's much publicized and eagerly pursued interview with Lewinsky went on like this.

"Did you or the president worry about somebody coming in and finding you? . . . Was this part of the thrill?" Walters asked next.

A moment later, she probed, "The impression that the president gave was that this was a one-way street, that he was gratified and you were not. But the truth is that you were gratified."

Then this: "And that there were things that were done that made you feel, as a woman, happy and contented?"

Walters also asked, "Throughout most of the relationship, the oral sex was not brought to completion for the president. Why not? What did he say?" [7]

Nearly half of ABC's two-hour interview pored over such questions as whether the president was a good kisser, a sensual man, and whether the danger of discovery was part of his psychological sexual motivation. Only in the second part did the program begin to probe questions of fact—and constitutional relevance—such as whether Lewinsky lied in an affidavit to protect the president and whether he had arranged a job for her in return.

The much-anticipated scoop/interview, in short, was produced as "Monica's Story," which coincidentally was the title of the book Lewinsky was using the interview to promote. In this case, news not only emphasized sex and emotion, it was also a form of commercial cross-promotion. ABC was using Lewinsky to build ratings. Lewinsky was using ABC to sell books.

Leo Braudy, an English professor at the University of Southern California who is the author of *The Frenzy of Renown* and an authority on the entertainment industry, says a key feature of infotainment journalism is to "somehow present the story as a secret. You have to be the knowing reporter and to let the audience in on it. And unfortunately, more and more as time goes on, the secret is something scandalous or salacious." This, in turn, creates "an audience that likes to think of itself as being in the know"—that needs the next salacious fix. [8]

These are the classic gimmicks of tabloidism: the news as revealed truth, as sex, or as celebrity scandal. A look at the content of the media bears out Braudy's argument that this is a major technique of turning news into entertainment and entertainment into news. One of the most interesting aspects of this is seeing how supposedly serious news organizations contend with the problem, much like ABC and the interview with Lewinsky. Consider the cover of *Newsweek* magazine in the first six months of the new century. An examination shows that seventeen of the twenty-two covers either featured entertainment figures, were about sex, or used the language of revealed secrets like "Eliãn: Behind the Custody Fight," "The Inside Story," or "The Truth About." Of those twenty-two covers, just two concerned politics, though it was a presidential primary year. Two concerned sexuality. Three concerned health. Two concerned technology. Two concerned business and two more concerned the case of the Cuban boy Eliān Gonzalez. Not one cover was about global affairs.

This marks a big change, for newsweeklies and arguably for the culture in general. In 1977, according to a study by the Project for Excellence in Journalism, the covers of *Time* and *Newsweek* concerned a political or international figure 31 percent of the time. At the same time, about half as many covers, 15 percent, concerned entertainment or celebrity figures. By 1997, the relationship had been effectively reversed. The number of political or international figures fell by more than 60 percent, to about one cover in ten, while the number of celebrity and entertainment covers increased 40 percent (to more than two in ten).[9]

Another set of numbers puts the shift in even clearer relief: taken together, the two major newsweeklies *Time* and *Newsweek* were seven times more likely to have the same cover story as *People* magazine in 1997 than in 1977.[10] As we have said before, news that only catalogues the significant is as stilted as news that leaves all the significance out. The inverse is also true.

At any given moment, we can find examples of where sensationalism sells. The Barbara Walters interview with Monica Lewinsky, for instance, was the highest-rated program ABC News had aired to that time. But history over a longer term suggests that the organizations that tip toward the information end of the spectrum tend to prevail over those that tip toward the entertainment end. While the celebrity/scandal tone of the Walters/Lewinsky interview was characteristic of more and more network news at the time it aired, that shift toward infotainment had done little to stem, and may well have contributed to, a steady decline in the audience for network news programming.[11] And it has always been thus.

As the immigrants of the 1890s moved into the middle class in the twentieth century, the sensationalism of yellow journalism gave way to the more sober approach of the *New York Times*. By the 1920s, Joseph

Pulitzer's *New York World*, for instance, had become quite a literary newspaper. As the delirium of the Roaring Twenties gave way to the severity of the Depression, the celebrity age of the tabloids and gossip-mongers like celebrity radio and newspaper columnist Walter Winchell gave way to a new seriousness that lasted through the Cold War. The survivors of the great newspaper wars of the 1960s, which saw most cities become one-newspaper towns, were not the mass-circulation tabloids but the serious papers in each city–the *Washington Post*, the *New York Times*, the *Los Angeles Times*, the *Philadelphia Inquirer*, the *Boston Globe*, and countless others. It was true in television as well. The dominant television network news operation has always been the one with the largest number of bureaus and greatest commitment to delivering serious news, whether it was *The Huntley-Brinkley Report* in the 1960s, *The CBS Evening News* with Walter Cronkite in the 1970s, or *World News Tonight* with Peter Jennings from the mid-1980s to the mid-1990s.

A Project for Excellence in Journalism study between 1998 and 2002 discerned a similar pattern even in local television news. Stories over 60 seconds that exhibited higher levels of significance, enterprise, balance, authoritativeness, community relevance, and lack of sensationalism had better viewership and retained more of its lead-in audience than a broadcast featuring lower-quality stories. [12]

The evidence suggests that attracting audiences by being merely engaging will fail as a business strategy for journalism over the long term, for three simple but indisputable reasons.

The first is that, if you feed people only trivia and entertainment, you will wither the appetite and expectations of some people for anything else. This is especially true of those people who, through inclination, time, or resources, are less likely to seek alternatives. This is the dilemma now faced by so much local television news. "Of those who do watch local news, more than half those surveyed no longer care which station they watch," according to data from Insite Research, a leading television audience research firm in California. [13]

The second long-term problem with the strategy of infotainment is that it destroys the news organization's authority to deliver more serious news and drives away those audiences who want it. This, too, has happened in local television news. A survey by Indiana University researchers for News Lab, for instance, found that five of the top seven reasons that people stopped watching local TV news is that it lacked substance (the other two top reasons were that people were not home or too busy).[14] This research is backed up not only by the intuition of many local newspeople but also by other survey research. "Avoidance of local news has doubled in the past ten years," say other data from Insite Research. One reason given was: "More than half of those surveyed feel that most stations spend too much time covering the same stories over and over again."

Finally, the infotainment strategy is faulty as a business plan because, when you turn your news into entertainment, you are playing to the strengths of other media rather than your own. How can the news ever compete with entertainment on entertainment's terms? Why would it want to? The value and allure of news is that it is different. It is based on relevance. The strategy of infotainment, though it may attract an audience in the short run and may be cheap to produce, will build a shallow audience because it is built on form, not substance. Such an audience will switch to the next "most exciting" thing because it was built on the spongy ground of excitement.

These challenges, like a distracted public, do not make journalism impossible, only difficult. They separate successful journalism from lazy, good from bad, the complete from the overly sensationalized.

Why do journalists miss this history? Lack of communication is one reason. After educational psychologists William Damon and Howard Gardner studied journalists, one of the most striking impressions was the degree to which journalists, compared with other professionals, failed to communicate the lessons of one generation to the next. In addition, not only has the apprenticeship system broken down, but also little or nothing has replaced it. Journalism education is held in generally low, or at least disputed, regard by working journalists.[15] Hairdressers have more continuing education than journalists.[16]

Perhaps most important, winning back audience through better storytelling is hard, time-consuming, and costly. As a consequence, when the news industry tries to address flagging audiences, it often emphasizes concerns that are easier to manage, boosting marketing budgets, cutting costs, changing anchorpeople, or building a new set for the news. When the newspaper industry in the 1980s began to address its readership losses, for instance, it emphasized layout, design, and color. Prototypes aimed at creating newspaper sections for non-readers developed by editors' groups in the 1980s literally would have copy in the place where the stories would go that said, "Text will go here. Text will go here. Text will go here. Text will go here." No one was rethinking the narrative approach to the news.

Individual journalists do succeed in making the news engaging and relevant, in making the significant interesting and the interesting significant. Yet as William Damon has found, they are usually self-taught, learned by trial and error or, secondarily, by borrowing ideas on their own from peers. The best ideas are not widely disseminated.

We cannot pretend to offer here an encyclopedia of methods to make storytelling more compelling and engaging—to make the significant more interesting. That is a different book. But we want to look at some more conceptual issues that may help citizens, citizen journalists, and professional journalists begin to think differently about storytelling.

First, it is useful to talk about what is lacking. Much of conventional journalistic storytelling tends to share some common weaknesses, according to journalists we have talked to. They include:

Character is missing—sources become templates, not real people.

Time is frozen so that everything happened yesterday or this evening.

Information is designed for a single audience, not multiple ones.

The news is presented as a conversation of insiders.

Stories don't illuminate a greater meaning.

There is little attempt to globalize the local or localize the global.

Storytelling is predictable and formulaic.

The Internet is used as a new place for old material rather than as a distinct technology.

SOME INNOVATIVE APPROACHES

If the journalism industry did seek out its best, collate their thinking, and search for uncommon ideas from across all media, it would discover some compelling new ideas.

The first idea is that better storytelling doesn't begin after you sit down to edit a story on video, write a script, or pull up to an empty screen to write a narrative story. It begins before you ever go out to report. And it involves reporting differently, going to different sources, and asking different questions.

WHO IS THE AUDIENCE AND WHAT DO THEY NEED TO KNOW?

Often journalists begin a story by "getting the clips," checking databases, getting up to speed, and then reporting on the newest development. This, however, can limit the story.

Several journalists now advocate a different approach. For any assignment, journalists should ask, and audiences be able to detect, the following questions:

1. What's this story really about?
2. Who is the audience for this story and what information do these people need to know to make up their own minds about the subject?
3. Who has the information?
4. What's the best way to tell this story?

These simple questions can make a big difference. They direct coverage toward the citizen—the audience first, away from interest groups, insiders, and other direct participants. They also may lead the journalism to a new set of sources, not found in the old clips, if the current sources the news organization is relying on cannot answer questions citizens need answered. These questions pull the coverage away from the routines of the previous story, which may already have limited the audience rather than expanded it.

A NEW DEFINITION OF WHO, WHAT, WHEN, WHERE, WHY, AND HOW

Journalists can rethink the basic elements of news—who, what, when, where, why, and how. Roy Peter Clark, writing professor at the Poynter Institute in St. Petersburg, Florida, has done just that. Years ago, Clark was struck by the ideas of Seattle writer and editor Rick Zahler, who argued that newswriting took dynamic events and froze them. Time sequences become simply yesterday. Place becomes a dateline. Zahler wanted to "thaw out" the news and put things in motion. Building on Zahler's ideas, Clark now talks often about how to do this.

"Who becomes character. What becomes plot. Where becomes scene or setting. Why becomes motivation or causation." Finally, "how becomes narrative," or the way all the elements fit together, Clark says.[17] At the beginning of *Romeo and Juliet*, Shakespeare tells in the first eight lines of a sonnet all the facts of the story, including the ending, Clark often points out. So what's left to tell? As he explains it, the next two hours of the play fill in all that missing detail. "We often give the news, but you still want to know how it happened. How did Monica Lewinsky get to the White House in the first place? Narrative is the way we answer the question 'How did that happen?'" says Clark.

If we think of *who* as character, *what* as plot, *where* as setting, and *how* as narrative, we can blend information and storytelling. News becomes not just data but also meaning. Doing so, not so incidentally, requires more reporting and more curiosity on the part of the reporter. Jack Hart, managing editor and writing coach at the *Oregonian*, says 15 to 30 inches is a reasonable length for a narrative that can be produced in a day. The idea is to follow a character through a complication and show how he resolves it. This can be done in a five-part narrative arc. First comes the exposition, in which the character and the complication are introduced. Then the rising action, which is the bulk of the piece showing the obstacles on the way to solving the complication. What follows are the point of insight, or the moment when the character has a revelation, and the resolution, when the complication is resolved. The ending is the denouement, a chance to tie up loose ends. [18]

EXPERIMENT WITH NEW STORYTELLING TECHNIQUES

The most common narrative structure used in journalism is remarkably limited. As journalism has grown more complex and the topics more vast, many of the best journalists have found it inadequate. "Sometimes just starting at A and going through to Z is not the best way to do it," William Whitaker of CBS News told our academic research partners. "Sometimes you grab L, M, N, O, P out of the middle and put it at the top because that's the point that makes the most sense and that's what's easiest for people to understand and that puts it in perspective." [19]

Todd Hanson, head writer at the weekly humor periodical the *Onion*, told the *Online Journalism Review* that much of his magazine's humor arises from the anachronistic quality that characterizes many newspapers. The magazine features such headlines as "Congress Approves $4 Billion for Bread" and "Circuses and Fairy Princess Ranks Depleting as Girls Aspire to Be Doctors, Lawyers." [20]

THE MOST ENGAGING APPROACH

Jacqui Banaszynski, a Pulitzer Prize winner, says one way to come up with different stories on a topic is to consider approaching it from seven distinctive paths and an eighth way. [21] They are not all going to be relevant on a particular topic, but this quick brainstorming exercise can produce a wealth of ideas for reporting a particular story:

1. *A profile.* Find the people behind a story, the characters driving the issue. You can profile not just a person but also a place, an event, even a building.
2. *Explanatory piece.* Show readers why something happens or how something functions.
3. *Issues and trend stories.* Ask yourself if there is a larger picture to explore. Trends are not exclusively related to culture or lifestyle; think crime or economy.
4. *Investigative.* Look into wrongdoing, "follow the money," analyze power struggles, and make use of available documents.
5. *Narrative.* A story with a character, scenes, and tension.
6. *Descriptive day in the life.* The alternative to a narrative, focusing on a particular moment, such as a ride-along with the police or a visit to the new museum.
7. *Voices or perspective story.* Have people tell a story in a unique way: Q&A, roundtable discussion, a rail of quotes, or vignettes.
8. *Visual story.* Photographs, graphics, or illustrations might be the best way to tell some stories.

THE HOUR GLASS

In the early 1990s, Clark noticed what he called the "hour glass" structure. "It isn't purely narrative. It isn't just the inverted pyramid. . . . It is a
form in which you begin by telling the news, telling what happened,
and then there is a break in the pyramid, and a line that begins a narrative, often chronologically, as in, 'The incident began when. . . .'" At
that point, the news is thawed out and put in more dramatic and often
genuine terms.

THE FUTURE OF THE Q&A

At a conference on exploring new ways to connect with citizens, Jay
Rosen, a New York University journalism professor and astute critic of
press culture, said that he considered the Q&A form to be a powerful
but underused method. It forces the journalist to frame the material
around things that citizens might ask. It also allows audiences to scan a
story and enter it wherever they want, rather than having to read it
from the top down. Interestingly, this has become a favored form on
websites, in the form of frequently asked questions (FAQs).

STORY AS EXPERIENCE

Michael Herr, whose book *Dispatches* is considered one of the best to
come out of the Vietnam War, added a new dimension to war reporting
by carrying Gay Talese's "fly on the wall" technique a step further. Not
only did Herr gather the copious detail that kind of reporting entailed,
but he also let the soldiers speak for themselves, selecting his material
not only to tell their story but also to capture their state of mind and
their thoughts. As Alfred Kazin wrote in a review of the book in *Esquire*,
"Herr caught better than anyone else the . . . desperate code in which
the men in the field showed that they were well and truly shit." [22]

BEING ON THE NOSE

Doug Marlette, award-winning editorial cartoonist, has also written
plays, movie scripts, and a novel and says that the biggest problem in
news is that too much of it is simply "boring."

"When you're bored," Marlette says, "you stop learning and communication fails."[23] The principal reason is that "you're never surprised." In the theater, there is a term for this boredom. It's called "being on the nose," which "is when you tell people what they already know."

In news, it is "telling not showing; lecturing; didacticism," Marlette says. "It is the moment in TV news when the correspondent tells the audience what they are already seeing." It is the moment a newspaper story belabors a point rather than moving on.

How do we keep news from being on the nose?

PICTURES OF THE MIND

One way is to help people build their own pictures in their minds, rather than drawing them for them. Annie Lang, who teaches telecommunications and runs the Institute for Communications Research at Indiana University, says academic research has clearly established the power of mental pictures, including metaphor. "There is nothing more scary than to say to someone, 'There is a snake behind you.' That is so much more powerful than to show them the snake."[24]

CONNECTING THE STORY TO DEEPER THEMES:
THE REVEAL

NBC News correspondent John Larson has suggested that surprise is key to storytelling. But, he adds, "surprise them in a meaningful way. Not just shock them and stun them."[25] At Larson's program, *Dateline,* they call this "the reveal." In Larson's mind, the best kind of reveal is when a story connects to some deeper unexpected themes. It's when stories "reach us on some elemental level. They talk about a mother's love for her children, a husband's pride in his country. Ambition. Avarice. Greed. There's something very important that's always going on in a very simple way in good stories."

These themes are not stated by the journalist but are shown, or revealed, in how the journalist treats the material—the right quote, the right shot on TV, or the look two people give each other when they are not talking. "Good stories lead you to the truth; they don't tell you the truth," as Larson puts it.

This connecting of material to larger themes is what Robert Caro did in *The Power Broker*, or David Halberstam did in *The Powers That Be*, or H. G. Bissinger did in *Friday Night Lights*, or Tom Wolfe did in *The Right Stuff*. Caro, the biographer of President Lyndon Johnson and New York power broker Robert Moses, says this notion has guided his life's work. When writing about Moses, a little-known bureaucrat who transformed New York City, Caro wanted to do something more than an exposé. "What I wanted to do was explain how political power worked, because I was a reporter and I was covering politics, and I felt that I wasn't really explaining what I had gone into the newspaper business to explain, which was how political power worked, and a lot of it led back to this man, Robert Moses, a lot of what I didn't understand. Now, here was a guy who was never elected to anything, and I was coming to realize that he had more power than anyone who was governor or mayor." [26]

CHARACTER AND DETAIL IN NEWS

Other journalists told us they consider character the key to pulling people into stories. Often this is found in the minor details that make someone human and real. When the father of the shipwrecked boy Eliãn Gonzalez came to America in 2000 to retrieve his son and take him back to Cuba, KARE-TV correspondent Boyd Huppert was struck most of all that in his interview with immigration officials, "the father knew [the son's] shoe size." For Huppert, this "put a whole new light on the man," revealing something about the father's relationship with the child, his involvement, and his character. [27]

Too much journalism fails to develop character. The people are cardboard; they are names and faces fit into a journalistic template–the investigating officer, the pro-life protester, the angry minority spokesman, the aggrieved mother. A major reason for this is that they are not allowed to speak the way people do in real life. Quotes are too often used as tools rather than as part of a deeper conversation between the subjects of a story and the audience. The way interviews are shot on TV is another major factor. Often people do not even look like real people when shot against artificial backgrounds in perfect light, or standing in front of a building surrounded by microphones. They exist only in an artificial world–the world of news–and seem more caricature than character.

To call someone "the investigating officer" is to describe a source.

But "Detective Lewis, a second-generation homicide cop, whose father had a similar case as this 20 years earlier," is a character. The first makes homicide investigator Lewis fit a fairly rigid template, one that is efficient for journalistic purposes but shallow, that turns him into a stick figure indistinguishable from any other investigating officer.

"The second-ranking Republican member of the House Ways and Means Committee" is a template. "The thirty-year veteran of the House, who has opposed nearly every tax cut except for mental health after becoming the grandfather to a disabled child," is already more interesting. Yet to get to the second level, to turn sources into people, involves thinking ahead about character. It involves asking different questions of the officer, looking for more things, and being curious about him as a potential character rather than merely a source. It may take more time, but not much more or as many questions as one might think. "Have you ever had any cases like this? Do you have any special style or method for investigating?" Most important, it involves looking at the officer as a person rather than merely looking for quotes or facts.

In a television context, it may also mean thinking differently about the photojournalism. David Turecamo, a filmmaker for ABC's *Nightline*, who shoots, interviews, writes, and edits his own pieces, always tries to photograph his subjects as they actually live—shopkeepers while behind the counter, salesmen while driving in their cars, businessmen while walking to meetings, usually in long takes. His pieces are small character studies, and the audience's view of the issue is changed because they suddenly see real people, businesspeople, and no longer "advocates" or part of a "lobby."

FINDING THE METAPHOR OR HIDDEN STRUCTURE IN EACH STORY

Perhaps no American journalist has been as inventive at making important topics interesting as ABC News correspondent Robert Krulwich. Krulwich says his method is to find the hidden material in each story that makes it memorable and genuine. This means avoiding formulas, treating each story as unique, and letting the material suggest its own structure. "I do a lot of abstract stories, so you have to find a metaphor that people will remember. It's like a hook in the sense of a hook where you hang your coat. If you have the hook, then, 'Well, that was the story about the chicken who sang, right? What was he talking about? Oh, yeah, currency devaluations.'"

Krulwich's metaphors are often quite unexpected. To reinforce the idea of the slowing Japanese economy, he slows down the video. To reinforce that people cannot spell the word *millennium*, he shows a stern schoolteacher slowly spelling the word.

USE THE POWER OF THE INTERNET

Many newsrooms have started to use the Web to enhance the power of their stories and make them more personal and interactive. It also increases transparency and allows readers to get a glimpse of how the reporting process works. Here's some popular added-value content for the online version of the story:

- Video of the story or about the story
- Audio of interviews, narration by the characters over a slideshow of photographs, or comments from the reporters themselves
- Chats with reporters or other ways to engage the readers in discussing the story
- Slideshow of photos
- Interactive graphics users can manipulate
- Full text of documents used and links to other sources mentioned in the story

Our list is only a sampling. We include it simply to suggest that newspeople can do more to experiment, treat each story as unique, and resist formula. The key is recognizing that making the significant interesting is a fundamental principle and requires more reflection.

NARRATIVE IN SERVICE OF TRUTH

Finally, a caution. In recent years, narrative newswriting has come to be viewed by editors as "writing with attitude." This is writing in which the journalist interjects his or her own feelings or opinions like a stage whisper, as is evident in self-referential lines like "There was an audible groan from the reporters when the candidate began to speak. . . ."

In some cases, an attitude can evolve that plays itself out through story after story, even in different publications—a kind of running meta-narrative that journalists share. Politicians are in it only for power. Newt Gingrich is a little crazy. Bill Clinton never keeps his promises. George W. Bush is a phony. The meta-narrative can become so powerful that it will cloud the truth.

As we discuss technique, it is vital to remember that form can never determine substance—technique should never alter the facts. The journalist's use of narrative forms must always be governed by the principles of accuracy and truthfulness, outlined earlier. Regardless of the form of presentation, the most engaging thing of all must be kept in mind: the story is true.

We have emphasized public affairs reporting in this discussion, but there is no subject for which the need for an engaging and relevant journalism does not apply. In many ways a story that helps the audience understand how the marketing strategy of Bill Gates affects their lives is as important as one that discusses the position of a presidential candidate on Internet policy. The celebrity profile that shows why Hollywood makes the films it does can be a major work illuminating American culture—or it can be press agent promotion. It depends on the treatment, not the subject matter. Thus citizens can use the principle of engagement and relevance to judge the value of any journalism they encounter.

The next principle puts this one in a broader context: how do we decide what stories get covered in the first place?

ENDNOTES

1. Diana Sugg, "Angels and Ghosts: Anatomy of a Story," *Poynter*, July 14, 2005; available at www.poynter.org.
2. Diana Sugg, interview by Cristian Lupsa, January 19, 2006.
3. Ray Suarez, interview by William Damon, Howard Gardner, and Mihaly Csikszentmihalyi, unpublished interviews conducted for the book *Good Work: When Excellence and Ethics Meet* (New York: Basic Books, 2001).
4. Howard Rheingold, interview by William Damon, Howard Gardner, and Mihaly Csikszentmihalyi, ibid.
5. "Project for Excellence in Journalism Local TV Project," *Columbia Journalism Review:* "Local TV News: What Works, What Flops, and Why," January 1999; "Quality Brings Higher Ratings, But Enterprise Is Disappearing," November 1999; "Time of Peril for TV News," November 2000; available at www.journalism.org.
6. Andy Smith, "A Touch of Glass," *Providence Journal*, April 14, 2005.

7. "Excerpts of Lewinsky Interviews," cnn.com, March 4, 1999.

8. Leo Braudy, at CCJ Forum, Los Angeles, March 4, 1998.

9. Project for Excellence in Journalism, "Changing Definitions of News," March 6, 1998, 4; available at www.journalism.org.

10. Ibid., 5.

11. Pew Research Center for the People and the Press, "Internet Sapping Broadcast News Audience, Investors Now Go Online for Quotes, Advice," June 11, 2000; available at http://people-press.org. Between 1987 and 2000, the percentage of Americans who reported that they regularly watched network evening news dropped to 50 percent from 71 percent. Between 1990 and 2000, the percentage of Americans who reported that they regularly watched network newsmagazine programs dropped to 31 percent from 43 percent.

12. Tom Rosenstiel, Walter Dean, Marion Just, Dante Chinni, and Todd Belt, "We Interrupt This Newscast" (Cambridge University Press, 2007).

13. Insite Research, Television Audience Survey, October 1999; available from Insite Research, 2156 Rambla Vista, Malibu, CA 90265.

14. News Lab Survey, "Bringing Viewers Back to Local TV News: What Could Reverse Ratings Slide?" September 14, 2000; available at www.newslab.org. People in the survey specifically answered that they got "local news elsewhere," there was "too much crime," "local news is always the same stuff," "too many fluff feature stories instead of real news," and "TV news seldom presents positive things that occur in your community."

15. Everette E. Dennis, "Whatever Happened to Marse Robert's Dream?: The Dilemma of American Journalism Education," *Gannett Center Journal* (Spring 1988), 3.

16. Betty Medsger, "Winds of Change: Whither Journalism Education," a Freedom Forum study, July 1996.

17. Roy Peter Clark, interview by author Rosenstiel, June 2000.

18. Jack Hart described this narrative arc in detail in an October 2004 article in *Above the Fold*, a newsletter on writing and editing published for the employees of the *Minneapolis Star Tribune*.

19. William Whitaker, interview by William Damon, Howard Gardner, and Mihaly Csikszentmihalyi.

20. Jim Benning, "Why Journalists Eat Up the Onion: World Media Shedding Tears of Joy Over the Onion," *Online Journalism Review,* May 2, 2000; available at www. ojr.org/ojr/workplace/1017964709.php.

21. Jacqui Banaszynski offers the seven paths (and an eighth way) to stories in writing workshops around the country.

22. Alfred Kazin, "Vietnam: It Was Us vs. Us: Michael Herr's Dispatches: More Than Just the Best Vietnam Book," *Esquire*, March 1, 1978, 120.

23. Doug Marlette, News Lab retreat on storytelling, Washington, DC, April 12 and 14, 2000.

24. Annie Lang, News Lab retreat, Washington, DC, April 12 and 14, 2000.

25. John Larson, News Lab retreat, Washington, DC, April 12 and 14, 2000.

26. *Booknotes,* C-Span, April 29, 1990.

27. Boyd Huppert, News Lab retreat, Washington, DC, April 12 and 14, 2000.

9

Make the News Comprehensive and Proportional

Valerie Crane, the head of Research Communications Limited, in Florida, likes to tell this story of how not to study audiences. It's about the head of market research at a major cable television network who was asked to include this question in a round of focus groups with young viewers: "What will be the next big trend for young people?"

The researcher felt that you could use tools such as survey research, psychographics, and focus groups to see how people react to things. You could even use them to learn more about how audiences live their lives and how they use the media. But they couldn't be used, or at least they shouldn't, to replace professional judgment.

The bosses wanted the question asked, however, so the researcher watched glumly as the focus group leader put the question to the teenagers gathered around a table on the other side of the one-way mirror: "What do you think the next trend will be?" To his delight the response came: "What do you mean, what will the next trend be? We rely on you to tell us what the next big trend will be."[1]

If the principle of engagement and relevance helps explain how journalists can more effectively approach their stories, the principle that follows informs what stories to cover.

What is news? Given the limits of space, time, and resources, what is important and what isn't, what is to be left in and what is to be left out? And in the age of Internet infinity, who is to say? These questions inform the eighth principle citizens require from their press:

Journalists should keep the news comprehensive and in proportion.

But how? In the age of exploration, cartography was as much art as science. The men who sat over parchment and drafted the pictures of the expanding world were able to do a fairly accurate job of drawing Europe and even the neighboring seas. As they moved west to the New World, however, to the regions that were so inflaming people's imaginations, they made mostly guesses. What was there? Gold? Fountains of youth? The end of the earth? Demons? The size of distant continents they sketched would swell and shrink according to which audience they thought might be purchasing their charts. In the faraway Pacific, they painted sea monsters, dragons, or giant whales to fill in what they did not know. The more fanciful and frightening their monsters, the more exotic the gold mines and Indians they depicted, the more their maps might sell, and the greater their reputations as cartographers might grow. Sensation made for popular maps, though they were poor guides for exploration or understanding.

Journalism is our modern cartography. It creates a map for citizens to navigate society. That is its utility and its economic reason for being. This concept of cartography helps clarify the question of what journalism has a responsibility to cover. As with any map, journalism's value depends on its completeness and proportionality. Journalists who devote far more time and space to a sensational trial or celebrity scandal than they know it deserves—because they think it will sell—are like the cartographers who drew England or Spain the size of Greenland because it was popular. It may make short-term economic sense, but it misleads the traveler and eventually destroys the credibility of the mapmaker. The journalist who writes what "she or he just knows to be true," without really checking first, is like the artist who draws sea monsters in the distant corners of the New World. A journalist who leaves out so much of the other news in the process is like the mapmaker who fails to tell the traveler of all the other roads along the way.

Thinking of journalism as mapmaking helps us see that proportion and comprehensiveness are key to accuracy. This goes beyond the single story. A front page, a Web page, or a newscast that is fun and interesting but by no reasonable definition contains anything significant is a distortion. At the same time, an account of the day that contains only the earnest and momentous, without anything light or human, is equally out of balance.

Obviously the limits of time and resources mean newspeople cannot cover everything. Still, as citizens, we can ask these questions: Can we see the whole community in the coverage? Do I see myself? Does the report include a fair mix of what most people would consider either interesting or significant?

THE FALLACY OF TARGETED DEMOGRAPHICS

The mapmaker concept also helps us better understand the idea of diversity in news. If we think of journalism as social cartography, the map should include news of all our communities, not just those with attractive demographics or strong appeal to advertisers. To do otherwise is to create maps with whole areas missing.

Unfortunately, this has proved a difficult principle to uphold. As we outlined in Chapter 3, on loyalty to citizens, news organizations throughout the 1980s began to focus more on affluent readers. This bears a little more discussion in the context of proportionality. There were several reasons for the strategy. After twenty-five years of losing audience and advertisers to television and other media, newspapers decided that there were structural limits to how much circulation they could have in the video age. Newspapers, in effect, decided they were a niche medium for the better educated. A second major reason had to do with costs. Newspapers sell each paper at a loss. The twenty-five cents or even a dollar paid covers roughly only a fraction of what it costs to report, print, and deliver each copy. The rest is made up in advertising revenue. Every copy of the paper sold to readers who didn't attract advertisers, in effect, cost money. The advertising business also decided to use newspapers mainly to reach the upper classes. It would use other media, especially television and radio, to reach blue-collar audiences. In time, newspaper business strategists rationalized that targeting circulation on the affluent was not a necessity but a virtue. Calculating cost per copy and revenue per subscriber could justify not appealing to the whole community in the name of economic efficiency. Writing off certain neighborhoods also meant not having to invest heavily to cover them.

It became difficult to argue with the economics, or even–given the loss of readership to television–the idea that these readers were not coming back. Bucking that trend would have meant believing in a long-term strategy that Wall Street and most conventional thinking disagreed with.

Television took a similar path, particularly after more stations began to do news, shrinking everyone's share of the pie. The pressure was intensified by the fact that stations, and Wall Street, were accustomed to enormous profitability–usually more than 40 percent–from news. To sustain the margins, stations kept surprisingly few reporters, and required most to produce at least a story a day.[2] Covering the whole community was impossible. The news was aimed instead at the most desirable segment–younger women.

The passage of time makes it possible to see serious problems with the economic logic of targeting demographics. One is that the new audiences being ignored starting in the late 1970s were the rising immigrant communities that were changing America's cities. This was precisely the population that became the backbone of journalism's success one hundred years earlier. Pulitzer, Scripps, and the rest of the penny-press barons made immigrants their core audience. Their prose was simple so immigrants could puzzle it out. The editorial pages taught them how to be citizens. New Americans would gather nights after work to talk about what was in the papers or to read to each other and discuss the highlights of the day.

As the immigrants of the 1880s and 1890s became more Americanized, the papers changed with them, becoming more middle class and more literary. The *New York World* of 1910 was a far more sober paper than the *World* of twenty years before. Eighty years later the journalism industry, now so tied to economic efficiency, did not make that same investment and establish a relationship with the newest Americans, as it had done a century before.

Nor, as journalism targeted itself to just the most profitable demographics, did it make much investment in the youngest Americans. Stories were long, sophisticated, and often required college degrees to follow. Critics such as Stephen Hess of the Brookings Institution began to talk about journalists writing for their sources.[3] On television, the emphasis on crime, and also titillation, transformed television news from something that families would gather to watch to something that parents would shield children from.[4] In the name of efficiency and profit margins, we did nothing to help create a new generation interested in news. Today, audience data from the Internet show that young people are interested in news, but not in any of the old forms of presentation in older technologies.[5] While the news business cannot take all the blame, it had in fact a business strategy that helped create non-news consumers.

The task of reaching out to all communities was doubtless harder to accomplish in 1990 than in 1890. Competition for people's time was much more intense, and the diversity of cultures more varied than a century earlier, when immigration was largely European. But there were now many more information sources to choose from, and news organizations mistakenly assumed that audiences would gravitate to the newspaper as they "Americanized." In Miami, the *Herald* was late in recognizing that its audience would not come to the *Herald,* that the *Herald* had to come to them. As a result, the paper had dramatically declined in circulation until the shifting demographics and the newspaper's need to respond became clear. The paper's circulation of more than 435,000 in 1984 had slumped to 357,000 by 1999. Innovations such as multiple newspapers, including *El Nuevo Herald, Jewish Herald,* and *¡Yo!* (a weekly aimed at young people), were begun. Interestingly, by the end of the century, the combined daily circulation of the *Herald* and *El Nuevo Herald* was 437,809–larger than that of the old *Herald* at its peak. By 2005 the combined circulation of the Miami papers, as reported in the *Editor and Publisher* yearbook, was 405,618.

Could it have been otherwise? Could journalism have avoided this disconnect with the broader audience and reached out successfully to a more diverse audience and a younger one? This is difficult to answer definitively. But as journalism companies aimed at elite demographics and cost efficiency, the industry as a general rule did not try. Or by the time they did, as in the case in Miami, it was very late. The concept of the mapmaker makes the error clear. We created a map for certain neighborhoods and not others. Those who were unable to navigate where they lived gave it up.

The newscasts and newspapers that ignored whole communities also created problems for those it did serve. First, it left its audiences poorly informed because so much was left out. This made citizens vulnerable to making poor decisions about contemporary trends and about their needs. Ultimately, the strategy threatened the livelihood of the news organization, the institution with the greatest need for an interested citizenry. In the memorable phrase of Wall Street analyst John Morton, we had "eaten our seed corn."[6]

With whole communities left out, there was also the reverse problem of offering too much detail to the demographic group journalism was serving. Stories became longer and more copious, though aimed at a narrower segment of the population. The papers were sometimes more than a hundred pages a day and could take a full day to read. In television, targeting had a similar effect. The daily health segments on local TV today, for instance, which cover every new medical study however preliminary, tend more to confuse citizens about health than inform them.

The mistake may be repairable. But journalism must act quickly to find ways to serve diverse communities—but as part of a whole community. There is also evidence that citizens agree. For several years, starting in 1998, the Project for Excellence in Journalism has studied what kind of local TV news builds ratings. A design team of local news professionals rated covering the whole community as the most important responsibility of a TV news station. The data found that viewers concurred. Stations that covered a wider range of topics were more likely to be building or holding on to their audience than those that did not.[7]

THE LIMITS OF METAPHOR

As with all metaphors, the mapmaking comparison has its limits. Cartography is scientific, but journalism is not. You can plot the exact location of a road and measure the size of a country, or even an ocean. The proportions of a news story are another matter. A big story for some is unimportant to others.

Proportion and comprehensiveness in news are subjective. Their elusiveness, however, does not mean they are any less important than the more objective roads and river features of maps. To the contrary, striving for them is essential to journalism's popularity—and financial health. It is also possible—not just an abstract notion—to pursue proportion and comprehensiveness despite their being subjective. A citizen and a journalist may differ over the choices made about what is important. But citizens can accept those differences if they are confident that the journalist is trying to make news judgments to serve what readers need and want. The key is that citizens must believe the journalists' choices are not exploitative—they are not simply offering what will sell— and that journalists aren't pandering. Again, people care less whether journalists make mistakes, or correct them well, or always pick the right stories. The key element of credibility is the perceived motive of the journalist. People do not expect perfection. They do expect good intentions, as we suggested in our discussion of allegiance to citizens. Concern for proportionality is a key way of demonstrating public interest motives.

Honest people can disagree about a story's importance, but citizens and journalists alike know when a story is being hyped. They may disagree on precisely when the line was crossed, but at a certain point they know it has happened. In recent times that point has been hit with depressing regularity.

THE PRESSURE TO HYPE

At moments when the news media culture is undergoing rapid change and disorientation, there seems to be pressure to hype and sensationalize. You might call it the principle of the "naked body and the guitar."

If you want to attract an audience, you could go down to a street corner, do a striptease, and get naked. You would probably attract a crowd in a hurry. The problem is, how do you keep people? How do you avoid audience churn? There is another approach. Suppose you went to the same street corner and played the guitar. A few people listen the first day. Perhaps more the second. Depending on how good a guitar player you are, how diverse and intriguing your repertoire, the audience might grow each day. You would not, if you were good, have to keep churning the crowd, getting new people to replace those who grew tired of repetition.

This is the choice, in effect, that the news media face at a time when new technology expands the number of outlets and each organization watches its audience shrink. When the future is uncertain, and it is unclear how long you can stay in business unless you generate audience fast, which approach should you pursue? A news organization has to operate, to some extent, according to a faith or philosophy, since empirical models of the past may not work in the future.

Some news organizations, even those with fairly serious histories, have resorted to the path of the naked. In part, this is driven by the idea that news has become a commodity that is in oversupply. As one Wall Street analyst, James M. Marsh Jr. of Prudential Securities, told the Committee of Concerned Journalists, "There is currently an overabundance of news programming, with supply easily outstripping demand."[8] In part, too, this is driven by the fact that producing a lot of original reporting is expensive and requires a web of correspondents, camera crews, and bureaus worldwide.

The consequence is that the networks have moved significantly away from the hard news business. Studies by the Project for Excellence in Journalism have repeatedly found that morning news programs, the economic engine of network TV, put a heavy focus on celebrity, entertainment, lifestyle, and product cross-promotion. The same is true for prime-time newsmagazines, which often largely ignore the news altogether.[9]

Even the nightly newscasts shifted during the 1990s to less reported news of the work of civic institutions to more entertainment and celebrity attraction, though that changed measurably after the terrorist attacks of September 11, 2001.[10]

Some in network television note that while the broadcast news divisions have moved away from covering beats and breaking news around the world, the entertainment divisions have moved in the direction of "reality-based" programming. Shows such as *Law and Order, CSI,* and *Without a Trace* strive for nuanced and complex stories that are "ripped from the headlines." "We've reached the point where the entertainment divisions are doing the news and the news divisions are doing the entertainment," mused ABC News correspondent Robert Krulwich in the spring of 2000.[11]

Within a few months, network programmers began staging "reality-based" entertainment shows, such as the blockbuster hit *Survivor* in the summer of 2000, and then inserting the stars as "guests" on their news programs to boost the ratings of both the entertainment and the news shows. CBS, for instance, turned over large segments of its morning show, which is produced by the news department, to promote *Survivor,* including interviews with the person kicked off the island the night before. Thus the entertainment division of the corporation stages news, which the news division then covers. The practice continued and even expanded as reality television grew even bigger, adding brands like *American Idol* or *The Apprentice.*

Within six years, it was obvious there was more than a grain of truth to what Krulwich said. By 2006, emotionalism in broadcast news was gaining new momentum. Increasingly TV newscasters were trying to connect with the audience by telling people how to feel about the news. A study by the Project for Excellence in Journalism in 2005, for instance, found that the morning news programs on the networks do this by lacing stories with emotional code words, words like "stunning . . . horrifying . . . horrific . . . " and phrases such as "a serious warning every parent needs to hear." On May 11, 2005, for instance, the three network shows used such words thirty times in introducing the first five stories alone, often in the anchor introduction or close, or sometimes by selecting sound bites in which sources used these words.[12]

This was accentuated further after Hurricane Katrina in 2005, when reporters at major events reacted not only with emotion, but sometimes with outrage. After Anderson Cooper did this in New Orleans in the aftermath of Hurricane Katrina, he was promoted to become CNN's main prime-time host, complete with an ad campaign showing him in moments of emotional interaction with the news.

Various observers have lauded the newfound passion of the fourth estate and some have even wondered whether it might be a sign of a newfound aggressiveness. The praise, however, has by no means been unanimous and many questioned whether a 100-year journalistic commitment to a dispassionate report of facts was in jeopardy.

The issue cuts to the heart of what it means to be a journalist. In a profession that promises to suppress self-interest to assure its credibility, are emotionalism and outrage ever appropriate? And if so, when is it crossing a line? It would be difficult to argue that emotions coming from journalists on the scene witnessing human suffering are always out of place. So, if emotionalism seems appropriate sometimes but not others, where is the line?

The first sensible rule of thumb would seem to be that it should come at those moments when any other reaction would seem forced—when emotion is the only organic response. When anchorman Walter Cronkite wiped his eyes after John Kennedy's assassination in 1963, or showed the sense of awe he felt over the space shots a few years later, it struck Americans as appropriate.

The second point is that emotionalism should disappear between the moment of discovery of a problem and the subsequent search for information meant to put the event into a broader and deeper context. Once journalists have reacted in a human way to what they have seen, they must compose themselves to search for answers, and that requires all of their skepticism, professionalism, and intellectual independence. Human emotion is at the heart of what makes something news. Once you try to manufacture it, or use it to bring attention to yourself, you have crossed the line into something there is already enough of—reality entertainment.

MARKETING VS. MARKETING

What is the answer to resisting sensationalism and keeping the news in proportion? As we have said, we do not think that it lies with isolating the journalist behind some wall to ignore the realities of the marketplace. A better understanding of changing tastes, needs, and trends in the community is an important part of the answer.

But much of the current thinking about the marketplace based on the most popular forms of market research may not work. Traditional market research asks consumers to choose between predictable alternatives. Do you prefer this sneaker in orange or blue? Your toothpaste in a squeeze bottle or tube? Paste or gel? "[People tend] to choose from a limited spectrum of options. You already have defined for people what the range of choices will be," Lee Ann Brady, then of Princeton Survey Research Associates, explained to us. "So they are not telling you what they like. They tend to be reacting to your limited choices and giving you a hierarchy."[13]

Consider a typical survey, 20 minutes long and probably with fifteen or eighteen questions. Usually only two of these questions allow the interviewee to come up with an independent answer. The rest either are multiple-choice or ask the respondent whether she agrees or disagrees with a statement offered by the survey.

News defies much of traditional market research—which tests a static universe of options—because it changes each day. Focus groups—one of the cheapest and most common forms of market research—allow for more open-ended questions. They are popular as well because they allow journalists to observe audiences talking about their products. But they, too, are enormously limited. "Occasionally, you will get a voice or thought from a focus group that had never occurred to you," says Brady. "So they can be helpful if you have a blank slate."[14]

Anyone who has monitored a focus-group session can readily see its limitations as a means of probing the news. To begin, focus groups are not very scientific. It is enormously difficult to make focus groups representative, or to have two focus groups replicate each other, a basic definition of objectivity. One or two people can sway the discussion, or the focus group leader can unconsciously lead the group toward a predetermined answer.

Probably most important, most people don't use focus groups to probe for open-ended ideas. Instead, groups are often conducted to test hypotheses or options the organization is already considering. "Focus groups first entered the scene as a way of evoking ideas that could then be taken out and examined in a properly done open survey and applied to a larger population," said the late media researcher Leo Bogart. "There was no expectation that anyone would draw conclusions or make projections from what a handful of people said." Today, "they are greatly misused."[15]

Beyond these structural limitations of traditional market research, researchers say audiences may not know precisely why they prefer one journalism over another. "If you ask people to compare gel versus paste toothpaste," says Larry McGill, former manager of news audience research for NBC News, "that is actually more concrete than trying to specify the essential difference between Tom Brokaw or Peter Jennings." At NBC, McGill says, he and his fellow researchers learned they had to be skeptical of this kind of image work. "There was a very healthy discounting of the numbers."[16]

Market research has been especially effective in revealing how best to structure stories in prime-time newsmagazines. NBC discovered that the single most significant way to deliver viewers to its affiliates at 11 P.M. was to show the picture of the day or picture of the week at the end of the broadcast. *Dateline* learned to time the material in such a way that it appeared when other networks were broadcasting their commercials. "It often was worth a 2 rating-point improvement, or more than 1.8 million households. We would do a 12 rating most of the show and deliver a 14 rating to our affiliates," McGill explained.

But when it comes to the content of news, how do you measure the response to a story you had not imagined and tested? Such is the experience of television news. The medium has gone well down the road in knowing what people watch through its minute-to-minute overnight ratings. It can even tell at what point in certain stories people began to click away. So the medium has begun to tailor newscasts to ensure that every story has wide viewership.

But this has been a strategy that has done little to forestall the declining audience. The share of households watching nightly network news has declined from 75 percent in 1980 to 37 percent in 2005. Local news viewership also began to decline in the late 1990s, though concrete numbers are not officially gathered.[17] This might be called the paradox of giving people only the news they want.

"News organizations have been hoist on their own petard," explained John Carey, a market researcher who has worked with NBC and other media clients.[18] "Over time they have followed those ratings numbers, doing more and more of those stories that get high numbers, and they get stuck in those patterns. . . . As a consequence, the newsmagazines are stuck with an older audience, a more sentimental one and a more sensational one." But most viewers have fled. "In a sense, the people at the network know it, but they don't know how to get out of it."[19]

But what if we return to the idea of the "interlocking public," to a news report that A. M. Rosenthal called "the smorgasbord of news and information" when he was executive editor of the *New York Times*? Or, as newspaper editor Dave Burgin used to say about how a page in a newspaper should be laid out: if no story may attract more than 15 percent of the audience, make sure there are enough stories so that everyone will want to read one of them. By choosing content this way, a news organization can be more assured of putting the news in proportion.

Or go back to the mapmaker analogy. If journalism provides people only with information they say in advance that they want to know about, we are telling them only about the part of the community they already know about.

A NEW MARKET RESEARCH FOR JOURNALISTS

So what kind of market research would be of value? Journalists, citizens, and researchers together offer this answer: research that helps journalists make judgments, not research that replaces their judgment. Put another way, we need to stop using market research that treats our audience as customers, asking them which products they prefer. We need to create a journalism market research that approaches people as citizens and tells us more about their lives. How do you spend your time? Take us through your day. How long is your commute? What are you worried about? What do you hope and fear for your kids? This is open-ended research on broad trends of interest—the kinds of questions that will allow editors to understand how to design a news package that is comprehensive and proportional to their community and their needs.

Butch Ward, a former managing editor at the *Philadelphia Inquirer* who now teaches at the Poynter Institute, says asking people what they want is asking the wrong question. "It's a marketing question. Think about it: On Monday, the man who started a diet wants more information on nutrition. By Thursday, the same man is eating potato chips again and asking for better television coverage."

Ward believes news organizations should rely instead on a journalistic question—one they can answer through reporting: what are people doing? "Find out what the community is doing," Ward says. "What are they talking about with friends at the dining room table? Why are they working two jobs? What are they eating? What decisions are they making about expenditures for health care, vacations, the kids' educations?"[20] Once you get those answers you can design coverage that responds directly to the people you're trying to reach.

This is the kind of research conducted by Valerie Crane at Research Communications Limited in Florida. Crane's research involves two broad approaches, neither of them strictly traditional. The first identifies through in-depth interviews and then larger survey samples what basic needs in people's lives are met by the news they get—a quantitative way of going back to the function of news. "For some people it is about connecting to community. For some it is about making their life better [healthier, safer, more comfortable]. For others it's about making up their own mind. For others it is a way of winning social acceptance," Crane says. She has identified a range of needs that vary depending on the type of media, the way news categories are defined, and the kind of audience that is studied.[21] Crane finds quantifying for news companies why people use news—rather than asking what kinds of topics people are interested in—is an important way to focus on the right issue. "Too rarely do people [in news companies] think about what citizens' needs are," she says of her clients.

Second, Crane studies how people in a given community are living their lives, using a version of what some people call lifestyle and trends research. This type of research tends to group populations into clusters based not just on demographics but on attitudes and behavior. She studies fifteen different areas, from health, religion, work, consumerism, family relations, education, and more, and identifies the top concerns and trends in a given place. Taken together, her research into why people use the news and her study of the deeper concerns and trends in their lives give journalists insight into how to apply their own professional judgment. But the research, she says, should augment, not supplant, that judgment.

Al Tompkins, a former news director who now teaches broadcasting at the Poynter Institute, believes Crane's research tells journalists "how communities live, where their loyalties are, and not just what are they watching but why are they watching."[22] Crane's work, Tompkins says, "guides the presentation of news but doesn't determine what stories you do." For instance, though a lot of research suggests people don't like politics, Tompkins said, "Crane's research shows us they do care about their community, but they don't trust the political institutions. . . . It wasn't the topic they were sick of, it was the approach to the topic."

This notion—that storytelling is more important than topic—has been largely lost in all the commotion surrounding ever more sophisticated market research. Yet for local TV, at least, it remains the key to newscast viewership.

An analysis of 33,000 stories from 2,419 newscasts on 150 stations over five years by the Project for Excellence in Journalism found that how a story is gathered and reported—the number, balance, and expertise of sources, whether its relevancy to the audience and importance to the community is established, whether the story is more complete—are *twice* as important as topic in determining audience ratings.[23] This finding is especially important if, as anticipated, the story—rather than the newscast—becomes the essential unit consumers will seek out in the new media marketplace.

This conclusion was strongly supported when the Pew Research Center conducted a nationwide poll that included the standard consultant question on politics. Only 29 percent said they would be very interested in that kind of reporting. Yet when people were asked whether they'd be interested in "news reports about what government can do to improve the performance of local schools," the percentage of "very interested" jumped to 59 percent. Similarly, when participants were asked whether they would be interested in reports on what government could do to ensure that public places were safe from terrorism, the percentage of "very interested" rose to 67 percent.[24] Similar interest-level percentages were tallied for stories about reducing health-care costs. All of these topics, from schools to health care to public safety, have everything to do with politics and government.

Journalists need to focus on people and their problems, not

politicians and theirs. Setting aside old-style consulting and doubtful research probably are key to navigating an increasingly difficult future. Scott Tallal at Insite Research in California developed technology to conduct phone surveys that involve more open-ended questions and that digitally records the interviews, rather than having the interviewer try to write down the responses verbatim.

John Carey at Greystone Communication did ethnographic market research. Ethnography, which is an outgrowth of anthropology, works through direct on-site observation. Carey literally sits in people's houses and watches how they interact with media and technology. He has sat in people's houses through mealtimes, at breakfast, dinner, early in the morning, and even late at night.

Carey's findings turned many of the conventional ideas about television on their head. For instance, though a good deal of social science research suggests what some academics have called the "supremacy of the visual," or the notion that pictures are more powerful than words in television, Carey's work found that "very often people are not watching but listening to television news. Many people are actually reading a newspaper while they have on TV news. They tend to turn to watch the television when they hear something that they think will have important pictures." Putting information out visually without reinforcing words can be a great mistake.

Carey's research also suggested that the concept of teasers, or tempting people to stay tuned a little longer for an important upcoming report, may be thoroughly misguided. "A big mistake is thinking that people are watching over a length of time. Teasers are a huge mistake. People don't wait." Those items that say, "Will it rain tomorrow? Well, tonight will be cold, and Jim will be back in seven minutes with the complete forecast"—those tend to drive people away. Indeed, Carey's observations show that anytime there is a commercial, most viewers immediately switch channels.[25] A better alternative, Carey believed, would be to provide key information like weather constantly, to pack information all over your newscast, even to scroll it during commercials. "You would grab people by the constancy of your information."

The late Carole Kneeland, a news director in Austin, Texas, who was also known for defying conventional wisdom, followed this approach. She repeated the weather forecast throughout the newscast on the assumption that people wouldn't stay for the whole half-hour, but if you could inform more people quickly, over time you would command the most loyal and largest audience. "I think in the future we will have to break away from thirty-minute and sixty-minute content," Carey suggested. "You could have programming that is five minutes long in cycles," with longer pieces at certain times, much like radio programs with news and weather repeating every eight or twelve minutes, or the National Public Radio broadcasts with repeating headlines intermixed with longer stories.

Yet these are concepts so far beyond the realm of traditional market research, or even traditional ratings and circulation data, that they amount to reinventing the nature of research and the package journalism comes in.

Many journalists resist market research. "It's what I call the myth of the golden gut," said Crane. Ironically, journalists have more of the skills needed to do the kind of observational research about people's lives than might be best suited for journalism. Journalists, however, have not developed any tradition of doing it. Nor do they appear close to trying.

If journalism has lost its way, the reason in large part is that it has lost meaning in people's lives, not only its traditional audience but the next generation as well. We have shown, we hope, that a major reason for this is that journalists have lost the confidence to try to make the news comprehensive and proportional. Like the ancient maps that left much of the world terra incognita, contemporary audiences confront a journalism with similar blank spaces in place of uninteresting demographic groups or topics too difficult to pursue.

If journalists are only nimble and creative enough to use it, the interactive nature of the Web offers opportunities to take dramatic steps in overcoming the problems created by shortsighted use of market research and demographic data. Using tools ranging from opening chat rooms with students to report a story on changes in curriculum to e-mailing recognized experts for their list of the least understood subjects, reporters can form deeper relationships with the public as stakeholders. This can create the kind of understanding that would allow the public itself to continuously fill in some of the blanks in the coverage of their world and to provide knowledge based on their own peculiar experiences that give them unique insights.

The answer is not to return to a day when journalists operate purely by instinct. We hope we have spotlighted a group of new cartographers who are developing tools to chart the way people live their lives today and the needs for news these lives create. They are providing one of the most important tools a news organization needs to design a more comprehensive and proportional news report that attracts rather than repels the audience. Now it is up to journalists to try.

With all this, there is still one more element that ties all the others together. It relates to what goes on in the newsroom itself.

ENDNOTES

1. Valerie Crane, interview by author Rosenstiel, June 2000.
2. Project for Excellence in Journalism Local TV Project, "Quality Brings Higher Ratings, But Enterprise Is Disappearing," *Columbia Journalism Review,* November 1999; available at www.journalism.org.
3. Several people have noted this phenomenon. Hess was one of the first, in *The Washington Reporters* (Washington, DC: Brookings Institution, 1981).
4. Various people have made this point, including the authors themselves, local newscasters, and viewers in focus groups and meetings with local broadcasters.
5. Carnegie Corporation of New York, "Use of Sources for News," May 1, 2005. A slideshow of the report is available online on the Carnegie Corporation website, www.carnegie.org/pdf/AbandoningTheNews.ppt.
6. John Morton, "When Newspapers Eat Their Seed Corn," *American Journalism Review* (November 1995), 52; available at www.ajr.org.
7. Project for Excellence in Journalism Local TV Project, "Quality Brings Higher Ratings."
8. "Transformation of Network News," *Nieman Reports,* special issue (Summer 1999).
9. Project for Excellence in Journalism, "Changing Definitions of News: A Look at the Mainstream Press over 20 Years," March 6, 1998, 5; available at www.journalism.org.
10. The trend has been reflected in data compiled by the Project for Excellence in Journalism in its annual State of the News Media reports beginning in 2004; available at www.journalism.org.
11. Krulwich made this remark at a gathering on storytelling in Washington, DC, organized by News Lab, a television think tank, on April 14, 2000.
12. Project for Excellence in Journalism, "State of the News Media 2006," March 2006; available at www.journalism.org.
13. Lee Ann Brady, interview by author Rosenstiel, June 2000.

14. Ibid.
15. Leo Bogart, interview by author Rosenstiel, June 2000.
16. Larry McGill, interview by author Rosenstiel, June 2000.
17. Nielsen Media Research, used under license and published in the Project for Excellence in Journalism "State of the News Media 2006" report. Data is for share data from November; available at www.journalism.org.
18. John Carey, interview by author Rosenstiel, June 2000.
19. Ibid.
20. Butch Ward, interview with Cristian Lupsa, December 1, 2005.
21. Crane, interview by author Rosenstiel, June 2000.
22. Al Tompkins, interview by author Rosenstiel, June 2000.
23. Tom Rosenstiel, Walter Dean, Marion Just, Dante Chinni, and Todd Belt, *We Interrupt This Newscast* (Cambridge University Press, 2007).
24. Tom Rosenstiel and Dave Iverson, "Politics and TV Can Mix," *Los Angeles Times*, October 15, 2002; available at www.latimes.com.
25. Carey, interview by author Rosenstiel, June 2000.

10

Journalists Have a Responsibility to Conscience

For three weeks in October 2002, Washington, D.C., was a community paralyzed by fear. With cunning stealth and deadly efficiency, someone stalked thirteen men, women, and children in the city and its Maryland and Virginia suburbs, shooting to death nine and seriously wounding four, including a twelve-year-old boy as he entered his school.

A nationwide manhunt ensued, with city, county, state, and federal law-enforcement officials taunted by notes left at the murder scenes, including one that warned "your children are not safe anywhere, anytime." The murders seemed frighteningly like the opening of a guerilla phase in the shadowy ill-defined "war against terror" declared by President George W. Bush thirteen months after hijacked jetliners became suicide bombs, killing thousands when they obliterated the World Trade Center buildings in New York City and destroyed a section of the Pentagon in Washington. Press coverage of the murders pushed other news, including that of American troops fighting in Afghanistan, off the front page as the world focused on the fear of hidden death that gripped America's capitol community.

For executive editor Howell Raines, the Washington story presented another opportunity to send a message to his staff and the competition that he was presiding over a new, super-charged *New York Times*, one that would "flood the zone" of a big story and dominate everybody else. Raines had been promoted to the top job in 2001, a few weeks before the September 11 attacks, and he had mobilized the staff to cover that historic event so well that it won the paper a record five Pulitzer Prizes. The Washington story was his opportunity to take on the *Washington Post* in its hometown with his brand of competition and try to erase the hurt many *Times* staffers still nursed over the way the *Post* had outreported them on the Watergate scandal thirty years earlier.

Although the *Times* had the largest bureau in Washington, with a cluster of a half-dozen of the paper's best investigative reporters, Raines kept direction of the coverage in New York. Among the people he dispatched to Washington was Jayson Blair, a twenty-seven-year-old former intern who had been a reporter for only twenty-one months. Within days the addition of Blair seemed an inspired choice. The new reporter was producing front-page stories with tantalizing details other Washington-area reporters were unable to match.

Just as quickly, more experienced reporters in Washington began raising questions about "this guy Blair," whose name began appearing in the paper but whom none of them saw in the bureau or in the field. One of those reporters, Eric Lichtblau, who covered the Department of Justice for the *Times*, became concerned as stories by Blair were routinely being questioned by officials he had come to trust in the Department of Justice. Other reporters were raising questions as well, and when one source in exasperation told Lichtblau he "didn't know who the anonymous sources this guy Blair is depending on was, but much of what he was writing is just not true," Lichtblau went to Rick Berke, the bureau's news editor. Berke reported his concerns to New York, where he said he was "brushed off" with suggestions that the complaints were prompted by jealousy. Raines, Berke was told, "had already decided Blair was a great shoe-leather reporter."[1]

What none of the people in the Washington bureau knew was that complaints about Blair's work had infected the newsroom in New York like a persistent fever for months before Blair was sent to Washington. Somehow, as Blair was moved from one supervising editor to another, the doubts about the quality of his work didn't travel with him, as if the editors worked on different continents rather than a few yards or miles from each other.

Washington reporters were considering an organized complaint to New York when two suspects were arrested and charged in the sniper shootings case. Coverage was reduced and the tension and doubts began to ease as Blair was reassigned to other stories. The dateline on his stories was no longer Washington but began to appear from Maryland, West Virginia, Ohio, even Texas, where Robert Rivard, the editor of the *San Antonio Express-News* saw something in a Blair story that troubled him. It concerned him enough to send an e-mail message to Raines and *Times* managing editor Gerald Boyd, telling them he had found an article written by Blair to be "disturbingly similar" to one his newspaper had published earlier.

This outside complaint from the editor of another newspaper couldn't be ignored, and Raines and Boyd confronted Blair with it. The young reporter quickly was caught up in a cascade of contradictions. After two days it became clear he had never visited the Texas home he wrote about and the "eyewitness" detail came from pictures in the *Times*'s photo archives; the other information came from stories by other reporters. On May 1, 2003, Blair resigned. News of his resignation had the effect of blasting open closed lines of communication inside the *Times*. One after the other, staff members realized that they were not the only ones who had complained about Blair's behavior and his work.

A full-scale investigation into Blair's work revealed what many on the staff had suspected: that he was not an aggressive, digging, dedicated reporter but a troubled young man relying on deceit, plagiarism, and fiction to further his career at the expense of everyone around him. Staffers started to air the feelings of resentment, even betrayal, they had long suppressed when they thought they were alone in feeling unappreciated. For the next two weeks Raines and Boyd met with individuals and groups in the newsroom and tried to reassure them. What they heard in those meetings were reporters and junior editors who vented their disillusion and anger that such basic violations of standards and values threatened to destroy their own credibility and that of the newspaper.

Instead of reassurance, staff discontent only became more intense and aggressive, and publisher Arthur Sulzberger Jr. announced that he and Raines and Boyd would meet with the newsroom in a "town hall" meeting to address questions and concerns. The meeting, which was closed to other journalists, was held in a nearby theater. The depth of suspicion and anger that focused on senior management during the session would later be described as "unusually raw, emotional and candid." Some of those who took part not only described the confrontation to reporters from other news organizations but also sent e-mail messages to journalism watch sites like Romenesko, where they were posted for everybody to see. Their message began to build a public bill of particulars against the leadership of Raines and Boyd.

The picture these messages painted was of a newsroom in which internal communications had become so dysfunctional that five years of warnings about the quality and reliability of Blair's work were ignored as he had steadily been assigned to more and more important stories until his byline adorned stories of national–even international–interest. Before the Blair episode concluded, both Raines and Boyd were forced out,[2] and more than two dozen newsroom employees engaged in a long-term reorganization of the newsroom's standards, structure, and operations.

By June the internal investigation had documented Blair's "frequent acts of journalistic fraud . . . widespread fabrication and plagiarism [that] represent a profound betrayal of trust and a low point in the 152-year history of the newspaper." As more information surfaced, it became clear to the staff that it had taken an outside voice to break open the dysfunctional lines of internal communication.

Much of the impetus for the collapse of the top newsroom managers was credited to the Internet on which many of the *Times* employees posted the complaints that had been ignored. Staff members who used the open architecture of the new medium to become "the outside voice" provided a check on internal behavior. Along with others, they realized that the Web had assumed an important role in opening new channels through which values and standards could be questioned and judged by a large community that depends upon the integrity of the press. In the end journalism is an act of character.

Since there are no laws of journalism, no regulations, no licensing, and no formal self-policing, and since journalism by its nature can be exploitative, a heavy burden rests on the ethics and judgment of the individual journalist and the individual organization where he or she works. This would be a difficult challenge for any profession. But for journalism there is the added tension between the public service role of the journalist—the aspect of the work that justifies its intrusiveness—and the business function that finances the work. Complicating things further, even in the age of the Internet, most journalists are still embedded in oligarchic institutions because of the prohibitive costs of assembling a comprehensive news organization.

The top-down structure of oligarchies usually makes it more difficult for individuals to be heard on abstract matters, such as ethics or questions of conscience—at least in their own newsrooms. In recent years, the rise of blogs and the democratization of content production have given voice to citizens monitoring politics, society, and the press, creating a new class of media pundits and critics. Some operate independently and some operate within organizations dedicated to watching the press, but what they all share is an unprecedented commitment to police "the MSM," or mainstream media. Today, if trouble is brewing inside a newsroom, it will leak. If the organization is skirting responsibilities, somebody will point it out. The tension and fear of having organizational issues discussed outside the newsroom have prompted some editors to stop sending memos or putting decisions down on paper.

Some of these new monitors have not only increased demands for transparency in newsrooms but, as was the case with Jayson Blair, also have helped expose ethical lapses and flaws in the hierarchical structure of the *New York Times*. It's true that much of the chatter in cyberspace does not rise above ideological accusations of the press being too conservative or too liberal, but when it does, and when it brings up serious issues in a newsroom, the credibility of that journalistic product can be greatly affected.

It's important to keep this consequence in mind because whether or not we are conscious of its importance, when all is said and done, what we are choosing when we select a magazine, a TV program, a website, or a paper is the authority, honesty, and judgment of the journalists who produce it. And it's part of the journalist's responsibility to encourage a transparent and open culture that won't allow critics to call the credibility of the product into question.

As a consequence, there is a final principle that journalists have come to understand about their work and that we as citizens intuit when we make our media choices. It is the most elusive of the principles, yet it ties all the others together:

Journalists have an obligation to exercise their personal conscience.

Every journalist, from the newsroom to the boardroom, must have a personal sense of ethics and responsibility—a moral compass. What's more, they have a responsibility to voice their personal conscience out loud and allow others around them to do so as well.

For journalists to be able to exercise their conscience, managers and owners have to create an open newsroom, an environment that is essential to fulfilling the principles outlined in this book. Innumerable hurdles make it difficult to produce news that is accurate, fair, balanced, citizen focused, independent minded, and courageous. But the effort is smothered in its crib without an open atmosphere that allows people to challenge one another's assumptions, perceptions, and prejudices. We need our journalists to feel free, even encouraged, to speak out and say, "This story idea strikes me as racist," or "Boss, you're making the wrong decision." Only in a newsroom in which all can bring their diverse viewpoints to bear will the news have any chance of accurately anticipating and reflecting the increasingly diverse perspectives and needs of American culture.

Simply put, those who inhabit news organizations must recognize a personal obligation to differ with or challenge editors, owners, advertisers, and even citizens and established authority if fairness and accuracy require they do so.

In turn, those who run news organizations must encourage and allow their staff to exercise this personal obligation. It would be naïve to assume an individual commitment is enough in an age of uncertainty about the future of the press. Many journalists are so worried that they might be swept by the next wave of layoffs that challenging authority and a flawed organizational culture is the last thing on their minds. So news organizations and, even more important in the conglomerated media world today, their parent companies need to build a culture that nurtures individual responsibility. And then managers have to be willing to listen, not simply manage problems and concerns away.

There is no separate section in this book on ethics. That is because of this moral dimension, this quality of judgment, tone, taste, and character that is implicit in why we choose one magazine, newscast, or website rather than another. Ethics are woven into every element of journalism, and we sense this as citizens often more acutely than do journalists themselves, who sometimes cordon ethics off as an isolated topic.

As Chicago newscaster Carol Marin told the Committee of Concerned Journalists at its first forum, "I think a journalist is someone who believes in something that they would be willing to quit over."[3]

In 1993, as NBC's *Dateline* was preparing a segment called "Waiting to Explode?" alleging that the gas tanks in General Motors trucks had a tendency to rupture and ignite in crashes, the reporter of the piece voiced concern. Though correspondent Michele Gillen had collected footage of actual accidents in which drivers wound up trapped inside burning cars, she knew that crash tests NBC had conducted had not produced the same results. A small fire broke out, but it lasted only 15 seconds before burning itself out. So when she learned that the network was setting up additional crash tests rigged to be more dramatic, Gillen did something she had not done in her seven months with the show. She called her boss, Jeff Diamond, at home and expressed her concerns. She wanted the new tests stopped.

Diamond told her that he thought the footage would be striking and would add to the report. The two went back and forth on the point for days, but Diamond in the end convinced Gillen to narrate the test crash when her producers assured her that her concerns would be noted in the final broadcast. The test would be labeled "unscientific" and any conclusions would be left to the experts.

The piece, however, didn't note all of Gillen's concerns. It never mentioned how long the fire lasted or that it went out on its own. In the end Gillen agreed to narrate the piece anyway, against her instinct, because, she said, "at some point, you have to have faith in your executive producer, and if he's telling me this is okay, and he's responsible for looking after my best interests and the show's best interests, then I'll trust him."[4] Gillen was wrong and the embarrassment of the rigged explosions was the low point in the history of NBC News.

The incident shows how delicate the question of moral compass can be. Conscience is not something to be assuaged, as it was in the *Dateline* case. It is something to be revered. The burden of protecting conscience cannot be laid entirely on the individual or it can be suffocated, just as Gillen's objections were. Had Gillen's objections been heeded, NBC News would have avoided the embarrassment that eventually led to the resignation of Michael Gartner as president of the news division.

If the Gillen incident happened today, the story might unfold in a similar fashion except that the conversation outside the newsroom would be much more spirited. The new press criticism and review made possible by the Internet would have likely championed Gillen and scoured NBC more vehemently and more immediately.

Consider an example of less importance than exploding vehicles. The morning of August 19, 2005, TVNewser, a blog on MediaBistro.com, a website providing journalism news and resources, broke the news that Bob Costas refused to host the previous night's edition of CNN's *Larry King Live* because he wasn't comfortable with the topic.[5] The show, on which Costas occasionally substituted for King, was to be primarily about Natalee Holloway, a teenager from Alabama who disappeared during a post-graduation trip to Aruba in May 2005. By August the Holloway story had become a media phenomenon, with some cable channels devoting hours on end to on-the-scene coverage.

Mediabistro's TVNewser blog said the information came from an "anonymous tipster, who applauds Costas 'for standing up for his principles in not dealing with trash stories'.... Costas hasn't responded to TVNewser's request for comment." The story was confirmed, and by the afternoon, it was on the Associated Press wire and everywhere else soon after. "I didn't think the subject matter of Thursday's show was the kind of broadcast I should be doing," Costas said in a statement. "I suggested some alternatives but the producers preferred the topics they had chosen. I was fine with that, and respectfully declined to participate."[6]

The AP story said the decision was one both Costas and CNN were comfortable with, but that did not prevent bloggers and critics from commenting on it for weeks to come. Most of them praised the journalist for his decision and their blog postings carried titles such as: "Finally, a Responsible Journalist!" and "Thank you, Bob Costas," or "The Integrity of Bob Costas."

EXERCISING CONSCIENCE IS NOT EASY

Introducing this need into the process of making journalism creates another tension. By necessity, newsrooms are not democracies. They tend to be unruly dictatorships. Someone atop the chain of command has to make the ultimate decision—to go with the story or not to go, to leave in the damning quote or take it out. Organizations as large as most newspapers, Web publishers, or TV stations simply could not meet their deadlines otherwise. Add to this the tendency in modern newsrooms to create a single corporate culture as the business and news sides increasingly work in team formats. This may make managing easier, but a newsroom monoculture is antithetical to this principle of individual conscience from which flow other values, such as accuracy, a commitment to citizens, and the intellectual diversity necessary to cover our communities. Managers need to understand that, though they have the final say, the door needs to be open to everyone along the way. As Bob Woodward says, his career has taught him one thing: "The best journalism is often done in defiance of management."[7]

In a sense, managers need to recognize the difference between their larger interests and their smaller ones. While a quiet and homogeneous newsroom may be easier to manage, the larger and more abstract interests of a news company require a culture that is more complex than that. Allowing individuals to voice their consciences in the newsroom makes running the newspaper more difficult. It makes the news more accurate.

This notion of moral conscience is something many, if not most, journalists we encountered believe in deeply. "Each individual reporter has to set his own rules, his own standards, and model his career for himself," Bill Kurtis told our academic research partners.[8]

When he began doing media criticism, Jon Katz sensed this about being a journalist and even more so about being a critic of journalists. Katz felt compelled to sit down and write his own personal code of ethics. "I think you have to have a moral context in the work you do for it really to have any meaning. Whatever you do, I think you have to do it in a way that is morally satisfying to you," he told our research partners.[9]

Most journalists are far less formal about it than Katz. They simply sense that journalism is a moral act and know that all of their background and values direct what they will do and not do in producing it. "My own instincts, and the way I was raised . . . and I suppose my own emotional and intellectual development, have led me to some pretty strong beliefs over the years, and I pay attention to them around here," Tom Brokaw told our research partners.[10]

For many journalists, this moral dimension is particularly strong because of what attracted them to the profession in the first place. When they initially became interested in news, often as adolescents or teenagers, many were drawn to the craft by its most basic elements–calling attention to inequities in the system, connecting people, creating community. In our survey of journalists with the Pew Research Center for the People and the Press, these factors outstripped all others by nearly two to one as distinguishing factors of journalism.[11] In short, for those who practice it, the craft has a moral aspect.

These journalists feel strongly about the moral dimension of their profession because without it they have so little to help them navigate the gray spaces of ethical decisions. As Carol Marin told us, since "there are no laws of news . . . it ends up being sort of your own guiding compass that will determine what you do and don't do."[12]

As audiences we are guided by the decisions journalists make about what to report and how it is reported, and we are guided in our choice of news packages by a subtle combination of reasons, but this moral sense is part of it. We are looking for information, but we are also looking for validation, for authority, for honesty, and for a sense that the journalists have our interests at heart.

Consider the experience Marin herself encountered in Chicago. Early in 1997, she was the anchor at WMAQ, the NBC-owned-and-operated station in the city. The man in charge of the news at the station, Joel Cheatwood, had an idea to sweeten the ratings of the struggling 6 P.M. newscast. Cheatwood, who had gained a kind of fame in Miami for turning a Fox affiliate into the number-one station by going to "All Crime All the Time," planned on turning the dial another notch in Chicago. He would hire Jerry Springer, the disgraced Cincinnati mayor turned talk-show host, to do commentaries at the end of the news. Springer was local. He taped his syndicated TV show about bizarre love triangles and violent confrontations right from WMAQ's studios.

When Cheatwood's plan was announced, the word sent WMAQ staff into depression. Were they in the shock-show business? They thought they were doing something important, something about public service. Finally, Marin decided enough was enough. She thought WMAQ was degenerating into sleaze. Management already had put her on probation once because she had refused to narrate health segments that were a collaboration between the station and a local hospital in exchange for buying ad time. Now came Springer. Marin had no illusions about herself. She was no saint. But journalists live and die by their reputation as people with ethics. It's all they have. She decided she would resign.

Marin's colleagues burst into loud applause when she announced her decision on camera. You could see them, right on the air. Many wept. It meant something that a public person would take such an ethical stand about her own job. Marin shifted to another station, and in the wake of her departure, WMAQ's viewers fled as well.

Afterward, Marin was "awestruck" by the response, especially the "quantity and the quality of the letters and e-mails. . . . People wrote long tracts, and they did three things in many of the letters. They explained their relationship to the news. . . . They described themselves in demographic terms. . . . They explained an ethical dilemma that had happened to them. . . . The fact of the matter is, and a lawyer that I know in Chicago wrote me and said, every one of us in our lives will face a so-called Springer decision. I talked to butchers who won't short-weigh meat, and one who got fired. A real estate banker who wouldn't pad assessments in Lake Forest and lost two critical accounts with Chicago banks."[13]

The questions of character that journalists face are not unfamiliar to us as we consume news, and we look for them in the judgments we make about who is credible and believable.

A CULTURE OF HONESTY

"The ability of journalists to exercise conscience is much more important than anything they believe or any beliefs they bring to their job," Linda Foley, the president of the Newspaper Guild, told us at a CCJ forum. "It's credibility, more than objectivity, that's important for us in our industry. . . . There has to be a culture in newsrooms that allows a journalist to have a free and open discussion."[14]

Donald Shriver, the president emeritus of Union Theological Seminary in New York City, not long ago reviewed four books on journalism ethics and offered this about the handbook on the subject prepared by the Poynter Institute in Florida: "The most useful piece of the Poynter schematic for journalistic ethics is its illustration of the transition from 'gut reaction' ethics to observation of rules to the maturity of reflection and reasoning. At the top of this hierarchy is their assertion that 'collaboration is essential.' That is, check the story with your colleagues. Given the rush to deadline and competition among reporters in most newsrooms, this is rare advice. Yet, if journalism is a medium of dialogue among citizens, it seems right for the dialogue to begin in the newsroom."[15]

Interestingly, some of the best and most difficult decisions in journalism history have come about through just the kind of elusive collaboration Shriver is talking about. When Katharine Graham made the decision to publish the Pentagon Papers in 1971, the process was extraordinarily open. Graham had to decide whether the *Washington Post* should risk legal sanction by publishing secret Pentagon documents after the Justice Department had already gone to court to block the *New York Times* from making them public. Here is how Graham herself described it in her autobiography:

> Ben [Bradlee] was beginning to feel squeezed between the editors and the reporters, who were solidly lined up for publishing and supporting

the *Times* on the issue of freedom of the press, and the lawyers, who at one point suggested a compromise whereby the *Post* would not publish the Papers on Friday but would notify the attorney general of its intention to publish on Sunday. Howard Simons, who was one hundred percent for publishing, summoned the reporters to talk directly with the lawyers.

[Don] Oberdorfer said the compromise was "the shittiest idea I've ever heard." [Chalmers] Roberts said the *Post* would be "crawling on its belly" to the attorney general; if the *Post* didn't publish, he would move his retirement up two weeks, make it a resignation, and publicly accuse the *Post* of cowardice. Murrey Marder recalled saying, "If the *Post* doesn't publish, it will be in much worse shape as an institution than if it does," since the paper's "credibility would be destroyed journalistically for being gutless." [Ben] Bagdikian reminded the lawyers of the commitment to [Daniel] Ellsberg to publish the Papers and declared, "The only way to assert the right to publish is to publish." . . . Gene Patterson . . . gave me the first warning of what was to come, saying that he believed the decision on whether to print was going to be checked with me and that he "knew I fully recognized that the soul of the newspaper was at stake."

"God, do you think it's coming to that?" I asked. Yes, Gene said, he did. . . .

Frightened and tense, I took a big gulp and said, "Go ahead, go ahead, go ahead. Let's go. Let's publish."[16]

As Anthony Lewis, then an editorial columnist for the *New York Times*, noted seventeen years later:

Examining that episode afterward, a law review article by Professors Harold Edgar and Benno Schmidt Jr. of the Columbia University Law School said it marked the "passing of an era" for the American press. It was an era, they said, in which there was a "symbiotic relationship between politicians and the press." But now, by printing the secret history of the Vietnam War over strenuous objections, establishment newspapers had "demonstrated that much of the press was no longer willing to be merely an occasionally critical associate [of the Government], devoted to common aims, but intended to become an adversary."[17]

A year after the Pentagon Papers, the *Washington Post* began looking into Watergate.

INTELLECTUAL DIVERSITY IS THE REAL GOAL

This notion of open dialogue in the newsroom is at the core of what a growing number of people who think about news consider the key element in the question of diversity and in the pursuit of a journalism of proportion.

"Is there a culture of the newsroom?" ABC newsman Charles Gibson asked at one of the CCJ forums. "Are you challenging each other, are you talking to each other, are you pushing each other?"[18]

"I'll tell you how it plays out for Christians in my newsroom," answered David Ashenfelder, a Pulitzer Prize winner at the *Detroit Free Press,* who is also a Christian and a member of a large weekly Bible study group in suburban Detroit. "They don't talk. They're afraid of being ridiculed. They're there. I know who a bunch of them are. We sort of have this little underground, and we talk to each other and we talk among ourselves. One thing we've been asking ourselves lately is, why are we just talking among ourselves?"[19]

Traditionally, the concept of newsroom diversity has been defined largely in terms of numerical targets that related to ethnicity, race, and gender. The news industry has belatedly recognized that its newsrooms should more closely resemble the culture at large. The American Society of Newspaper Editors, for instance, in 1978 formally targeted that the number of minorities working at American newspapers should reflect the percentage in the general population—a goal it has still not met. These targets, and the failure to meet them, are important. The numerical quotas are matters of justice as well as a necessary step to making journalism, and therefore citizenship and democracy, something available to everyone.[20]

Seen in the broader context of personal conscience, however, this conventional definition of diversity, important as it may be, is too limited. It risks confusing means with ends. Getting more minorities in the newsroom is a target, but not the goal, of diversity. The goal is a more accurate and representative news organization. Ethnic, gender, and racial quotas are a means of approaching that. But they will accomplish nothing in themselves if the newsroom culture then requires that these people from different backgrounds all adhere to a single mentality. The local newspaper or TV station may "look like America," as President Bill Clinton was fond of saying, but it won't think like the community and it won't understand it or be able to cover it.

The goal of diversity should be to assemble not only a newsroom that might resemble the community but also one that is as open and honest so that this diversity can function. This is not just racial or gender diversity. It is not just ideological diversity. It is not just social class or economic diversity. It is not just numerical diversity. It is what we call intellectual diversity, and it encompasses and gives meaning to all the other kinds.

Increasingly, people who have fought for diversity are coming to precisely this conclusion. "We have defined ... diversity too often in gender and genetic terms as people who look a little different but basically sound the same," Mercedes de Uriarte, who teaches journalism at the University of Texas, told us at another committee forum. "We extend that too often to sources, who echo the thing that we're comfortable in hearing on both sides of a very narrow spectrum of debate." But, said de Uriarte, "it is intellectual diversity that we still have difficulty including in the news. Intellectual diversity is, according to scholars of American culture, among the most difficult for Americans to accept."[21]

Unfortunately, this concept of intellectual diversity is also difficult for managers. The tendency, for many reasons, is to create newsrooms that think like the boss.

THE PRESSURES AGAINST INDIVIDUAL CONSCIENCE

Various factors pull toward making newsrooms homogeneous. One is simply human nature. "Editors have a tendency to create people in their own image. If the editor doesn't like you for some reason, you don't rise. So there's a self-selection process that goes on within the profession," Juan Gonzalez, a columnist at the *New York Daily News,* told us at one committee forum.[22]

"We have hiring systems in this country that make it very difficult to take risks on people. The people who are outside the mainstream as we would define it ... are precisely the people who don't get a chance," Tom Bray, then a conservative columnist for the *Detroit News,* told us.[23]

Another problem is a kind of bureaucratic inertia that sets in at any organization. Inertia pushes people to do in any circumstance that which is normally done. Routines become safe havens. This occurs because news organizations–with their business, community, production, and other interests–are complex and hierarchical. It becomes easy to fall into a process of what might be called cascading rationalization, which can undermine and discourage acts of individual conscience. The story "has to" go now, even if it's not completely checked out, because the deadline won't wait. Maybe it's better not to pursue that lead at this sensitive moment of the debate. Our production capacity won't allow a story that long in this edition. And so forth.

Some journalists have always worked outside organizations. Guided only by their sense of personal commitment, these individuals pursue stories with single-minded, sometimes idiosyncratic, purpose and regularly reveal unpopular truths others have ignored, avoided, or simply did not see–people like Thomas Paine, George Seldes, I. F. Stone, or more recently, David Burnham and Charles Lewis.

It is also simpler, as we have said, to run a newsroom in which people operate and think alike. Newsrooms are, in the end, governed by the requirements of the production facilities. They need to fill a certain amount of airtime, or Web space, or newsprint. In this atmosphere it is easy to conclude that a good story is any story that is finished. To the degree that the daily work of putting out the paper or getting the show on is an assembly line, there is pressure to make that process as smooth and efficient as possible.

BUILDING A NEWSROOM WHERE CONSCIENCE AND DIVERSITY CAN THRIVE

Maybe the biggest challenge for the people who produce the news is to recognize that their long-term health depends on the quality of their newsroom, not simply its efficiency. The long-term interest pulls one toward a more complex and difficult newsroom culture. The quality of an owner, an editor, or any manager is defined to a large extent by the degree to which the individual manages for that long haul.

As difficult as the obstacles are, the history of journalism is filled with cases where collaboration and even confrontation occurred, and even where it was nurtured. Some in the news business seem to naturally gravitate to a culture where people feel free and encouraged to operate according to conscience.

One model is to have this culture flow down in clear demonstrations from the top, in public, where they set a tone for others to see. Maybe the best example is the story David Halberstam tells of his first meeting with Orville Dryfoos, who had only recently been made publisher of the *New York Times*:

> It was in early 1962, maybe February. I had been in the Congo only since the previous July and had been called back to New York to receive an award. A man walked up to the desk where I was sitting and introduced himself as Orville Dryfoos. "I heard you were here," he said, "and I wanted to let you know how much I admire what you do, how much we are all aware of the risks you take. It is what makes this paper what it is." As much as anything else it was that attitude and the ease with which that conversation could occur between the publisher and a reporter that set that newsroom apart from any other.[24]

In the end, most newsroom people feel that communicating to fellow citizens is a mission that transcends the institution where they work. It is something of a calling, and everyone who works in a newsroom is a steward of that mission. For their part, managers need to help their journalists fulfill that mission to their best potential. Gregory Favre, former editor of the *Sacramento Bee*, vice president of news for the McClatchy chain, and later a faculty member at the Poynter Institute, often talks to journalists about this larger sense of mission.

> You help people whether it's a time of calm or whether it is a time of crisis. You help them speak to each other, allowing many voices to be heard, and providing them with information necessary to function as productive citizens. You help them build a bridge across their gulf of differences. And you have an obligation to question yourselves, just as you question others. An obligation to live and work by the same set of values that you ask of those you cover. An obligation to help bring about a change in the culture throughout our business, a culture that

has a sense of caring, that demands diversity in our ranks, that has a human touch, internally and externally, a culture that is wrapped in a moral fabric that won't be ripped apart in the moments of tough times.[25]

Indeed, Favre tells people in newsrooms that this mission is so significant that journalists have an obligation to preserve it and strengthen it, for both those who came before and those who will come after.

THE ROLE OF CITIZENS

The final component in the equation is how the members of the community, the citizens, become part of the process. What responsibilities do they have? One frequent response of journalists is that if the press is failing—if it is overly sensational or biased toward infotainment—then these are ultimately failures of the citizenry. If people wanted better journalism, they say, the market would provide it. The problem with this rationalization, as we have seen, is that journalism is not shaped by a perfect market. The kind of local news we get in television, for instance, owes a great deal to the level of profitability required by Wall Street. The nature of a newspaper, we have learned from news executives, is heavily influenced by the values of the ownership. The quality of the decisions journalists make from day to day is heavily influenced by editors and the culture of the newsroom. The way the business of news is organized also plays a role. Newspapers are by and large monopolies. TV stations, which are licensed on the public airways, are largely an oligarchy. At this point, the Internet is still too young to predict what market reality it will come to represent.

The market does not, as it is so often said, provide citizens simply with the news they want. They also get the news that Wall Street, ownership, journalism training, and the conventions of news dictate be made available to them. If this is to change and if the principle that the journalist's primary allegiance to the citizens is to have meaning, a new relationship between the journalist and the citizen must evolve. It is the newest element of journalism, one that has always been at play, but in the new century is becoming more palpable, and more vital. It is the role of the citizen.

ENDNOTES

1. This account comes from interviews with Lichtblau and Berke conducted by author Kovach, March 2006.
2. CNN.com, "Top New York Times Editors Quit," March 1, 2004; available at www.cnn.com/2003/US/Northeast/06/05/NYTimes/resigns/.
3. Carol Marin, at CCJ Forum, Chicago, November 6, 1997.
4. Benjamin Weiser, "Does TV News Go Too Far? A Look Behind the Scenes at NBC's Truck Crash Test," *Washington Post*, February 28, 1993; available at www.washingtonpost.com.
5. "Did Bob Costas Refuse to Fill in for Larry King on Thursday?" *TVNewser*, August 19, 2005.
6. Bill Carter, "Bob Costas says no to Hour on Amba," *New York Times*, August 24, 2005, E1.
7. Bob Woodward, Nieman Fellows seminar, Harvard University, Fall 1998.
8. Bill Kurtis, interview by William Damon, Howard Gardner, and Mihaly Csikszentmihalyi; unpublished interviews for the book *Good Work: When Excellence and Ethics Meet* (New York: Basic Books, 2001).
9. Jon Katz, interview by William Damon, Howard Gardner, and Mihaly Csikszentmihalyi, ibid.
10. Tom Brokaw, interview by William Damon, Howard Gardner, and Mihaly Csikszentmihalyi, ibid.
11. CCJ and the Pew Research Center for the People and the Press, "Striking the Balance: Audience Interests, Business Pressures and Journalists' Values," March 1999, 6; available at www.journalism.org.
12. Marin, at CCJ Forum, Chicago, November 6, 1997.
13. Ibid.
14. Linda Foley, at CCJ Forum, Ann Arbor, MI, February 2, 1998.
15. Donald W. Shriver Jr., "Meaning from the Muddle," *Media Studies Journal* (Spring/Summer 1998), 138.
16. Katharine Graham, *Personal History* (New York: Alfred A. Knopf, 1997), 449.
17. Anthony Lewis, Eleventh Annual Frank E. Gannett Lecture, Capitol Hilton Hotel, Washington, DC, November 28, 1988.
18. Charles Gibson, at CCJ Forum, Ann Arbor, MI, February 2, 1998.
19. David Ashenfelder, at CCJ Forum, Ann Arbor, MI, February 2, 1998.
20. American Society of Newspaper Editors, "1999 Newsroom Census: Minority Employment Inches Up at Daily Newspapers"; available at www.asne.org.
21. Mercedes de Uriarte, at CCJ Forum, St. Petersburg, FL, February 26, 1998.
22. Juan Gonzalez, at CCJ Forum, New York City, December 4, 1997.
23. Tom Bray, at CCJ Forum, Ann Arbor, MI, February 2, 1998.
24. David Halberstam, interview by author Kovach, June 10, 2000.
25. Favre delivered a version of this speech at the Portland *Oregonian*'s annual Fred Stickel Award ceremony in April 2006.

11

The Rights and Responsibilities of Citizens

O n the morning of July 7, 2005, three bombs exploded in the London subway, followed shortly by an explosion on a double-decker bus. The suicide bombings killed fifty-two people in an attack evocative of the 2004 train explosions in Madrid.

The British Broadcasting Corporation, or BBC, understood that this was a most important story and threw its staff at it, trying to get information first and, as Richard Sambrook, director of the news division, wrote, "get things right."[1] On that day, the BBC received unprecedented help from London residents. Six hours after the attack, the organization counted more than 1,000 photographs, twenty video clips, 4,000 text messages, and 20,000 e-mails–all sent in by citizens.

The BBC had always encouraged citizen involvement in the news, but this level of participation was new. "The quantity and quality of the public's contributions moved them beyond novelty, tokenism or the exceptional and raises major implications that we are still working through," recalled Sambrook.

Despite the surprise response, the BBC made good use of the material, going as far as to open a newscast with video footage received from citizens. Sambrook called the reporting of the London story a partnership, and noted that his organization learned that "when major events occur, the public can offer us as much new information and we are able to broadcast to them."

Technology has enabled citizens to be players in the news and become partners of traditional media in times of crisis. But the BBC model of interacting with citizens proves that dramatic events are not the only time when citizen journalism can or should be used.

Other BBC citizen initiatives include:

- The Digital Storytelling Project, started in 2001, involves local workshops in which BBC professionals teach ten people at a time to craft scripts, record audio, and edit stills and video. More than 500 people have been trained so far, and many of the stories they produced were used on the air.

- A participatory media project called Island Blogging was started by local authorities on the islands off the coast of Scotland with the help of BBC Scotland. Islanders were issued a personal computer and a narrowband Web connection, which they put to use posting pictures and stories, and sparking debate on numerous community issues. They even broke news, such as the beaching of a whale, later picked up by mainstream Scottish media.

- The BBC Action Network is an attempt to reconnect citizens with the political process by offering them a forum to discuss issues relevant to them.

The BBC has other ideas in store, including Global Conversation, which Sambrook sees as a "global public space" where people from different countries can interact with each other. These initiatives are possible because of advances in technology that have empowered citizens like never before. Journalism is only beginning to explore ways in which it can better involve the public in the issues of the day. This effort will take time and will likely frustrate both the public and the journalists, who will need to negotiate a middle ground.

"As someone who supports this new direction, I don't suggest the BBC staff abdicate their responsibility for accuracy, fairness or objectivity," Sambrook wrote. "As we open up to contributions from the public, we must do so in a way that is consistent with our editorial values. However, I believe that truth, accuracy, impartiality and diversity of opinion are strengthened by being open to a wider range of opinion and perspective, brought to us through the knowledge and understanding of our audience."

It took some two hundred years for the diffusion of knowledge that began with the discovery of mechanical printing to engender the structural transformation of western society. This transformation was powered by the spread of knowledge via the printed word, and it enabled the people to become a public sufficiently empowered with knowledge to form a public opinion that could take part in its own social, economic, and political systems. Much of this information came to be distributed to the broad mass of the people by what came to be known as journalism. It was that information that helped them become informed citizens, and it would be in this climate that public opinion would be formed. Public opinion, in turn, made possible the rise of self-government.

In this sense journalism and democracy were born together. In the first phase of development the role of the press was simply to provide the people with information about the activities and institutions of power that controlled their lives. Today, when the world is awash in information, the role of the press becomes different. When information is abundant and available all the time everywhere, a new relationship between the press and the public needs to be formed. And just as the values of journalism do not change in this new competitive atmosphere, the role does not change much, either. Where once the role was simply providing information as a tool of self-governance, it now becomes a role to provide citizens with the tools they need to extract knowledge for themselves from the undifferentiated flood of rumor, propaganda, gossip, fact, assertion, and allegation the communications system now produces. Thus the journalist must not only make sense of the world but also make sense of the flood of information as it is being delivered to citizens.

To do this, journalists must first invite their audience into the process by which they produce the news. As we detailed in Chapter 4, on verification, they should take pains to make themselves and their work as transparent as they insist on making the people and institutions of power they cover.

This sort of approach is, in effect, the beginning of a new connection between the journalist and the citizen. It is one in which individuals in the audience are given a chance to judge the principles by which the journalists do their work. They are equipped with information that invites them to compare this with other choices available. Most important, it gives the public a basis on which to judge whether this is the kind of journalism they wish to encourage.

In this sense citizens bear some responsibility. Consider it the tenth element of journalism, one growing with the advent of new empowering technology.

Citizens have rights, but also responsibilities when it comes to news.

They must set aside prejudice and judge the work of journalists on the basis of whether it contributes to their ability to take an informed part in shaping their society. But the way journalists design their work to engage the public must provide not only the needed content but also an understanding of the principles by which their work is done. In this way, the journalists will determine whether or not the public can become a force for good journalism.

Market demand is clearly the most powerful force shaping society today. It would seem obvious that it is in the interest of journalists to do what they can to create a market for the kind of journalism this book attempts to describe: a journalism that recognizes and applies principles that help assure reliable, timely, proportional, comprehensive news to help make sense of our world and our place in it. The first step in that direction has to be developing a means of letting those who make up that market finally see how the sausage is made—how we do our work and what informs our decisions.

What does this mean to citizens? More precisely, what should we as citizens expect from a news organization? And what should we do if we believe we are not getting it? These questions are important. The elements of journalism belong to citizens as much as they do to journalists for the simple reason, as we said at the beginning, that these principles grow out of the function news plays in people's lives, not out of some professional ethos.

In that sense, the elements of journalism are a citizen's bill of rights as much as they are a journalist's bill of responsibilities. And with rights naturally come responsibilities for citizens as well—responsibilities that in the twenty-first century are growing along with the increased ability of the citizen to interact with the news. Thus, it is useful to enumerate how we as citizens can recognize whether the elements of journalism are evident in the news we receive.

A CITIZEN'S BILL OF RIGHTS AND RESPONSIBILITIES

1 • ON TRUTHFULNESS

We have the right to expect that the evidence of the integrity of the reporting be obvious. This means that the process of verification—how newspeople made their decisions and why—should be transparent. There should be a clear indication of open-minded examination. We should be able to judge the value and bias of the information for ourselves.

To live up to this responsibility, what elements would such a piece of reporting contain? A story should make clear the sources of information and the basis of the knowledge. The story's relevance should be clearly stated. Important unanswered questions should be noted. If the story raises a point of controversy, we should expect follow-up. Other stories would continue the public discussion over time so the sorting-out process that leads to truthfulness can take place. News, in other words, should not only engage us but also challenge us and make us think.

This, in turn, implies a two-way process. The citizen has an obligation to approach the news with an open mind and not just a desire that the news reinforce existing opinion.

2 • ON LOYALTY TO CITIZENS

We should expect to see evidence that the material has been prepared for our use above all. This means stories should answer our needs as citizens and not just the interests of the players and the political or economic system. It also means that there is a demonstrated effort to understand the whole community.

Perhaps the best way to judge this is how well the news over time avoids stereotypes. In news, stereotypes are usually characterizations that may be true in some cases but are not in the specific case being reported. A story about local crime that focuses on only one part of the community when the facts show that crime is spread generally throughout the whole community is an example. Usually, stereotyping is a failure of execution. Stereotypes of this type can almost always be avoided by more reporting and more specific reporting, both of which should be recognizable in any story carefully done.

We should also expect to see clear cases in which the news company will, at times, put its own interests at risk in order to bring us important information through its news, artistic and commercial reviews, and consumer and retail coverage. Katharine Graham did this when she chose to print the Pentagon Papers, but countless others do it every day when they print a critical review of a restaurant that is also an advertiser or a tough-minded report on an important local industry.

Loyalty to citizens also means disclosure of any synergy, connecting partnerships, or conflicts of interest as they relate to a particular story. This would include reporting on their own lobbying efforts, the organized pressure they put on government that is favorable to their own business interests. There is every reason we should expect our news providers be as transparent in their operations as we expect them to demand of other institutions of power.

3 • ON INDEPENDENCE

We have a right to expect that the commentators, columnists, and journalists of opinion are serving the interests of citizens' debate rather than the narrow interests of a faction or a predetermined outcome.

Independence is not to be found in commentaries that are in lockstep with factions or vested interests. This implies, for example, that we can expect to see Republicans at times criticized by conservative commentators and Democrats at times by liberals. Recalling that the journalist's primary allegiance is to the citizen's needs also implies that, while journalists need not be neutral, we can expect them not to have divided loyalties. We can expect that they are not writing speeches or secretly counseling those they cover or opine about. Because we look to opinion writers to help us sort through the complex and competing issues confronting citizens, we should expect to see evidence in the body of their writing or reporting that they have examined the ideas of others on the subject.

4 • ON MONITORING POWER

We have a right to expect monitoring on the most important and difficult centers of power. While this includes government, there are other institutions and individuals in society that wield economic, coercive, social, moral, and persuasive powers equal to or exceeding that of government.

Since its investigatory role vests considerable power in the press itself, we can expect to see great care and discretion in its use. This means that the news organizations have a responsibility to lead—to uncover things that are important and new and that change community paradigms. We have a right to expect that the watchdog role will demonstrate the news organization's public-interest obligation. This implies that we can expect that power will not be frittered away on minor or pseudo-scandals such as safe levels of bacteria in frozen yogurt or harmless amounts of dirt in hotel bedding. Instead, news organizations should focus their time and resources on major issues, unexpected scoundrels, and new perils, such as when the *New York Times* went back months later to examine how the GOP grossly manipulated the counting of absentee ballots in Florida during the 2000 presidential election.

5 • A PUBLIC FORUM

We should expect our news providers to create several channels through which we may interact with them. Such channels could include letters, e-mail, phone contacts, chat room discussions, space to write guest opinion columns, opportunities to make story suggestions, and ombudsmen. These channels should also include regular public appearances by members of the staff in public gathering venues such as forums, civic clubs, PTA meetings, and panel discussions, as well as interactive radio and television appearances.

And, as new technology and the Internet empower the citizens and reduce some of the space constrictions of traditional media, we should expect to be allowed to produce content or add to the news report (as the BBC example illustrates).

Through all these contacts, we should, over time, expect to see our views and values reflected in the news coverage and not just those of the most polarized positions on important issues. If the democratic ideal of compromise is to be reached, we should expect the media's public forum to build toward community understanding on which compromise can be realized.

Implicit in these rights is also responsibility. We as citizens have an obligation to approach the news with open minds, willing to accept new facts and examine new points of view as they are presented. We as citizens also have a responsibility to show up at the public forums or to send e-mails or letters to the editors. In short, the elements of journalism are principles that apply to citizens as well as to members of the news business, and citizens have to do their part to sustain the relationship.

6 • ON PROPORTIONALITY AND ENGAGEMENT

We have a right to expect journalists to be aware of our basic dilemma as citizens: that we have a need for timely and deep knowledge of important issues and trends in our community, but we lack both the time and the means to access most of this crucial information.

Being aware of this, we have a right to expect journalists to use their unique access to events and information to put the material they gather in a context that will engage our attention and, over time, see these trends and events in proportion to their true significance in our lives. We should not find matters of transitory importance overplayed and distorted for commercial purpose. For weeks in 1997 the national and local press across the country was riveted by the assault trial of a basketball announcer named Marv Albert, a case that focused more on sexual habits and a bad hairpiece than on anything of national consequence. To cover stories like this merely to attract ratings is to exploit the audience rather than serve it, and over time usually alienates people.

So that we as citizens may make sound and well-informed decisions about the many issues that touch our lives, we have a right to news reports that reflect the true nature of threats to our community, such as crime, as well as those aspects of community life that are functioning well. Our successes should be as apparent as our failures.

A close reader will notice two elements of journalism discussed in this book—verification and conscience—missing from this list of citizen's rights. This is because, when restated from the standpoint of how a citizen should recognize these rights, some elements are best understood as part of others. In this context, the journalist's process of verification becomes a hallmark of adherence to a truthful account of the news and is covered under the heading of truthfulness. By the same token, conscience becomes part of the interaction that occurs between citizen and news provider in the public forum function of a news organization and is covered under the heading a public forum.

What do we do as citizens if these rights are not met? What action, for instance, can and should we take if a newspaper reports on a case of business or political fraud but doesn't follow up on the controversial issues that it raises? First, of course, such contact works best if it comes constructively, as advice and information rather than condemnation. Second, if it is ignored it should be offered again, perhaps through more than one means. If, for example, an e-mail is not acknowledged, send it again, and then pick up the phone or write a letter, with a copy to the editor in chief. If you want to make other citizens aware of your complaint, keep a public record of your attempts to contact the organization and their reactions on a blog.

What can we do if as citizens we offer news organizations this feedback and our contributions, ideas, or criticisms are ignored? Rights mean something only if they are viewed as rights. At that point, withhold your business. Drop the subscription. Stop watching. Most important, write a clear explanation of why you have done so and send it to the editor or media critics, or post it on your own site. The marketplace fails if we as citizens are passive, willing to put up with a diminishing product. It used to be that there was no alternative, but today traditional news organizations don't hold a monopoly on some of the content. They will probably listen and engage in dialogue if we act with a voice and a reason. And if they don't, they failed their purpose.

. . .

In the end it may be that, as Carol Marin says, "there are no laws of news." But our research and our conversations with journalists and citizens have told us that there are certain enduring ideas about the flow of news and the role of journalism in providing it that can be identified. These ideas have ebbed and flowed, been misunderstood and abused—usually by those working in their name. Still, they are not artificial creations. The elements of journalism have been forged and tempered in three hundred years of experience and testing in the marketplace of competing forms of information. They stem from the function that news plays in people's lives. Those who produce journalism must use these elements to steer an ethical course in their work. Time suggests we vary from them at our peril.

The elements of journalism we have outlined here, the theory of journalism we have inherited, form the basis of the journalism of the new century, a journalism of sense making based on synthesis, verification, and fierce independence. They also hold the only protection against the force that threatens to destroy journalism and thus weaken democratic society. This is the threat that the press will be subsumed inside the world of commercialized speech or the undifferentiated world of broad communication. The only way to avoid this threat is for journalists to have a clearer and more rigorous understanding of the elements that make journalism a thing of value. A transparent enterprise that creates its own demand by inviting citizens into the process, reconnecting journalism and citizen in a conversation and not a lecture hall. This shift is not only something citizens and journalists have in their own control; it is something for which both bear some responsibility.

History has taught us by bloody experience what happens to a society in which the citizens act on the basis of self-interested information—whether it is the propaganda of a despotic state or the edicts of a sybaritic leisure class substituting bread and circuses for sovereignty.

The public continues to be troubled. There are heightened concerns about bias and whether the news media really protects democracy. But it would be an overstatement to suggest the country has reached some new crisis point, or even that public confidence in the press is on a worsening downward course. While public attitudes toward the press had been in general decline since the 1980s by some measures—among them whether the press is professional and moral—Americans are more confident than they were before September 11, 2001, or in the aftermath of the impeachment of Bill Clinton.

The number of Americans who had a "favorable" view of the press rose—across party lines.[2] And nearly three-quarters of Americans continue to believe in the idea of an independent nonpartisan news media. There is no magic formula embedded in these numbers. What seems consistent, and clearer, is that the public appreciates the idea that the press is aspiring to work in the public interest, trying to get it right, trying to be aggressive. What people have serious doubts about is whether journalists live up to those ideals and whether the companies that own the news still believe in them.

Civilization has produced one idea more powerful than any other: the notion that people can govern themselves. And it has created a largely unarticulated theory of information to sustain that idea, called journalism. The two rise and fall together. This book is an attempt to articulate that theory. Our best hope is not a future that returns to the past, which was never as sweet as people remember it. Our freedom in a digital century does depend on not forgetting that past, or the theory of news it produced, in a surge of faith in technological and corporate rebirth. We fought two conventional world wars and a largely covert Cold War in the last century against such technological utopianism. We may not survive another.

ENDNOTES

1. Richard Sambrook, "Citizen Journalism and the BBC," *Nieman Reports* (Winter 2005), 13–16; available at www.nieman.harvard.edu/reports/05-4NRwinter/Sambrook.pdf.
2. The number of Americans who viewed the press favorably rose from 43 percent in December 2004 to 53 percent in February 2006. These numbers are from Pew Research Center for the People and the Press, "Bush a Drag on Republican Midterm Prospects," February 9, 2006.

ACKNOWLEDGMENTS

This book is not ours alone. It is the fruit of the years of work of the Committee of Concerned Journalists and the 1,200 journalists who gave their names, their time, and their care to its creation. It is also informed by the more than 300 people who came to our forums to give us their thoughts, by the hundreds who answered our surveys, and by the roughly one hundred more who sat for hours for interviews by our academic partners. Our goal with this book was not to offer an argument of what journalism should be, but to outline the common ground on which journalists already stand. Since journalists are so independent, they have always resisted putting these ideas in one place, or even working through them consciously. But in a time of confusion and doubt about the differences between journalism and all the other forms by which information is communicated, we believe clarity of purpose and professional theory are more crucial than ever before. It is important for journalists who are coming to doubt themselves. It is important to a generation new to the newsroom. It is important to members of the public who express a longing for news they can trust. This was our intention. If we have succeeded in some measure, it is because of their help. If we have failed, it is because we have let them down.

We owe a special debt to some in particular. That list begins with Dante Chinni, who served as our partner, researcher, and counsel on the first edition. For the second paperback edition, we want to thank Cristian Lupsa, who served as our researcher, sounding board, and critic. Amy Mitchell is the person most responsible for operating the committee in its early days, organizing the forums, supervising the survey research, and all other activities of the committee. This work bears the stamp of her professionalism, organization, and good humor. Tom Avila took over for Amy in shepherding the committee in its next phase and caring for it as if it were his own creation. Carrie Brown, Wally Dean, Brett Mueller, and a strong cohort of superb journalists served as trainers in newsrooms for the committee's traveling curriculum; their work informed many of the new insights in this new edition. In addition, we want to thank Howard Gardner, Mihaly Csikszentmihalyi, and William Damon for sharing their research with us. Damon also became our partner in training journalists. A few key friends played a vital role in encouraging, counseling, editing, and guiding this book, including James Carey, who never failed to elevate our thinking and excite our imagination, Roy Peter Clark, Tom Goldstein, David Halberstam, Richard Harwood, John Kovach, Jim Naughton, Geneva Overholser, Sandra Rowe, Matthew Storin, and Mark Trahant.

The staff of the Project for Excellence in Journalism was critical: that list includes Nancy Anderson, Jennifer Fimbres, Stacy Forster, Chris Galdieri, Carl Gottlieb, and John Mashek. Important help, too, was provided by Julie Dempster at the Nieman Fellowship program at Harvard. Our steering committee played a pivotal role in guiding us along the way. We owe a great thanks to the universities, newspapers, and individuals who co-hosted, organized, and in several cases financed our forums, including the Park Foundation. The many hours of conversation with journalists in newsrooms around the country that informed this revision of the book was made possible by a generous grant from the John S. and James L. Knight Foundation, a foundation committed to improving journalism worldwide. We thank our agent, David Black, for his confidence and his passion, and our editors at Crown, first Bob Mecoy, then Annik Lafarge, and now Lindsey Moore, for their belief in this project.

None of this would have been possible, too, without the support, both financial and personal, of Rebecca Rimel and Don Kimelman at the Pew Charitable Trusts, whose faith in us to embark on this voyage was constant. They deserve much credit.

Finally, we owe a debt to those journalists who came before us, who helped create the First Amendment and then gave it its meaning. Their legacy imposes on us the obligation to accept the responsibility of a free and independent press and realize its promise to a self-governing people.

INDEX

Bill Kovach is the former Washington bureau chief of the *New York Times*, editor of the *Atlanta Journal-Constitution*, and curator of the Nieman Fellowships at Harvard. He is currently the founding chairman of the Committee of Concerned Journalists, as well as the senior counselor to the Project for Excellence in Journalism. He has won the Elijah Parish Lovejoy Award and the Richard M. Clurman Award for Mentoring. His writing has appeared in *The New York Times Magazine*, the *Washington Post*, *The New Republic*, and many other newspapers and magazines in the United States and abroad.

Tom Rosenstiel is director of the Project for Excellence in Journalism and vice chairman of the Committee of Concerned Journalists. A former media critic for the *Los Angeles Times* and chief congressional correspondent for *Newsweek*, he is the coeditor of *Thinking Clearly: Cases in Journalistic Decision Making* and author of *Strange Bedfellows: How Television and the Presidential Candidates Changed American Politics* and the upcoming *We Interrupt This Newscast: How to Improve TV News and Win Ratings, Too*. His writing has appeared in such publications as *Esquire*, *The New Republic*, the *New York Times*, *The Columbia Journalism Review*, and *The Washington Monthly*. A former media critic for MSNBC's *The News with Brian Williams*, he is a frequent commentator on radio and television and in print.

Together, Bill and Tom are the authors of *Warp Speed: America in the Age of Mixed Media*. Both live in Washington, D.C.